NEWTON'S PRINCIPIA, SECTIONS I, II, III, WITH NOTES AND ILLUSTRATIONS. ALSO A COLLECTION OF PROBLEMS

Published @ 2017 Trieste Publishing Pty Ltd

ISBN 9780649657537

Newton's Principia, Sections I, II, III, with Notes and Illustrations. Also a Collection of Problems by Sir Isaac Newton & Percival Frost

Except for use in any review, the reproduction or utilisation of this work in whole or in part in any form by any electronic, mechanical or other means, now known or hereafter invented, including xerography, photocopying and recording, or in any information storage or retrieval system, is forbidden without the permission of the publisher, Trieste Publishing Pty Ltd, PO Box 1576 Collingwood, Victoria 3066 Australia.

All rights reserved.

Edited by Trieste Publishing Pty Ltd.
Cover @ 2017

This book is sold subject to the condition that it shall not, by way of trade or otherwise, be lent, re-sold, hired out, or otherwise circulated without the publisher's prior consent in any form or binding or cover other than that in which it is published and without a similar condition including this condition being imposed on the subsequent purchaser.

www.triestepublishing.com

SIR ISAAC NEWTON & PERCIVAL FROST

NEWTON'S PRINCIPIA, SECTIONS I, II, III, WITH NOTES AND ILLUSTRATIONS. ALSO A COLLECTION OF PROBLEMS

NEWTON'S PRINCIPIA.

SECTIONS I. II. III.

WITH

NOTES AND ILLUSTRATIONS.

ALSO

A COLLECTION OF PROBLEMS

PRINCIPALLY INTENDED AS EXAMPLES OF NEWTON'S METHODS.

BY

PERCIVAL FROST, M.A.
LATE FELLOW OF ST JOHN'S COLLEGE;
MATHEMATICAL LECTURER OF KING'S COLLEGE.

Principiis enim cognitis, multo facilius extrema intelligetis.—CICERO.

Cambridge and London:
MACMILLAN AND CO.
1863.

Cambridge:
PRINTED BY C. J. CLAY, M.A.
AT THE UNIVERSITY PRESS.

PREFACE TO THE SECOND EDITION.

In publishing the following work, my principal intention is to explain difficulties, which may be encountered by the student on first reading the *Principia*, and to illustrate the advantages of a careful study of the methods employed by Newton, by showing the extent to which they may be applied in the solution of problems. I have also endeavoured to give assistance to the student who is engaged in the study of the higher branches of Mathematics, by representing in a geometrical form several of the processes employed in the Differential and Integral Calculus, and in the analytical investigations of Dynamics.

In my version of the first section and the beginning of the second I have adhered as closely as I could to the original form; and, in the cases in which sections have been interpolated, or the form of demonstration changed, I have indicated such changes and interpolations by brackets.

Although it is generally advisable not to deviate from Newton's words in the demonstrations of the Lemmas, yet in many cases, I suppose, purposely, he expressed himself very concisely, as in Lemmas IV. and X.; and he was contented with simply giving the enunciation of Lemma V.; in these cases, therefore, interpolations are made which, I believe, are in accordance with Newton's plan of demonstration.

Throughout the Problems and Theorems which depend upon the sixth proposition, the variations are replaced by equations; by this method of treating the subject, I conceive that clearer ideas of the meaning of each step are obtained by the student.

PREFACE TO THE SECOND EDITION.

I take this opportunity to acknowledge the great assistance which I have derived in the preparation of my notes, from the study of Whewell's *Method of Limits*, from which the Articles 55—60 have been almost entirely taken; I have also made use of several editions of Newton, and especially of Carr's.

The Problems are principally selected from the papers set in the examinations for the Mathematical Tripos, and in the course of the College examinations; the results of these problems are given either in the statements or at the end of the work, but I have not thought it advisable to supply hints for the solution, because I imagine that the student would have been deprived thereby of the advantages which it is the object of a problem to secure. It is only necessary to add that I have been careful to introduce no problems which are not capable of solution by methods given in the work.

I desire to express my thanks to Mr Hadley of St John's College for several valuable suggestions, and also to Mr Cockshott of Trinity College, and to Mr King of Jesus College, for their kindness in correcting the errors of the press, and in testing the accuracy of the problems, which, I believe, are nearly free from mistakes.

PERCIVAL FROST.

CAMBRIDGE,
November 13, 1863.

CONTENTS.

SECTION I.

ON THE METHOD OF PRIME AND ULTIMATE RATIOS.

	PAGE
LEMMA I.	1
Variable quantities	"
Continuity	2
Equality	3
Notes on the Lemma	4
Limits of variable quantities	6
Ultimate ratios of vanishing quantities	7
Investigation of certain limits	8
Problems	14
LEMMA II.	17
LEMMA III.	18
Notes on the Lemmas	19
Volumes of revolution	"
Sectorial Areas	20
Surfaces of revolution	21
Centers of gravity	22
General extension	"
Notes on Corollaries	23
Investigation of certain Areas, Volumes, &c.	"
Parabolic area	"
Paraboloid, Volume of	25
Spherical segment, volume of	26
Cone, surface of	27
Rod of variable density, mass of	28
Hemisphere, center of gravity of	29
Equiangular spiral, area of	30
Problems	31
LEMMA IV.	34
Notes on the Lemma	35

CONTENTS.

	PAGE
Application of Lemma IV., to find	
Elliptic area	36
Parabolic area	37
Paraboloid, volume of	,,
Paraboloid, center of gravity of	38
Cycloidal area	39
Rod of variable density, center of gravity and mass of	40
Circular arc, center of gravity of	41
Attraction of uniform rod	42
Problems	43
LEMMA V.	45
Notes on the Lemma	46
Criteria of similarity	,,
Centers of similitude	48
Similar continuous arcs, having coincident chords, have a common tangent	49
Centers of similitude of two circles	,,
Conditions of similarity of two conic sections	50
Parabolas are all similar	51
Cycloids are all similar	,,
Construction of curves under given conditions	52
Instruments for drawing on altered scales	,,
Volume of conical figure of any form	53
Problems	54
LEMMA VI.	56
Tangents to curves	,,
Notes on the Lemma	57
Subtangents	58
Subtangent of parabola	59
Surface of spherical segment	,,
Center of gravity of spherical belt	60
Volume of spherical sector	,,
Center of gravity of spherical sector	61
$SY^2 = SP \cdot SZ$	,,
Problems	62
LEMMA VII.	63
Notes on the Lemma	64
Exterior curve greater than interior	66
Polar subtangent	67
Inclination of tangent to radius vector	,,
Cardioid	68
Problems	,,
LEMMA VIII.	70
Notes on the Lemma	,,
LEMMA IX.	72
Notes on the Lemma	73

CONTENTS.

	PAGE
LEMMA X.	75
Finite force	77
Notes on the Lemma	,,
Space described under action of constant force	79
Geometrical representations of	
Space in given time, velocity variable	,,
Velocity in given time, force variable and depending on the time	81
Square of velocity, force depending on the position	82
Motion of a particle under various circumstances:	
Space when velocity varies as square of time	83
Space when force varies as m^{th} power of time	84
Velocity from rest, force varying as distance	85
Time of describing given space, force varying as the distance	86
Cycloidal oscillation, time of	87
Path of particle acted on by a force tending to a point and varying as the distance	88
Problems	90
LEMMA XI.	91
Scholium	93
Curvature of curves	96
Curvature of circle constant	97
Curvatures of different circles vary inversely as the radii	98
Measure of curvature	,,
Circle of curvature	
Has closer contact than other circles	100
Generally cuts the curve	,,
Evolute of a curve	101
Properties of evolute	,,
Involute	102
Diameters and chords of curvature	,,
Parabola	103
Ellipse	104
Hyperbola	106
Ratio of radius of curvature to normal in any conic section	,,
Common chord of conic section and circle of curvature	107
Radius and chord of curvature of a curve referred to a pole	108
Tangents to a curve, from the same point, ultimately equal	,,
Equiangular spiral, radius and chord of curvature	109
Catenary, radius and vertical chord of curvature	110
Cardioid, chord of curvature through the focus	111
Problems on circles of curvature	112
Notes on the Lemma	113
Sagitta	114
Example of wrong reasoning	,,
Relation between sagitta and subtense	115
Parabola of curvature	117
Problems	118

SECTION II.

CENTRIPETAL FORCES.

	PAGE
PROP. I.	120
Notes on the Proposition	123
Force in parallel lines	127
Effect of sudden change of force	128
Apses	129
Apsidal line divides an orbit symmetrically	,,
Only two different apsidal distances	130
Illustrations	,,
Problems	131
PROP. II.	135
Notes on the proposition	137
Relative motion	,,
Possibility of description of a curve, forces tending to any point	139
PROP. III.	141
Illustration from moon's motion	142
PROP. IV.	144
Symbolical representation of areas, lines, &c.	149
Notes on the proposition	151
Centrifugal force	,,
Examples of circular motion	153
Conical pendulum	154
Problems	155
PROP. V.	157
Problems	158
PROP. VI.	159
Notes on the proposition	161
Dimensions of symbols, homogeneity	163
Tangential and normal forces	,,
Velocity in an orbit, any forces acting	164
Radial and transversal forces	165
Angular velocity	166
Examples of constrained motion	167
Problems	171
PROP. VII.	174
Notes on the proposition	176
Velocity in circular orbit	179
Absolute force	,,
Periodic time	181
Illustrations	,,
Problems	182

CONTENTS.

	PAGE
PROP. VIII.	181
Scholium	185
Notes on the proposition	186
Extension of Scholium to any curve	,,
Application to the case of	
Cycloid, force parallel to the axis	187
Catenary, force perpendicular to the directrix	,,
Problems	188
PROP. IX.	189
Notes on the proposition	,,
Velocity in the equiangular spiral	,,
Time of describing a given arc	,,
Problems	190
PROP. X.	191
Velocity in an ellipse about the center	193
Hyperbola, repulsive force from the center	,,
Time in an elliptic arc	,,
Orbit described under given circumstance of projection, force tending to a point, and varying as the distance from it	194
Geometrical construction of the orbit	195
Equations for determining the position and magnitude of the orbit,	
Attractive force	,,
Repulsive force	196
Resultant of forces tending to different centers	197
Examples of orbits described under various circumstances	199
Variation of elements for a given small change of velocity	201
Problems	204

SECTION III.

ON THE MOTION OF BODIES IN CONIC SECTIONS, UNDER THE ACTION OF FORCES TENDING TO A FOCUS.

PROP. XI.	207
PROP. XII.	208
PROP. XIII.	209
Notes on the propositions	211
PROP. XIV.	212
PROP. XV.	,,
Notes on the propositions	213
Periodic time in an ellipse	,,
Time in an elliptic arc	214
Eccentric, true, and mean anomalies	,,
Time in a parabolic arc	215

CONTENTS.

	PAGE
Kepler's laws	216
Deductions from Kepler's laws	,,
Law of gravitation	217
PROP. XVI.	218
Velocity in the different conic sections	220
Hodograph	221
PROP. XVII.	223
Notes on the proposition	226
Direct investigation for the orbit described under given circumstances of projection, force tending to a point and varying inversely as the square of the distance from it	227

Equations for determining the elements of

Elliptic orbit, $V^2 < \dfrac{2\mu}{SP}$ 229

Hyperbolic orbit, $V^2 > \dfrac{2\mu}{SP}$ 230

Parabolic orbit, $V^2 = \dfrac{2\mu}{SP}$ 231

Hyperbolic orbit, repulsive force............ ,,

Examples of orbits described under various circumstances .... ,,
Variation of elements for given changes of direction of motion 234
Velocity in ellipse compounded of two uniform velocities 235
Change of eccentricity and position of apsidal line for a given small change of velocity .... ,,
Problems............ 236

APPENDIX I.

SECTION VII.

ON RECTILINEAR MOTION.

PROP. XXXII. and XXXVI.	241
Notes	242
PROP. XXXVIII.	243

SECTION VIII.

PROP. XL.	244
Problems	245

APPENDIX II.

ON THE GEOMETRICAL PROPERTIES OF CERTAIN CURVES.

Cycloid	247
Tangent	,,

CONTENTS.

	PAGE
Length of arc	247
Area	248
Evolute	249
Time of oscillation in	250

Pendulum.

To count a large number of oscillations	251
Force of gravity determined by means of	,,
Height of mountains determined by	252
Epicycloid and Hypocycloid	253
Radius of curvature	,,
Evolute	254
Area	,,
Length of arc	256
Equiangular spiral	257
Length of arc	,,
Catenary	258
Tension at any point	,,
Length of arc	260
Tangent, construction for	,,
Lemniscate	,,
Inclination of curve to radius	261
Relation between radius and perpendicular on tangent	,,
Chord of curvature through center	,,
Radius of curvature	262
Area	,,
Law of force tending to the center	,,
Velocity	,,
Time in any arc	,,
Poles	,,
Problems	263
General Problems	266
Solutions of Problems	282

NEWTON'S FIRST BOOK

CONCERNING THE MOTION OF BODIES.

SECTION I.

ON THE METHOD OF PRIME AND ULTIMATE RATIOS.

LEMMA I.

Quantities, and the ratios of quantities, which, in any finite time, tend constantly to equality, and which, before the end of that time, approach nearer to each other than by any assigned difference, become ultimately equal.

If not, let them become ultimately unequal, and let their ultimate difference be D. Hence, [since, throughout the time, they tend constantly to equality,] they cannot approach nearer to each other than by the difference D, contrary to the hypothesis, [that they approach nearer than by *any* assigned difference. Therefore, they do not become ultimately unequal, that is, they become ultimately equal].

Variable Quantities.

1. The *Quantities*, of which Newton treats in this Lemma, are variable magnitudes, described by a supposed law of construction, the variation of these magnitudes being due to the arbitrary progressive change of some element of the construction employed in the statement of the law.

When, in the progressive change of this element, it receives the last value which is assigned to it in any proposition, the hypothesis is said to arrive at its ultimate form, or to be indefinitely extended.

Thus, if ABP be a semicircle, ACB its diameter, BP any arc, PM the ordinate perpendicular to ACB, as the arc BP gradually diminishes, AM is a variable magnitude, continually increasing, and BP is the element of the construction, to the

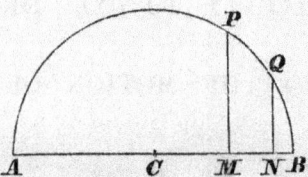

arbitrary change of which the variation of AM is due; and, if BP may be made as small as we please, AM may be made to approach to AB nearer than by any difference that can be named, and the hypothesis approaches its ultimate form.

Again, if ABC be a triangle, and AB be divided into a number of equal portions, Aa, ab, bc,... and a series of parallelograms be inscribed upon those bases, whose sides $a\alpha$, $b\beta$, $c\gamma$,... are parallel to BC and terminated in AC, the sum of the areas of the parallelograms will be a variable magnitude, defined by that construction, and changing in a progressive manner, if the

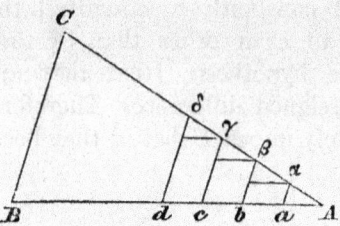

number of parts into which AB is divided is continually increased. In this case the number of parts is the variable element of the construction. In the ultimate form of the hypothesis, it will be shewn (Lemma II.) that the sum of the parallelograms is the area of the triangle, when the number is increased indefinitely.

2. The variation of a magnitude is *continuous*, when in the passage from *any* one value to *any* other, throughout its change,

it receives every intermediate value, without becoming infinite. When this is not the case the variation is *discontinuous*.

According to the hypothesis in the last illustration, the number of parts into which AB is divided being exact, the magnitude varies discontinuously, i.e. the sum of the areas does not pass through all the intermediate values between any two states of the progress.

If the hypothesis be changed, equal portions being set off commencing from B, and Aa remaining over and above after ba, the last of the portions for which there is room, these equal portions could be made to diminish gradually, and the sum of the areas would in that case vary continuously.

Tendency to Equality.

3. Quantities are ultimately equal, when they are ultimately in a ratio of equality.

4. Quantities, which always remain *finite*, throughout the change of the hypothesis, by which they are described, tend continually to equality, when their difference continually diminishes.

Thus, if BQ be an arc, always half of BP, in fig. 1, page 2, and QN be the corresponding ordinate; as BP continually diminishes, AM and AN remain finite, and, since their difference continually diminishes, they tend continually to equality.

5. Quantities, which may become *indefinitely small*, or *indefinitely great*, as the hypothesis is indefinitely extended, tend continually to equality, when the ratio of their difference to either of them continually diminishes.

To illustrate this test of a tendency to equality, let us suppose, in fig. 1, page 2, that the chord BP is double of the chord BQ, then, since (chord $BP)^2 = AB \cdot BM$,

and (chord $BQ)^2 = AB \cdot BN$;

∴ $BM : BN :: $ (chord $BP)^2 : $ (chord $BQ)^2$
  $:: 4 : 1$;

∴ $MN : BN :: 3 : 1$,

hence, we observe that BM and BN have a difference, which tends continually to become $3BN$, the ratio of which to either is finite, so that, although both tend to become indefinitely small, as the hypothesis tends to its ultimate form, BM and BN do not satisfy the condition requisite for a tendency to equality.

Observations on the Lemma.

6. We will now proceed to examine the force of the other important terms employed in the statement of the first Lemma.

The expression "in any finite time" (tempore quovis finito), signifies what has been called the indefinite extension of the hypothesis from some definite state to its ultimate form*.

The law of the variation of the magnitudes under consideration is obtained by the examination of their construction while the element, to which the change is due, is at a finite distance from its final value, and the finite time is the supposed time occupied in the passage from this definite to the ultimate state.

In the first illustration (Art. 1), it denotes the progressive diminution of BP, from being a *finite* magnitude to the point of evanescence.

In the second, the progress from *any* finite number of equal portions to an indefinite number.

7. The expression, "which *constantly* tend" (quæ constanter tendunt), signifies that, from the commencement of the *finite time* to the limit of the extension of the hypothesis, the differences continually diminish.

To illustrate this mode of expression, let BC be a quadrant

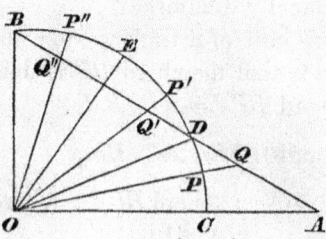

---
* Vide Whewell's *Doctrine of Limits*.

LEMMA I. 5

of a circle whose bounding radii are OB, OC, and let BDA be a straight line cutting the arc BDC and the radius OC in D and A, and let OP be a radius revolving from OC to OB, and cutting BA in Q, E the point of bisection of the arc BD.

OP and OQ twice tend *to* equality, viz. from OC to OD and from OE to OB, and once *from* equality from OD to OE; it is only from OE to OB that OP'' and OQ'' tend to equality constantly, during the progress, and it is from such a position as OE that the finite time must be considered to commence.

8. "Before the end of that time," (ante finem temporis,) implies that however small the given difference may be, a less difference than that difference is arrived at, while the distance from the ultimate state is still finite, however near to the final state it may be necessary to proceed.

Thus, if, in the last figure, the angle BOD be 60°, the radius one inch, and the given difference $\frac{35}{100000}$ or $\frac{18}{100000}$ of an inch, the difference between OP and OQ is less than the given difference, if the revolving radius be 2' or 1', respectively, from the ultimate position; and so on, however small the difference which is chosen.

9. In the proof of the Lemma, if the ultimate difference be D, the quantities cannot approach nearer than by that given difference; otherwise, they would, in one part of the progression, have been tending *from* equality in order to arrive ultimately at that difference, contrary to the statement of the proposition in the words, "ad æqualitatem constanter tendunt."

The nature of the proof, which is more difficult than may at first sight appear, can be illustrated as follows, by examining the effect of the omission of some of the points in the statement of the Lemma.

Draw Oy, Ox at right angles, AB any straight line meeting Oy in A, CED a curve touching AB in E and meeting Oy in C, CD' another touching a straight line parallel to AB in C, $MQPP'$ a common ordinate.

As OM diminishes until it becomes indefinitely small, $MQPP'$ moves up to Oy.

In both curves, the ordinates MQ and MP or MP' have an ultimate difference CA, equal to D suppose.

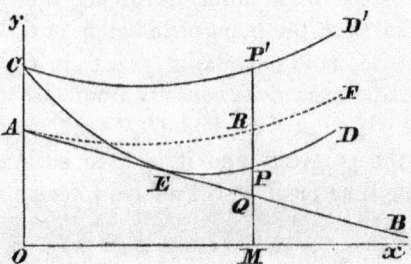

Omit the word "constanter," and the curve CED is admissible in a representation of the approach of the quantities; because the ordinates approach, before the end of the time, nearer than by any assignable difference, as at E, although the condition of continual tendency to equality is not satisfied.

Omit the words "ante finem temporis, &c." and CD' is sufficient; for, in this case, they tend continually to equality, but before the end of the time they do not approach nearer than by any assignable difference, and they are ultimately unequal.

In the case of the dotted line ARF touching AB at A, all the conditions are satisfied. QM and RM tend continually to equality, and their difference may be made less than any given difference before OM vanishes.

Limit of a variable quantity.

10. When a variable quantity tends continually to equality with a certain fixed quantity, and approaches nearer to this quantity than by any assignable difference, as the hypothesis determining its variation is approaching its ultimate form, this fixed quantity is called the *Limit of the variable quantity*.

The tests are,—that there should be a tendency to equality;—that this tendency should be continued from some finite condition;—and that the approach should, during the progression to the ultimate form, be nearer than by any assignable difference.

Thus, as is mentioned in the Scholium at the end of the section, the variable quantity does not become equal to, or surpass the limit, before the arrival at the ultimate form.

Limiting ratio of variable quantities.

11. If two quantities continually diminish or increase, and the ratio of these quantities tends continually to equality with a certain fixed ratio, and may be made to differ from that ratio by less than any assignable difference, as the hypothesis determining their variation is indefinitely extended; this fixed ratio is called the *limiting ratio* of the varying quantities.

Ultimate ratio of vanishing quantities.

12. When the ultimate form of the hypothesis brings the quantities to a state of evanescence, they are called *vanishing quantities;* and the limiting ratio, or the limit of the ratio, is the *ultimate ratio of the vanishing quantities.*

The expression, "Vanishing quantities," does not imply that the quantities *are* indefinitely small while under examination, but only that they *will be* so in the ultimate form; which observation implies that *the ratio of the vanishing quantities* is not an equivalent expression with *the ultimate ratio of the vanishing quantities*, the former being taken "ante finem temporis."

"Ultimæ rationes illæ quibuscum quantitates evanescunt, revera non sunt rationes quantitatum ultimarum." See Scholium, at the end of the section.

Thus,

Let GC, FC be two straight lines intersecting AB in G, F, ADE, MPQ, perpendicular to AB.

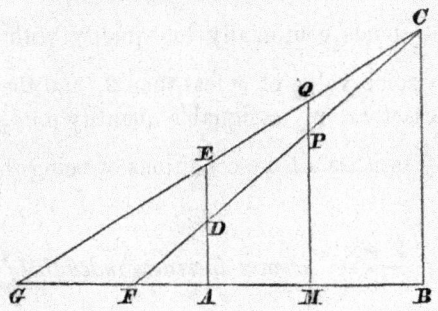

Let α, β be the areas $AMPD$, $AMQE$, then it is easily found that
$$\alpha : \beta :: AD + MP : AE + MQ;$$
now, let MPQ be supposed to move up to ADE, then, in the ultimate form of the hypothesis, α and β vanish, and are called vanishing quantities from this circumstance.

Also, the *ultimate ratio* of the vanishing quantities is $AD : AE$.

In this case, since $MP : MQ$ is not equal to $AD : AE$, the ratio of the vanishing quantities, viz. $AD + MP : AE + MQ$, is different from $AD : AE$ the ultimate ratio.

Prime Ratios.

13. If the order of the change in the form of the hypothesis be reversed, or the varying quantities be tending from equality, having started into existence from the commencement of the time, the quantities are called *nascent quantities;* and the ratio with which they commence existence is called the *prime ratio* of the nascent quantities.

Application of Lemma I to the investigation of certain Limits.

1. *Limit of* $\dfrac{1+x}{2-x}$, *as* x *gradually diminishes, and ultimately vanishes.*

Since the difference between $\dfrac{1+x}{2-x}$ and $\dfrac{1}{2}$ is $\dfrac{3x}{2(2-x)}$, this difference continually diminishes as x gradually diminishes, and, by diminishing x sufficiently, may be made less than any assignable difference.

Hence, $\dfrac{1+x}{2-x}$ tends continually to equality with $\dfrac{1}{2}$, if we commence from some value of x less than 2, and the difference may be made less than any assignable quantity *ante finem temporis*, therefore $\dfrac{1}{2}$ satisfies all the conditions of being the required limits.

2. *Limit of* $\dfrac{2+x}{5+3x}$, *when* x *increases indefinitely.*

LEMMA I.

Since the difference $\frac{2+x}{5+3x} - \frac{1}{3} = \frac{1}{3(5+2x)}$, which continually diminishes as x increases, and may be made less than any assignable difference; therefore, as before, $\frac{1}{3}$ satisfies all the conditions of being a limit of $\frac{2+x}{5+3x}$.

3. *Tangents are drawn to a circular arc, at its middle point, and at its extremities. Shew that the area of the triangle formed by the chord of the arc, and the two tangents at the extremities, is ultimately four times that of the triangle formed by the three tangents.*

Let C be the middle point of the arc, AB the chord, FA, FB, DCE the three tangents,

$$\triangle FDE : \triangle FAB :: FC^2 : FG^2.$$

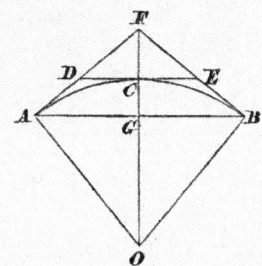

Now $\quad FC(FC + 2CO) = FA^2 = FO \cdot FG$;

$$\therefore FC : FG :: FO : FC + 2CO;$$

therefore, since FC vanishes in the limit, $FC : FG :: CO : 2CO$ ultimately;

$$\therefore FG = 2FC \text{ ultimately,}$$

and $\triangle FDE : \triangle FAB :: 1 : 4$.

4. *Limit of* $\frac{x^m - 1}{x - 1}$, *when* x *differs from* 1 *by an indefinitely small quantity,* m *being any number, fractional or integral, positive or negative.*

1st, where m is a positive whole number

$$\frac{x^m - 1}{x - 1} = x^{m-1} + x^{m-2} + \ldots + x + 1,$$

which may be made to differ from m by less than any assignable difference by taking x sufficiently near to unity;

therefore m is the limit of $\dfrac{x^m - 1}{x - 1}$.

2ndly, Let $m = \dfrac{p - q}{r}$, p, q, and r being positive whole numbers, and let $x = y^r$;

$$\therefore \frac{x^m - 1}{x - 1} = \frac{y^{p-q} - 1}{y^r - 1}$$

$$= \frac{1}{y^q} \cdot \frac{y^p - y^q}{y^r - 1}$$

$$= \frac{1}{y^q} \cdot \frac{y^p - 1 - (y^q - 1)}{y^r - 1}$$

$$= \frac{1}{y^q} \cdot \frac{\dfrac{y^p - 1}{y - 1} - \dfrac{y^q - 1}{y - 1}}{\dfrac{y^r - 1}{y - 1}}.$$

This may be made to differ from $\dfrac{p - q}{r}$ by a quantity less than any assignable quantity by taking x, and therefore y, sufficiently near to unity;

therefore m or $\dfrac{p - q}{r}$ is the limit required.

When we divide the numerator and denominator by $y - 1$, y is not equal to 1, the time chosen being *ante finem temporis* while the difference is finite: see the direction in the Scholium referred to above; "Cave intelligas quantitates magnitudine determinatas, sed cogita semper diminuendas sine limite."

5. *Limit of* $\dfrac{1^p + 2^p + 3^p + \ldots + n^p}{n^{p+1}}$, *when* n *is indefinitely increased,* p *being any positive number.*

LEMMA I.

Since this sum is the arithmetic mean of the n fractions

$$\left(\frac{1}{n}\right)^p, \left(\frac{2}{n}\right)^p, \ldots\ldots \left(\frac{n}{n}\right)^p,$$

therefore, for all positive values of p, integral or fractional, it lies between $\left(\frac{1}{n}\right)^p$ and $\left(\frac{n}{n}\right)^p$ or 1, therefore its ultimate value lies between 0 and 1.

This being an important limit, we will investigate it first for the particular case in which p is integral and positive, and then generally, when p is any positive quantity.

Let $\qquad S_n = 1^p + 2^p + \ldots\ldots + n^p$.

Then $\qquad S_{n+1} = 1^p + 2^p + \ldots\ldots + n^p + (n+1)^p$;

$$\therefore S_{n+1} - S_n = (n+1)^p.$$

If therefore we assume that

$$S_n = An^{p+1} + Bn^p + \ldots\ldots + Ln + M,$$

then $S_{n+1} = A\,\overline{n+1}\,|^{p+1} + B\,\overline{n+1}\,|^p + \ldots\ldots + L\,\overline{n+1}\,| + M$,

$$\therefore (n+1)^p = A\,(\overline{n+1}\,|^{p+1} - n^{p+1}) + B\,(\overline{n+1}\,|^p - n^p) + \ldots\ldots$$
$$+ \&c.$$

$$= A\left\{(p+1)\,n^p + (p+1)\cdot\frac{p}{2}\,n^{p-1} + \ldots\ldots\right\}$$

$$+ B\left(pn^{p-1} + p\cdot\frac{p-1}{2}\,n^{p-2} + \ldots\ldots\right) + \ldots\ldots$$

$$+ \&c.$$

we obtain, by equating the coefficients, $p+1$ equations for determining the values of the $p+1$ constants $A, B, \ldots\ldots L$, which reduce the equation to an identity.

The first of these equations is

$$1 = (p+1)\,A;$$

$$\therefore S_n = \frac{1}{p+1}\cdot n^{p+1} + Bn^p + \ldots\ldots$$

and $\dfrac{S_n}{n^{p+1}} = \dfrac{1}{p+1} + \dfrac{B}{n} + \dfrac{C}{n^2} + \ldots\ldots + \dfrac{M}{n^{p+1}}$,

the number of the terms following $\dfrac{1}{p+1}$ being finite.

Hence, if n be increased, we may make the difference between
$$\dfrac{S_n}{n^{p+1}} \text{ and } \dfrac{1}{p+1}$$
diminish until it becomes less than any assignable quantity;

therefore $\dfrac{1}{p+1}$ is the limit required.

Next, let p be any positive quantity, and let l be the limit of
$$\dfrac{1^p + 2^p + \ldots\ldots + n^p}{n^{p+1}},$$

$\therefore 1^p + 2^p + \ldots\ldots + n^p = ln^{p+1} + Bn^\beta + Cn^\gamma + \ldots\ldots$

in which $p+1, \beta, \gamma \ldots\ldots$ are in descending order, and
$$\dfrac{Bn^\beta + Cn^\gamma + \ldots\ldots}{n^{p+1}}$$
vanishes, when n is made infinitely large.

$\therefore 1^p + 2^p + \ldots\ldots + \overline{n+1}\,]^p = l\,\overline{n+1}\,]^{p+1} + B\,\overline{n+1}\,]^\beta + \ldots\ldots$

$\therefore \overline{n+1}\,]^p = l\,(\overline{n+1}\,]^{p+1} - n^{p+1}) + B\,(\overline{n+1}\,]^\beta - n^\beta) + \ldots\ldots$

$\therefore \left(1 + \dfrac{1}{n}\right)^p = l \cdot \dfrac{\left(1 + \dfrac{1}{n}\right)^{p+1} - 1}{1 + \dfrac{1}{n} - 1} + \dfrac{Bn^\beta}{n^{p+1}} \cdot \dfrac{\left(1 + \dfrac{1}{n}\right)^\beta - 1}{1 + \dfrac{1}{n} - 1}$

$+ \ldots\ldots\ldots\ldots\ldots\ldots$

therefore, observing that, when n is increased indefinitely,
$$\dfrac{\left(1 + \dfrac{1}{n}\right)^q - 1}{1 + \dfrac{1}{n} - 1} = q,$$

LEMMA I.

$$1 = (p+1)\,l + \text{limit of } \frac{\beta(1+\epsilon)\,Bn^\beta + \gamma(1+\epsilon')\,Cn^\gamma + \ldots\ldots}{n^{p+1}};$$

where $\epsilon, \epsilon', \ldots$ vanish ultimately. If now ϵ_1 be the greatest of the quantities $\epsilon, \epsilon', \ldots$ and all the terms be positive, which is the most unfavourable case,

$$\frac{\beta(1+\epsilon)\,Bn^\beta + \ldots\ldots}{n^{p+1}} \text{ is less than } (1+\epsilon_1)\,\beta \times \frac{Bn^\beta + \dfrac{\gamma}{\beta}\,Cn^\gamma + \ldots}{n^{p+1}};$$

and, since $\dfrac{\gamma}{\beta}, \dfrac{\delta}{\beta} \ldots\ldots$ are each < 1, this is less than

$$(1+\epsilon_1)\,\beta \times \frac{Bn^\beta + Cn^\gamma + \ldots\ldots}{n^{p+1}}$$

which vanishes in the limit, hence, $1 = (p+1)\,l$ ultimately;

therefore $\dfrac{1}{p+1}$ is the limit required.

Cor. $\dfrac{1}{p+1}$ is evidently also the limit of the sum

$$\frac{1^p + 2^p + \ldots\ldots + \overline{n-1}|^p}{n^{p+1}}, \text{ since } \frac{n^p}{n^{p+1}} \text{ vanishes in the limit.}$$

6. *If a straight line of constant length slide with its extremities in two straight lines, which intersect at a given angle* A, *and* BC, *bc be two positions of the line intersecting in* P, *which become ultimately coincident, find the limits of the ratios* Cc : Bb *and* PC : PB.

By hypothesis, $BC^2 = bc^2$,

but $BC^2 = BA^2 + CA^2 - 2BA \cdot CA \cos A$,

and $bc^2 = bA^2 + cA^2 - 2bA \cdot cA \cos A$;

$\therefore CA^2 - cA^2 = bA^2 - BA^2$

$\qquad\qquad + 2\,\{BA\,(cA + Cc) - (BA + Bb)\,cA\}\cos A;$

$\therefore Cc\,(CA + cA) = Bb\,(BA + bA)$

$\qquad\qquad + 2\,(BA \cdot Cc - cA \cdot Bb)\cos A;$

$\therefore Cc : Bb :: BA + bA - 2cA \cos A : CA + cA - 2BA \cos A$
$:: BA - CA \cos A : CA - BA \cos A$ ultimately.

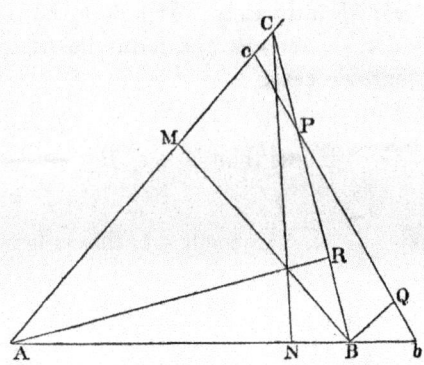

Draw CN, BM perpendicular to AB, AC, therefore the limit of the ratio $Cc : Bb$ is $BN : CM$.

Again, let BQ, drawn parallel to AC, meet bc in Q,

then $\qquad PC : PB :: Cc : BQ$.

And $\qquad Cc : Bb :: BN : CM$ ultimately,
also $\qquad Bb : BQ :: Ab : Ac$;

$\therefore Cc : BQ :: BN . AB : CM . AC$ ultimately.

Draw AR perpendicular to BC, then $BN . AB = BR . BC$ and $CM . AC = CR . BC$;

$\therefore PC : PB :: BR : CR$;

$\therefore PC = BR$ and $PB = CR$.

I.

1. Are the limits of the ratios $y^2 : x$ equal in any of the three equations,

(1) $y^2 = ax^2$, (2) $y^2 = ax - b^2$, (3) $y^2 = ax - x^2$,

when x is indefinitely diminished?

2. Find the limit of $\dfrac{x+3}{1+3x}$,

   (1) when x is indefinitely diminished,

   (2) when x is indefinitely increased.

3. Find the ultimate ratio of the vanishing quantities $ax + bx^2$, $bx + ax^2$, when x is made indefinitely small.

4. Prove that $a - bx$ and $b - ax$ tend to equality as x diminishes to zero, and yet have not their limits equal.

5. BAC, bAc are two triangles, in which AB, Ab and AC, Ac are coincident in direction, and BC, bc intersect in P; prove that if the areas of the triangles are equal, as B, C and b, c approach, each to each, P is ultimately in the point of bisection of BC.

6. If in the right-angled triangles ABC, Abc the perimeters be equal, shew that the ultimate ratio of the vanishing quantities Bb and Cc is $AC + BC : AB + BC$.

Also shew that the ultimate ratio of the areas BPb and CPc is $(BC + AC)(BC - AB) : (BC - AC)(BC + AB)$.

7. ABC is an isosceles triangle, base BC; P, Q are points on the straight lines CA, CB such that AP is always twice BQ; prove that, if PQ and AB intersect in R, and R' be the ultimate position of R, when AP is indefinitely diminished,

$$R'B : AC :: AC : 2BC - AC.$$

8. The extremities of a straight line slide upon two given straight lines, so that the area of the triangle, formed by the three straight lines, is constant; find the limiting position of the chord of intersection of two consecutive positions of the circle described about that triangle.

9. Tangents are drawn to a circular arc at its middle point, and at its extremities, and the three chords are drawn. Prove that the triangle contained by the three tangents is ultimately one half of that contained by the three chords, when the arc is indefinitely diminished.

10. In the last construction shew that one of the triangles contained by two tangents and a chord is eight times either of the two other triangles, when the arc is indefinitely diminished.

11. APQ is a parabola, PM, QN ordinates to the axis AMN, with centres M and N and radii PM, QN two circles are drawn;

prove that, when N approaches indefinitely near to M, if the two circles intersect, the distance of their point of intersection from PM is ultimately equal to the semi-latus rectum. What is the condition that the circles may intersect?

12. PN is an ordinate, and PT a tangent to an ellipse, cutting the axis major in N and T respectively; A being the vertex, shew that as P approaches A, NT is ultimately bisected in A.

13. Two concentric and coaxial ellipses have the sum of the squares of their axes equal; if the curves approach to coincidence with each other, shew that the ratio of the distances of one of their points of intersection from the axes is ultimately equal to the inverse ratio of the squares of the axes.

14. APQ, ABC are two straight lines which are intersected by two fixed lines BP, CQ, prove that, as APQ moves up to ABC, PC and QB intersect in a point whose ultimate position divides BC in the ratio of $AB : AC$.

15. ABC, APQ are drawn to cut a circle from an external point A; BU, CT are tangents at B and C to the circle, meeting APQ in U, T; shew that the ultimate ratio of $PU : QT$, when APQ moves up to ABC, is $AB^2 : AC^2$.

16. PSp, QSq are focal chords of a parabola, prove that, ultimately, when P moves up to Q,

$$PQ : pq :: SP^{\frac{3}{2}} : Sp^{\frac{3}{2}}.$$

17. Find the limit of $\left(1 + \dfrac{1}{n}\right)^n$ when n is indefinitely increased.

18. Find the limit of $\dfrac{1}{n} l_e (1 + n)$ when n is indefinitely diminished.

LEMMA II.

If, in any figure AacE, *bounded by the straight lines* Aa, AE *and the curve* acE, *any number of parallelograms* Ab, Bc, Cd, &c. *be inscribed, upon equal bases* AB, BC, CD, &c., *and having sides* Bb, Cc, Dd, &c. *parallel to the side* Aa *of the figure; and the parallelograms* aKbl, bLcm, cMdn, &c. *be completed; then, if the breadth of these parallelograms be diminished, and the number increased indefinitely, the ultimate ratios which the inscribed figure* AKbLcMdD, *the circumscribed figure* AalbmcndoE, *and the curvilinear figure* AabcdE, *have to one another, are ratios of equality.*

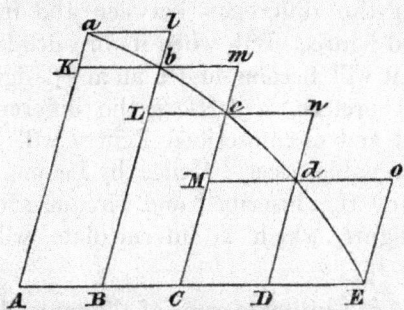

For the difference of the inscribed and circumscribed figures is the sum of the parallelograms *Kl, Lm, Mn, Do*, that is, (since the bases of all are equal) a parallelogram whose base is *Kb*, that of one of them, and altitude the sum of their altitudes, that is, the parallelogram *ABla*. But this parallelogram, since its breadth is diminished indefinitely, [as the number of parallelograms is increased indefinitely,] becomes less than any assignable parallelogram, therefore (by Lemma I), the inscribed and circumscribed figures, and, *a fortiori*, the curvilinear figure, which is intermediate, become ultimately equal.

LEMMA III.

The same ultimate ratios are also ratios of equality, when the breadths of the parallelograms AB, BC, CD, ... *are unequal, and all are diminished indefinitely.*

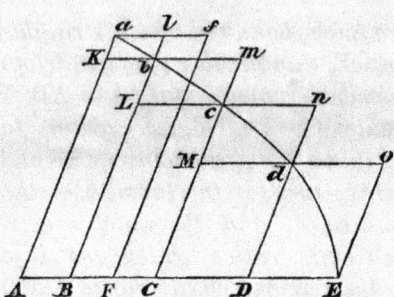

For, let AF be equal to the greatest breadth, and the parallelogram $FAaf$ be completed. This parallelogram will be greater than the difference between the inscribed and circumscribed figures. But, when its breadth is diminished indefinitely, it will become less than any assignable parallelogram. [Therefore, *a fortiori*, the difference between the inscribed and circumscribed figures will become less than any assignable areas. Hence, by Lemma I, the ultimate ratios of the inscribed and circumscribed and the curvilinear figure, which is intermediate, will be ratios of equality.]

COR. 1. Hence the ultimate sum of the vanishing parallelograms coincides [as to area] with the curvilinear figure.

COR. 2. And, *a fortiori*, the rectilinear figure which is bounded by the chords of the vanishing arcs ab, bc, cd, &c. ultimately coincides [as to area] with the curvilinear figure.

COR. 3. As also the rectilinear circumscribed figure, which is bounded by the tangents at the extremities of the same arcs.

COR. 4. And these ultimate figures, with respect to their perimeters acE, are not rectilinear figures, but curvilinear limits of rectilinear figures.

Observations on the Lemmas.

14. The statements of the propositions concerning limits of quantities and their ratios contain:

I. The hypothesis by which the quantities are defined.

II. The manner in which the hypothesis approaches its ultimate form.

III. The ultimate property when the hypothesis is thus indefinitely extended.

The strength of the proofs lies in the examination of the quantities, while the hypothesis is in a finite state, before arrival at the ultimate form, and the deduction of properties by which the relations of the quantities can be pursued accurately to the ultimate state.

If in this manner we analyse the statements of Lemmas II and III: the hypothetical constructions are given in the manner of describing the parallelograms; the extension of the hypothesis towards its ultimate form is the continual increase of the number of parallelograms *in infinitum;* the ultimate property is the equality of the ratio of the sums of the parallelograms and the curvilinear area.

In the proof of the Lemmas, the continual decrease of the parallelograms Al or Af, shews that the conditions of ultimate equality of two quantities are all satisfied, *viz.*, that the sums of the two series of parallelograms, since they are finite, tend continually to equality, and that they approach nearer to each other than by any assignable difference "ante finem temporis," while the number of the parallelograms still remains finite.

Volumes of Revolution.

15. In a manner exactly similar to Lemma II, it may be shewn, that, if Aa be perpendicular to AE, and the whole figure revolve round AE as an axis, the ultimate ratios which the sums of the volumes of the cylinders, generated respectively by the rectangles $Ab, Bc, \ldots\ldots$ and $aB, bC, \ldots\ldots$ and the volume of revolution generated by the curvilinear area AEa have to each other, are ratios of equality.

The figure represents the cylinders generated by the inscribed rectangles.

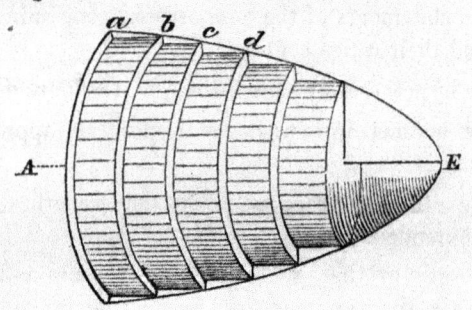

Thus, the difference of the cylinders generated by Ab and aB is the annulus generated by the rectangle ab, and the difference of the two series of cylinders, which have all equal heights AB, BC, ..., is the sum of such annuli, and is easily seen to be the cylinder generated by aB, which, since the height continually diminishes, may be made less than any assignable volume, hence the conditions that the two series may have the same limit are satisfied, and hence also the volume of revolution, which is greater than one sum and less than the other, is ultimately in a ratio of equality to either sum.

The same argument applies, if the revolution be only through a certain angle instead of being complete; in which case the cylinders are replaced by sectors of cylindrical volumes.

Sectorial Areas.

16. The Lemmas may be extended to sectorial areas.

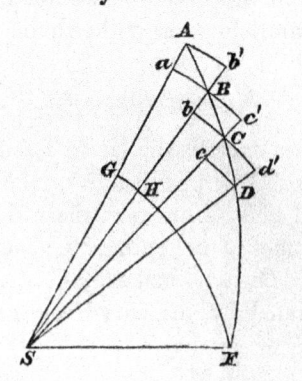

Thus, if $SABCF$ be a sectorial area, and the angle ASF be divided into equal portions ASB, BSC, ... and the circular arcs Ab', aBc', bCd', ... be drawn with center S; then, since the difference of the two series of circular sectors is the sum of the areas ab', bc', ... it is equal to the difference of the greatest and least of the sectors, viz. $AGHb'$, therefore the two areas $SAb'Bc'$...... and $SaBbC$ ...... tend continually to equality as the number of angles is increased, and their magnitudes diminished, and the ratios which these areas have to each other and to the area $SABF$ are ultimately ratios of equality.

Similarly for Lemma III, if ASB, BSC, ... be unequal.

Surfaces of Revolution.

17. The following proposition is the extension of the principles of the Lemmas to the determination of a method for finding the area of a surface of a solid of revolution.

Let CD be a plane curve which generates a surface of revolution by its revolution round AB, a line in its plane.

CD is divided into portions of which PQ is one, PM, QN are perpendicular to AB; Pp, Qq are drawn parallel to AB, and each equal to PQ in length, pm, qn are perpendicular to AB. The surface generated by CD shall be the limit of the sum of the cylindrical surfaces generated by such portions as Pp or Qq.

For, the cylindrical surfaces generated by Pp and Qq are one less, and the other greater than that generated by PQ, since every portion of Qq is at a greater, and every portion of Pp at a less distance from the axis, than the corresponding portions of PQ.

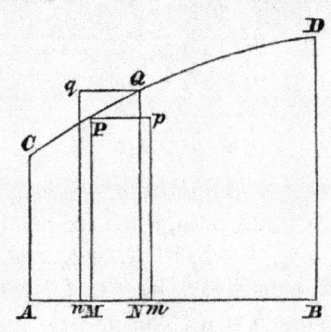

But these surfaces are respectively $2\pi PM \cdot Pp$ and $2\pi QN \cdot Qq$, and their difference is $2\pi (QN - PM) PQ$, and the ratio of this difference to the surfaces themselves is $QN - PM : PM$, or QN, which ratio is ultimately less than any given ratio.

Hence the sums of the surfaces generated by the lines corresponding to Pp and Qq have the ratio of their difference to either sum less than the greatest value of the ratio $QN - PM : PM$, which may be made less than any finite ratio. Therefore the sums of the cylindrical surfaces, and the curved surface, which is intermediate in magnitude to these sums, are ultimately in a ratio of equality.

Centers of Gravity.

18. It is easily seen how the same methods are applicable to determine the position of the center of gravity of any body, since it is known that, if a body be divided into any number of portions, the distance of the center of gravity of the body from any plane is equal to the sum of the moments of all the subdivisions divided by the sum of all the subdivisions.

General Extension.

19. The most general extension may be stated as follows. If any magnitude A be divided into a series of magnitudes $A_1 A_2 \ldots\ldots A_n$, each of which, when their number is increased indefinitely, becomes indefinitely small, and two series of quantities $a_1 a_2 \ldots\ldots a_n$ and $b_1 b_2 \ldots\ldots b_n$ can be found such that

$$a_1 > A_1 > b_1,$$
$$a_2 > A_2 > b_2,$$
$$\ldots\ldots\ldots\ldots\ldots$$
$$a_n > A_n > b_n,$$

and also such that each of the ratios $a_1 - b_1 : a_1, a_2 - b_2 : a_2 \ldots\ldots$ becomes less than any finite ratio, when the number is increased; then $a_1 + a_2 + \ldots\ldots + a_n$, $b_1 + b_2 + \ldots\ldots + b_n$ and A will be ultimately in a ratio of equality. For, let $l : 1$ be equal to the greatest of the ratios $a_1 - b_1 : a_1$, &c.

$$\therefore a_1 - b_1 + a_2 - b_2 + \ldots\ldots : a_1 + a_2 + \ldots\ldots$$

is a ratio less than $l : 1$, and may therefore be made less than any assignable ratio by increasing the number. Therefore the two series $a_1 + a_2 + \ldots\ldots$ and $b_1 + b_2 + \ldots\ldots$ tend continually to equality, and the difference may be made, before the end of the time, less than any assignable magnitude; therefore the three magnitudes are ultimately in a ratio of equality.

20. COR. 1. "Omni ex parte" has not been adopted from the text of Newton, because it requires limitation, for the perimeters do not coincide with the perimeter of the curvilinear area.

In the figure for Lemma II, the perimeter of the inscribed series of parallelograms is

$$AK + Kb + bL + Lc + \ldots\ldots + DA = 2AK + 2AD,$$

and the limit of this perimeter is $2Aa + 2AE$.

The perimeter of the other series of parallelograms being also $2Aa + 2AE$ is constant throughout the change, and has properly no limit.

21. COR. 2. The perimeter of the figure bounded by the chords $ab, bc, \ldots\ldots$ ultimately coincides with that of the curvilinear figure. This coincidence will be discussed under Lemma V.

22. COR. 3. The same is true for the figure formed by the tangents.

23. COR. 4. Instead of "propterea," as in Newton, it is advisable to *state*, as in Whewell's *Doctrine of Limits*, that, if a *finite* portion of a curve be taken, and many successive points in the curve be joined, so as to form a polygon, the sides of which are chords, taken in order, of portions of the curve, when the number of those points is increased indefinitely, the curve will be the limit of the polygon.

Application to the determination of certain areas, volumes, &c.

1. *Area of a parabola bounded by a diameter and an ordinate.*

Let AB, BC be the bounding abscissa and ordinate. Complete the parallelogram $ABCD$.

Let AD be divided into n equal portions, of which suppose AM to contain r and MN to be the $(r+1)^{th}$, draw MP, NQ parallel to AB, meeting the curve in P, Q, and Pn parallel to MN; the curvilinear area ACD is the limit of the sum of the series of parallelograms constructed, as PN, on the portions corresponding to MN.

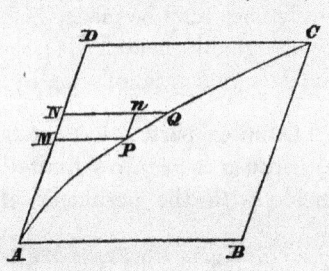

But, parallelogram PN : parallelogram $ABCD$

$$:: PM.MN : CD.AD,$$

and, by the properties of the parabola,

$$PM : CD :: AM^2 : AD^2$$
$$:: r^2 : n^2,$$
$$\text{and } MN : AD :: 1 : n;$$
$$\therefore PM.MN : CD.AD :: r^2 : n^3;$$

therefore, parallelogram $PN = \dfrac{r^2}{n^3} \times$ parallelogram $ABCD$;

hence, the sum of the series of parallelograms

$$= \frac{1^2 + 2^2 + \ldots\ldots + \overline{n-1}|^2}{n^3} \times \text{parallelogram } ABCD,$$

$$\text{and } \frac{1^2 + 2^2 + \ldots\ldots + \overline{n-1}|^2}{n^3} = \frac{1}{3},$$

when the number of parallelograms is increased indefinitely, therefore, proceeding to the ultimate form of the hypothesis,

the curvilinear area $ACD = \dfrac{1}{3}$ of the parallelogram $ABCD$,

and the parabolic area $ABC = \dfrac{2}{3}$ of the parallelogram $ABCD$.

LEMMA II, III.

COR. 1. If we had inscribed the series of parallelograms in ABC, AB being divided into n portions, we should have arrived at the result

$$\frac{1^{\frac{1}{2}}+2^{\frac{1}{2}}+ \ldots\ldots +\overline{n-1}\rceil^{\frac{1}{2}}}{n^{\frac{3}{2}}},$$

for the ratio of the series of parallelograms to the parallelogram $ABCD$, which might thus have been shewn to be ultimately $\frac{2}{3}$.

COR. 2. If BC had been divided into n equal portions, the parallelogram corresponding to PN would have been

$$\frac{n^2-r^2}{n^3} \times \text{parallelogram } ABCD,$$

and the ratio of the area ABC to the parallelogram $ABCD$, the limit of

$$\frac{n^2-1^2+n^2-2^2+ \ldots\ldots +n^2-\overline{n-1}\rceil^2}{n^3},$$

of $1-\dfrac{1^2+2^2+ \ldots\ldots +\overline{n-1}\rceil^2}{n^3}=1-\dfrac{1}{3}=\dfrac{2}{3}$.

2. *Volume of a paraboloid.*

Let AKH be the area of a parabola cut off by the axis AH

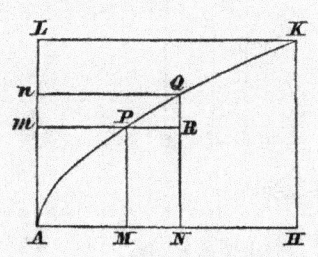

and an ordinate HK, which by its revolution round the axis generates a paraboloid.

Let AH be divided into n equal portions, and on MN the $\overline{r+1}^{\text{th}}$, as base, let the rectangle $PRNM$ be inscribed.

Cylinder generated by PN : cylinder by $AHKL$

$$:: PM^2 . MN : HK^2 . AH.$$

But, $\quad PM^2 : HK^2 :: AM : AH,$
$$:: r : n,$$
and $\quad MN : AH :: 1 : n;$
$$\therefore PM^2 . MN : HK^2 . AH :: r : n^2.$$

Hence cylinder generated by $PN = \dfrac{r}{n^2} \times$ cylinder by $AHKL$; therefore the sum of the cylinders inscribed is

$$\dfrac{1 + 2 + \ldots\ldots + (n-1)}{n^2} \times \text{circumscribed cylinder},$$

but, when n is indefinitely increased,

$$\dfrac{1 + 2 + \ldots\ldots + \overline{n-1}]}{n^2} = \dfrac{1}{2} \text{ ultimately,}$$

and the paraboloid is the limit of the series of inscribed cylinders; hence the volume of the paraboloid is half the cylinder on the same base and of the same altitude.

3. *Volume of a spherical segment.*

Let AHK generate, by its revolution round the diameter AB, the spherical segment whose height is AH.

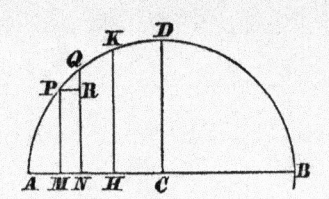

Divide AH, as before,

$$\therefore AM = \dfrac{r}{n} AH,$$

and $PM^2 = AM . MB$

$$= AM . (AB - AM)$$

$$= \dfrac{r}{n} AH . AB - \dfrac{r^2}{n^2} AH^2.$$

LEMMA II, III.

Volume of cylinder generated by PN

$$= \pi PM^2 \cdot MN = \pi \cdot \frac{AH}{n} \cdot PM^2$$

$$= \pi AH^2 \cdot \left(\frac{r}{n^2} AB - \frac{r^2}{n^3} AH\right),$$

whence as before, the limit of the sum

$$= \pi AH^2 \left(\frac{AB}{2} - \frac{AH}{3}\right),$$

which is the volume proposed.

Cor. 1. If $AH = \frac{1}{2} AB = AC$, the segment is a hemisphere whose volume is

$$\pi AC^2 \left(AC - \frac{AC}{3}\right) = \frac{2\pi AC^3}{3},$$

which is two-thirds of the cylinder on the same base and of the same altitude.

Cor. 2. If $AH = 2AC$, the volume of the whole sphere

$$= 4\pi AC^2 \left(AC - \frac{2AC}{3}\right) = \frac{4\pi AC^3}{3}.$$

4. *Area of the surface of a right cone.*

As an illustration of the method of finding surfaces given above, suppose AHK to be a right-angled triangle, which revolves round AH, a side containing the right angle, then the hypothenuse AK generates a conical surface.

Let MN be the $\overline{r+1}|^{\text{th}}$ portion of AH, after division into

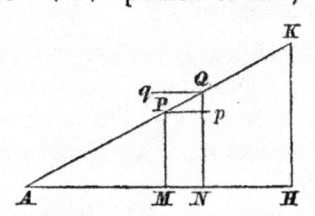

n equal portions, MP, NQ ordinates parallel to HK, Pp, Qq each equal to PQ and parallel to AH.

The areas generated by Pp and Qq respectively are
$$2\pi PM \cdot Pp, \text{ and } 2\pi QN \cdot Qq,$$
and $PM : HK :: AM : AH :: r : n,$
$QN : HK :: AN : AH :: r+1 : n,$
$PQ : AK :: MN : AH :: 1 : n;$

therefore, the areas are $\dfrac{r}{n^2} \cdot 2\pi HK \cdot AK$, and $\dfrac{r+1}{n^2} 2\pi HK \cdot AK$, respectively; and the conical surface is intermediate in magnitude to
$$2\pi HK \cdot AK \times \frac{1+2+\ldots\ldots+(n-1)}{n^2},$$
and $2\pi HK \cdot AK \times \dfrac{1+2+\ldots\ldots+n}{n^2}$,

each of which have for their limit $\pi HK \cdot AK$, which is therefore the area of the conical surface.

The reader may notice the following method of obtaining the conical surface by development, although it is not related to the method of limits.

If a circular sector KAK', traced on paper, be cut out, the bounding radii AK, AK' can be placed in contact, so that the boundary KLK' forms a circle.

The figure so formed will be conical, AK will be the slant side, and HK in the last figure will be the radius of the circular base whose length will be the arc of the sector KAK'.

Hence, the area of the conical surface is equal to that of the sector $KAK' = \dfrac{1}{2} AK \cdot 2\pi HK = \pi HK \cdot AK$.

5. *Mass of a rod whose density varies as the* m^{th} *power of the distance from the extremity.*

Let AB be the rod, and let MN be the $\overline{r+1}\,^{th}$ portion, when its length has been divided into n equal parts; and let $\rho \cdot AM^m$ be the density at M, or the quantity of matter contained in an unit of length of the rod supposed of the same substance as the rod at the point M.

The quantity of matter in MN is intermediate between
$$\rho \cdot AM^m \cdot MN, \text{ and } \rho AN^m \cdot MN,$$

the ratio of the difference of these to either of them being less than any assignable ratio when n is indefinitely increased.

Therefore, since $AM = \dfrac{r}{n} AB$, and $MN = \dfrac{1}{n} AB$, the mass of the whole rod is the limit of

$$\rho \cdot \frac{1^m + 2^m + \ldots + \overline{n-1}|^m}{n^{m+1}} AB^{m+1}$$

$$= \frac{1}{m+1} \times \rho \cdot AB^{m+1}$$

$= \left(\dfrac{1}{m+1}\right)^{th}$ of the mass of a rod of length AB, and of uniform density equal to that of the rod AB at B.

6. *Center of gravity of the volume of a hemisphere.*

Let CAB be a quadrant which by its revolution round the radius CA generates the hemisphere.

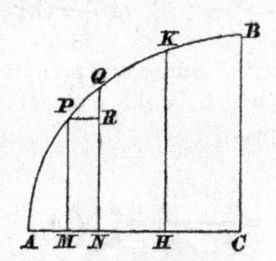

Let MR be the rectangle which generates the rth inscribed cylinder, so that $CM = \dfrac{r}{n} \times CA$, and $MN = \dfrac{1}{n} \times CA$.

If the mass of an unit of volume be chosen as the unit of mass, the mass of the cylinder generated by MR will be

$$\pi PM^2 \cdot MN = \pi (CA^2 - CM^2) MN$$

$$= \left(1 - \frac{r^2}{n^2}\right) \pi CA^2 \cdot \frac{CA}{n}$$

$$= \frac{\pi CA^3}{n} - \frac{(r+1)^2}{n^3} \pi CA^3;$$

hence, the mass of the series of inscribed cylinders will be

$$\pi CA^3 - \frac{1^2 + 2^2 + \ldots\ldots + n^2}{n^3} \pi CA^3;$$

and the mass of the hemisphere

$$= \pi CA^3 - \frac{1}{3} \pi CA^3 = \frac{2}{3} \pi CA^3.$$

Again, the moment of the mass of the cylinder generated by MR, with respect to the base of the hemisphere, will be

$$\pi PN^2 . MN . \frac{CM + CN}{2},$$

which differs from $\pi PN^2 . MN . CM$ by a quantity which vanishes compared with it, and is therefore ultimately

$$\left(\frac{r}{n^2} - \frac{r^3}{n^4}\right) \pi CA^4;$$

therefore the moment of the hemisphere, with respect to its base, is

$$\left(\frac{1}{2} - \frac{1}{4}\right) \pi CA^4, \text{ or } \frac{1}{4} \pi CA^4;$$

hence, the distance of the center of gravity of the volume of the hemisphere from C, which is the moment with respect to the base divided by the mass,

$$= \frac{\frac{1}{4} \pi CA^4}{\frac{2}{3} \pi CA^3} = \frac{3}{8} . CA.$$

7. *Area of an equiangular spiral, between bounding radii* SA, SL.

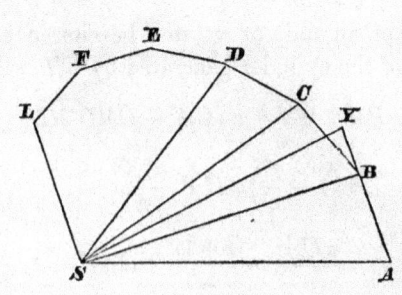

LEMMA II, III.

Let ABC be the polygon whose curvilinear limit is the equiangular spiral (Appendix II.), in which

$$\angle SAB = \angle SBC = \ldots\ldots = \alpha.$$

Draw SY perpendicular to AB.

Then, $\quad SB^2 = SA^2 + AB^2 - 2AB \cdot AY,$

and $\triangle SAB = \tfrac{1}{2} AB \cdot SY$

$\qquad\qquad = \tfrac{1}{2} AB \cdot AY \tan \alpha$

$\qquad\qquad = \tfrac{1}{4} \tan \alpha (SA^2 - SB^2 + AB^2).$

Similarly $\triangle SBC = \tfrac{1}{4} \tan \alpha (SB^2 - SC^2 + BC^2),$

and $\triangle SCD = \tfrac{1}{4} \tan \alpha (SC^2 - SD^2 + CD^2),$

....

$\therefore$ area $ASL = \tfrac{1}{4} \tan \alpha (SA^2 - SL^2 + AB^2 + BC^2 + \ldots).$

But $\quad BC : AB :: CD : BC :: \ldots\ldots :: \lambda : 1,$

where $\lambda : 1$ is a constant ratio, $\lambda < 1$;

$\therefore AB^2 + BC^2 + \ldots\ldots : AB^2 :: 1 + \lambda^2 + \lambda^4 + \text{to } n \text{ terms} : 1,$

$\qquad\qquad\qquad :: 1 - \lambda^{2n} : 1 - \lambda^2;$

$\qquad\qquad\qquad :: SA^2 - SL^2 : SA^2 - SB^2;$

$\therefore AB^2 + BC^2 + \ldots\ldots : SA^2 - SL^2 :: AB^2 : 2AB \cdot AY - AB^2$

$\qquad\qquad\qquad :: AB : 2SA \cos \alpha \text{ ultimately};$

therefore $AB^2 + BC^2 + \ldots\ldots$ vanishes in the limit,

and the curvilinear area $= \tfrac{1}{4} (SA^2 - SL^2) \tan \alpha.$

II.

1. Illustrate the terms "tempore quovis finito" and "constanter tendunt ad æqualitatem" employed in Lemma I, by taking the case of Lemma III, as an example.

2. Shew from the course of the proof of Lemma II, that the ultimate ratio of vanishing quantities may be indefinitely small or great.

3. Shew that the ratio of the area of the parabolic curve, in which $PM^3 \propto AM$, to the area of the circumscribing parallelogram, of which one side is a tangent to the curve at A, is $3 : 4$.

4. Prove that the areas of parabolic segments, cut off by focal chords, vary as the cubes of the greatest breadths of the segments.

5. Shew that the volume of a right cone is one-third of the cylinder on the same base and of the same altitude.

6. Find the center of gravity of the volume of a right cone, by the method of Lemma II.

7. AHK is a parabolic area, AH the axis and HK an ordinate perpendicular to the axis. $AHKL$ the circumscribing rectangle. Shew that the volumes generated by the revolution of AHK round AH, KL, AL and HK are respectively $\frac{1}{2}$, $\frac{8}{5}$, $\frac{4}{5}$ and $\frac{8}{15}$ of the cylinder generated by the rectangle.

8. Find the mass of a rod whose density varies as the distance from an extremity. Find also its center of gravity, and shew that it is in one of the points of trisection of the rod.

9. Find the mass of a circle whose density varies as the mth power of the distance from the center.

10. Find the volume of the solid of revolution generated by the curve in which $a \cdot PM^2 = b^2 \cdot AM - AM^3$, round the line along which AM is measured, PM being perpendicular to AM.

11. Find the area of an hyperbola intercepted between the curve, an asymptote, and two ordinates parallel to the other asymptote.

Shew that, if OAB be the first asymptote, AD, BC the bounding ordinates, O the center, the area required is $OA \cdot AD \, l_e \dfrac{OB}{OA}$.

12. In the curve ACD, BE is an ordinate perpendicular to AD, and FC is the greatest value of BE, and

$$BE : FC :: \sin\left(\pi \cdot \frac{AB}{AD}\right) : 1.$$

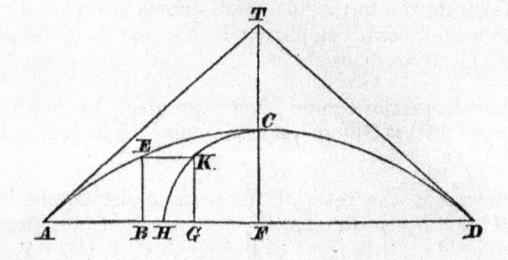

Shew that the area ABE varies as HG, where GK is the ordinate equal to BE of the circle CH, whose centre is F, and radius FC.

13. In the curve of the last problem, shew that the ratio of the area ACD to the triangle whose sides are AD, and the tangents AT, DT at the extremities, is $8 : \pi^2$.

14. In the curve APC, in which the relation between any rectangular ordinate PM, and abscissa OM, is

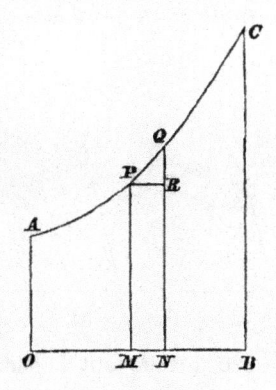

$$OM : OA :: \log \frac{PM}{OA} : 1 ;$$

prove that the area contained between the curve, the abscissa OB, and ordinate BC, is $OA\,(BC - AO)$.

15. Shew that the center of gravity of a paraboloid of revolution is distant from the vertex two-thirds of the length of the axis.

16. Shew that the abscissa and ordinate of the center of gravity of a parabolic area, contained between a diameter AB and ordinate BC, are $\frac{3}{5} AB$ and $\frac{3}{8} BC$, respectively.

17. The limiting ratio of a hyperboloid of revolution, whose axis is the transverse axis, to the circumscribing cylinder, is $1 : 2$, when the altitude is indefinitely diminished, and $1 : 3$, when it is indefinitely increased.

18. The volume of a spheroid is two-thirds of the circumscribing cylinder.

NEWT.   D

LEMMA IV.

If in two figures AacE, PprT, *there be inscribed (as in Lemmas* II, III*) two series of parallelograms, the number in each series being the same, and if, when the breadths are diminished indefinitely, the ultimate ratios of the parallelograms in one figure to the parallelograms in the other be the same, each to each; then, the two figures* AacE, PprT *are to one another in that same ratio.*

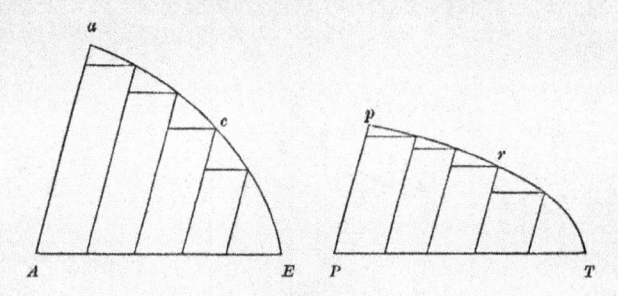

[Since the ratio, whose antecedent is the sum of the antecedents, and whose consequent is the sum of the consequents of any number of given ratios, is intermediate in magnitude between the greatest and least of the given ratios; it follows that the sum of the parallelograms described in $AacE$ is to the sum in $PprT$ in a ratio intermediate between the greatest and least of the ratios of the corresponding inscribed parallelograms; but the ratios of these parallelograms are ultimately the same, each to each, therefore the sums of all the parallelograms described in $AacE$, $PprT$ are ultimately in the same ratio, and so the figures $AacE$, $PprT$ are in that same ratio; for, by Lemma III, the former figure is to the former sum, and the latter figure to the latter sum in a ratio of equality.] Q.E.D.

Cor. Hence, if two quantities of any kind whatever, be divided into any, the same, number of parts; and those parts, when their number is increased, and magnitude diminished indefinitely, assume the same given ratio each to each, viz. the first to the first, the second to the second, and so on in order, the whole quantities will be to one

LEMMA IV.

another in the same given ratio. For, if, in the figures of this Lemma, the parallelograms be taken each to each in the same ratio as the parts, the sums of the parts will be always as the sums of the parallelograms: and, therefore, when the number of the parts and parallelograms is increased, and their magnitude diminished indefinitely, the two quantities will be in the ultimate ratio of parallelogram to parallelogram, that is, (by hypothesis) in the ultimate ratio of part to part.

Observations on the Lemma.

24. The general proposition contained in the Corollary may be proved independently in the following manner:

Let A, B be two quantities of any kind, which can be divided into the same number n of parts, viz. $a_1, a_2, a_3 \ldots\ldots a_n$, and $b_1, b_2, b_3 \ldots\ldots b_n$ respectively; such that, when their number is increased and their magnitudes diminished indefinitely, they have a constant ratio $L : 1$ each to each, so that

$$a_1 : b_1 :: L(1+a_1) : 1,$$
$$a_2 : b_2 :: L(1+a_2) : 1,$$
$$\ldots\ldots\ldots\ldots\ldots$$

where $a_1, a_2, \ldots\ldots$ vanish when n is increased indefinitely.

Then, $a_1 + a_2 + \ldots\ldots : b_1 + b_2 + \ldots\ldots$ being a ratio which is intermediate between the greatest and least of these ratios, each of which is ultimately $L : 1$, we have, if we proceed to the limit,

$$A : B :: L : 1,$$

that is, A and B are in the ultimate ratio of the parts.

25. The proof given in the *Principia* is as follows: "For, as the parallelograms are each to each, so, componendo, is the sum of all to the sum of all, and so the figure $AacE$ to the figure $PprT$, for, by Lemma III, the former figure is to the former sum, and the latter figure to the latter sum in a ratio of equality."

The proof given in the text is substituted for this, because the state of things is not followed up from a finite time to the ultimate form.

D 2

In the last article the ratio $a_1 + a_2 + \ldots : b_1 + b_2 + \ldots$ is

$$L \left(1 + \frac{a_1 b_1 + a_2 b_2 + \ldots}{b_1 + b_2 + \ldots}\right) : 1,$$

and reason ought to have been given why $\dfrac{a_1 b_1 + a_2 b_2 + \ldots}{b_1 + b_2 + \ldots}$ vanishes in the limit.

Application of Lemma IV *to the comparison of certain areas, and the determination of certain volumes, masses, &c.*

1. *Area of an ellipse.*

Let ACa be the major axis of an ellipse, BC the semi-minor axis, ADa the auxiliary circle, and let parallelograms be inscribed whose sides are common ordinates to the two curves.

Let $PMNR$, $QMNU$ be any two corresponding parallelograms. The ratio of these parallelograms is $PM : QM$ or $BC : AC$.

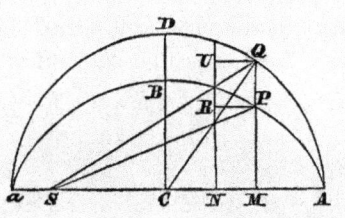

Hence, by Lemma IV,

area of ellipse : area of circle :: $BC : AC$
:: $\pi AC \cdot BC : \pi AC^2$,

but area of circle $= \pi AC^2$.

Therefore, area of ellipse $= \pi AC \cdot BC$.

COR. *Area of a sector of an ellipse, pole in the focus.*

If S be a focus of the ellipse, and SP, SQ be joined,

$\triangle SPM : \triangle SQM :: BC : AC$,

and area APM : area $AQM :: BC : AC$,

hence, area ASP : area $ASQ :: BC : AC$,

but area $ASQ = \triangle SCQ +$ sector ACQ
$$= \tfrac{1}{2} SC . QM + \tfrac{1}{2} AC . \text{arc } AQ;$$
therefore area $ASP = \tfrac{1}{2} \{SC . PM + BC . \text{arc } AQ\}$.

2. In the following proposition it is asserted that when a chord PQ is drawn to a curve from a point P, as Q moves up to P, PQ assumes as its limiting position that of the tangent at P, which is deducible from the idea of a tangent being in the direction of the curve at the point of contact.

Area of a parabolic curve cut off by a diameter and an ordinate to the diameter.

Let AB, BC be the diameter and ordinate, AD the tangent at A, CD parallel to AB, P, Q points near each other, PM, QN and Pm, Qn parallel respectively to AD and AB.

Let QP produced meet BA in T, and complete the parallelograms $TMPS$, $TNQU$.

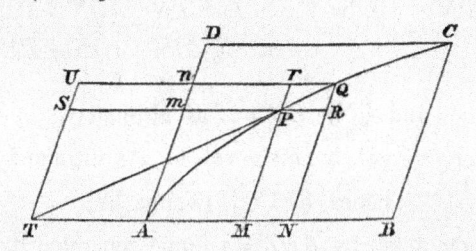

Then since QP is ultimately a tangent at P, $AT = AM$ ultimately, and the parallelogram PU is ultimately double of the parallelogram Pn, and the complements PN, PU are equal; therefore the parallelograms PN, Pn are ultimately in the ratio $2 : 1$.

Hence, in the curvilinear areas ABC, ACD, two sets of parallelograms can be inscribed which are ultimately in the ratio $2 : 1$, each to each; therefore area ABC is ultimately double of area ACD, and is therefore two-thirds of the parallelogram $ABCD$.

3. *Volume of a paraboloid of revolution.*

Let AH be the axis of the parabola APK, $AHKL$ the circumscribing rectangle. Also let PN, Pn be rectangles inscribed in the portions AHK, AKL.

Volume generated by PN
$$= \pi PM^2 . MN = \pi . PM . PN.$$

Volume generated by Pn
$$= \pi QN^2 . AM - \pi PM^2 . AM$$
$$= \pi AM . (QN + PM) . mn$$
$$= \pi (QN + PM) . Pn ;$$

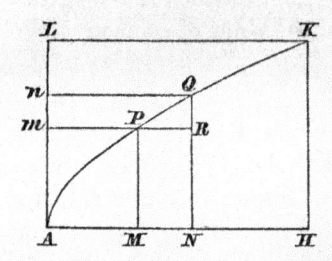

∴ vol. by PN : vol. by Pn :: $PM . PN$: $(QN + PM) Pn$
:: $PM . 2Pn$: $(QN + PM) Pn$, ultimately ;

and $QN + PM = 2PM$ ultimately ;

therefore vol. by PN = vol. by Pn, ultimately ;

hence, by Cor., Lemma IV,

volume generated by AHK = volume generated by AKL,

therefore the volume of paraboloid is half the volume of the circumscribing cylinder.

4. *Center of gravity of a paraboloid of revolution.*

Since the volumes generated by PN and Pn are ultimately equal, the moment of the volume generated by PN with respect to the tangent plane at A

: moment of that generated by Pn

:: distance of the center of gravity of PN

: distance of center of gravity of Pn, ultimately ;

:: AM : $\tfrac{1}{2} Pm$, ultimately,

:: 2 : 1 ;

LEMMA IV. 39

hence the moment of volume generated by AHK
: that of the volume generated by AKL
:: 2 : 1, ultimately,

and the moment of the paraboloid

$$= \frac{2}{3} \text{ moment of the cylinder}$$

$$= \frac{2}{3} \text{ volume of cylinder} \times \frac{AH}{2}:$$

$$\therefore = \frac{2}{3} \text{ volume of paraboloid} \times AH;$$

hence the distance of the center of gravity of the paraboloid from the vertex is two-thirds of the height of the paraboloid.

5. *Area of a cycloid.*

Let P, P' be two points very near each other in a cycloid, Q, Q' corresponding points in the generating circle, p, p' in the evolute, R, R' the intersections of the base with normals Pp, $P'p'$, T, S the intersections of BQ' and $P'p'$ with PQ.

Then $pR = PR = BQ$ (see Appendix II),

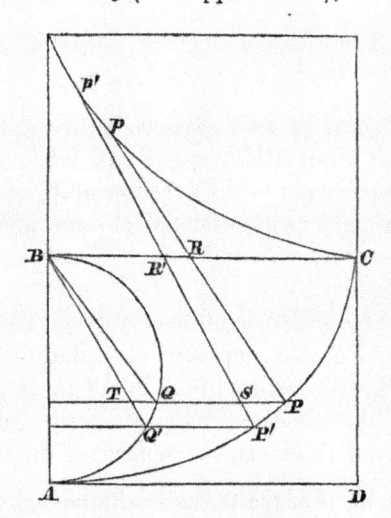

and triangle $p'RR'$: triangle $p'PS$ :: 1 : 4, ultimately.

Also $BQT = p'RR'$, ultimately, since BQ, BT are equal and parallel to pR, $p'R$;

$$\therefore \triangle BQT : \triangle p'PS :: 1 : 4,\text{ ultimately},$$
and $\triangle BQT$: trapezium $PRR'S :: 1 : 3$, ultimately,

and the same being the ultimate ratio of all the inscribed triangles, and trapeziums, whose sums are ultimately the areas of the semicircle and semicycloid; therefore by Cor., Lemma IV,

$$\text{area of semicircle : area of semicycloid} :: 1 : 3,$$

hence the area of the cycloid is three times the generating circle.

6. *Center of gravity and mass of a rod whose density varies as the distance from an extremity.*

Let AB be the rod, MN a small portion of it, then the density at $M \propto AM$.

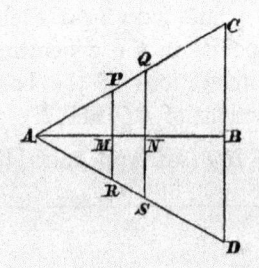

Construct on AB as axis an isosceles triangle CAD, whose base is CD, and draw PMR, QNS parallel to CD; then PR, QS, CD are proportional to the densities at M, N, and B; therefore the mass of MN is proportional to a rectangle intermediate to the rectangles PR, MN and QS, MN, which are ultimately in a ratio of equality.

Hence the mass of MN is ultimately proportional to the mass of the rectangle PR, MN, supposed of uniform density, and the moment of MN, with respect to the line CD, is proportional to the moment of the same rectangle, since their distance is the same; hence, by the Lemma, the moment of the whole rod

: the moment of the triangle with respect to CD
:: the mass of the rod : the mass of the triangle;

therefore the distances of the centers of gravity of the rod and triangle from CD being the same, the center of gravity of the rod is at a distance $\frac{1}{3}AB$ from B.

Also, the mass of MN being proportional to the area PRN, the mass of the rod is proportional to the area of the triangle ACD, and the mass of a rod of uniform density equal to that at B, and of length AB, being in the same proportion to the rectangle AB, CD, is therefore double of the mass of the rod.

7. *Center of gravity of a circular arc.*

Let O be the center of a uniform circular arc ABC, OB the bisecting radius, aBc a tangent at B, OD parallel to ac, and Aa, Cc parallel to OB.

Let QR be the side of a regular polygon described about the

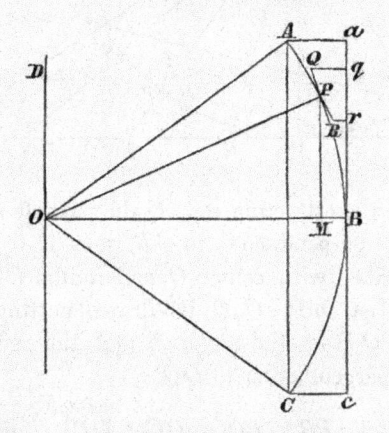

arc, P the point of contact, Qq, Rr perpendicular to ac, and PM to OB. Then, since OP, OB are perpendicular to QR, qr,

$$qr : QR :: OM : OP$$
$$:: OM : OB;$$

but since OM, OB are the distances of the centers of gravity of QR and qr from OD, and $QR \cdot OM = qr \cdot OB$, the moments of QR and qr with respect to OD are in a ratio of equality, and the same is true of every side of the circumscribing polygon; therefore, by Cor., Lemma IV, the moment of the arc, which is ultimately that of the polygon, is equal to the moment of $ac = ac \cdot OB =$ chord $AC \cdot$ radius OB.

Hence, the distance of the center of gravity of the arc from O

$$= \frac{\text{radius} \times \text{chord}}{\text{arc}}.$$

8. *To find the direction and magnitude of the resultant attraction of a uniform rod upon a particle, every particle of the rod being supposed to attract with a force which varies inversely as the square of its distance from the attracted particle.*

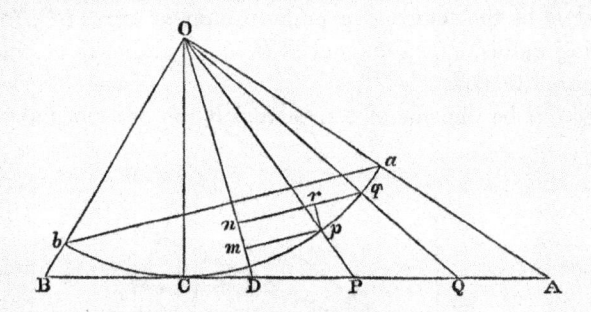

Let AB be the attracting rod, O the particle attracted by the rod; draw OC perpendicular to AB, join OA, OB, and let a circle be described with center O and radius OC meeting OA, OB in a, b. Let OpP, OqQ be drawn cutting off the small portions pq, PQ from the arc aCb and the rod, respectively: and draw PR perpendicular to OQ.

Then, $\quad PR : PQ :: OC : OP \quad$ ultimately,

and $\quad pq : PR :: Op : OP \quad$ ....

$\therefore pq : PQ :: Op^2 : OP^2, \quad$ ....

and if aCb be of the same density as the rod, and attract according to the same law,

attraction of pq on O : attraction of PQ

$$:: \frac{pq}{Op^2} : \frac{PQ}{OP^2} \text{ ultimately.}$$

Therefore, the portions PQ, pq of the rod and arc attract O in the same direction, with forces which are ultimately equal.

Hence, by the Corollary to Lemma IV, the resultant attraction of the rod is the same as that of the arc aCb, which by symmetry is in the direction OD, bisecting the angle AOB.

Again, if qn be perpendicular to OD, pr to qn,

$$pq : qr :: Oq : On;$$

$$\therefore \frac{pq}{Oq^2} \cdot \frac{On}{Oq} = \frac{qr}{OC^2};$$

that is, the resultant attraction of pq in the direction OD is the same as that of qr at the distance OC; hence the whole resultant attraction of AB is

$$\frac{\mu \cdot ab}{OC^2}, \text{ or } \frac{2\mu}{OC} \sin \frac{1}{2} AOB,$$

where μ is the attraction of an unit of mass at the unit distance.

III.

1. Find the volume of a hemisphere, by comparing the volumes generated by the quadrantal sector, and the portion of the circumscribing square which is the difference between the square and the quadrantal sector.

2. Shew that the area of the sector of an ellipse contained between the curve and two central distances, varies as the angle of the corresponding sector of the auxiliary circle.

3. Find the volume of a paraboloid by comparison with the area of a triangle whose vertex and base are those of the generating parabola.

4. Find the center of gravity of the paraboloid by reference to the same triangle.

5. Find the mass of a straight rod, whose density varies as the square of the distance from the extremity, by comparison with a cone whose axis is the rod.

6. Find the volume of a paraboloid generated by the revolution of a semi-cubical parabola, in which $PM^2 \propto AM^3$, by means of a cone on the same axis.

7. Shew that the orthogonal projection of any plane area on another plane is the given area × the cosine of the inclination of the two planes.

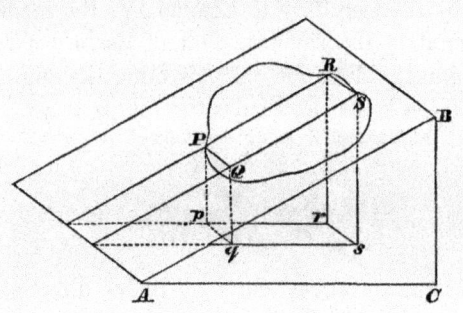

Prove that, *pqsr* being the projection of the inscribed parallelogram *PQSR*,

$$pqsr : PQSR :: \cos BAC : 1,$$

and deduce the proposition by Lemma IV.

8. P is any point of a curve OP, OX, OY any lines drawn at right angles through O, PM, PN perpendicular to OX, OY respectively. Prove that, if area OPM : area $OPN :: m : 1$, and the whole system revolve about OX, volumes generated by OPM, OPN will be as $m : 2$.

9. Prove that the surface generated by the revolution of a semi-circle round its bounding diameter is to the curved surface generated by the revolution of the same semicircle round the tangent at the extremity of the diameter, in the ratio of the length of the diameter to the length of the arc of the semicircle.

10. Common ordinates MPP', NQQ' are drawn to two ellipses which have a common minor axis, and the outer of which touches the directrices of the inner; shew that the area of the surface generated by the revolution of PQ about the major axis bears a constant ratio to the area $MP'Q'N$.

11. Two catenaries touch at the vertex, and the inner one is half the linear distance of the outer; from the directrix of the outer are drawn two ordinates MPQ, $M'P'Q'$, shew that the area of the surface generated by the arc PP' about the directrix is equal to $2\pi \times$ area $MQQ'M'$.

LEMMA V.

All the homologous sides of similar figures are proportional whether curvilinear or rectilinear, and their areas are in the duplicate ratio of the homologous sides.

[Similar curvilinear figures are figures whose curved boundaries are curvilinear limits of corresponding portions of similar polygons.

Let $SABCD$ ......, $sabcd$ ...... be two similar polygons of which $SA, AB, BC,$ ...... are homologous to $sa, ab, bc,$ ...... respectively.

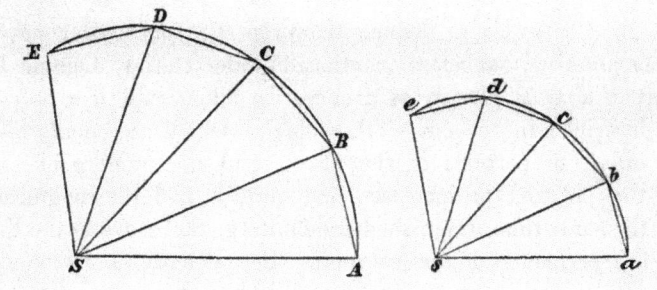

Then, $\quad AB : ab :: SA : sa.$

Similarly, $\quad BC : bc :: AB : ab :: SA : sa$

$\quad\quad\quad\quad CD : cd :: BC : bc :: SA : sa,$

....

Therefore, componendo,

$\quad AB + BC + CD + \ldots : ab + bc + cd + \ldots :: SA : sa.$

Now this, being true for all similar polygons, will be true in the limit, when the number of the sides $AB, BC, \ldots$ and $ab, bc, \ldots$ is increased, and their lengths diminished indefinitely; if, therefore, AE, ae be curves which pass through the angular points $A, B,$ ...... and $a, b,$ ...... of the polygons, these curves are the curvilinear limits of $AB + BC + \ldots$ and $ab + bc + \ldots$ and are the boundaries of similar curvilinear figures: and therefore

$\quad\quad$ the curved line AE : the curved line ae

$\quad\quad\quad\quad :: SA : sa :: SE : se.$

Again,   polygon $SABC \ldots$: polygon $sabc \ldots$ :: $SA^2 : sa^2$, and this being true always, is true in the limit;

$\therefore$ (Lemma III, Cor. 2),

curvilinear area SAE : curvilinear area sac
:: $SA^2 : sa^2$
:: $AE^2 : ae^2$
:: $SE^2 : se^2$.

Q. E. D.]

Observations on the Lemma.

26. In order to deduce the properties of similar curves, it is premised as before mentioned under Cor. 4, Lemma III, that, if a *finite* portion of a curve be taken, and if a polygon be inscribed in the curve, the sides of which are chords taken in order, of portions of the curve, and the number of sides of the polygon be increased indefinitely, and the magnitudes at the same time diminished indefinitely, the curve is the limit of the perimeter of the polygon. See Whewell's *Doctrine of Limits*.

It is *not* assumed that each chord is equal to the corresponding arc ultimately: this is afterwards proved for a continuous curve in Lemma VII.

Criteria of Similarity.

27. From the *definition* of similar curve lines, that they are curvilinear limits of homologous portions of similar polygons, the following criteria of similarity can be deduced, which are each very convenient in practice; namely,

(1) One curve line is similar to another when, if *any* polygon be inscribed in one, a similar polygon can be inscribed in the other.

(2) If two curves be similar, and any point S be taken in the plane of one curve, another point s can be found in the plane of the other, such that, *any* radii SP, SQ being drawn in the first, radii sp, sq can be drawn in the second, inclined at

the same angle as the former, and such that the following proportion will hold,
$$sp : sq :: SP : SQ.$$

(3) If two curves be similar, and in the plane of one curve *any* two lines OX, OY be drawn, two other lines ox, oy can be drawn in the plane of the other curve, inclined at the same angle, having the property that the abscissa and ordinate OM, MP of any point P in the first being taken, the abscissa and ordinate om, mp of a corresponding point p in the second will be proportional to the former, viz.,
$$om : mp :: OM : MP.$$

And the converse propositions can also be deduced, that if these proportions hold, the curves will be similar.

28. In order to illustrate test (1), let the arcs AB, ab of two circles have the same center C, and let the bounding radii be coincident in direction.

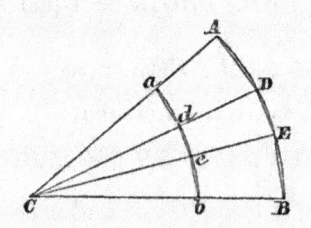

Let $ADEB$ be *any* polygon inscribed in AB, and let CD, CE cut ab in d, e; join ad, de, eb; these are parallel to AD, DE, EB, respectively, and $ad : de : eb :: AD : DE : EB$, hence, $adeb$ is similar to $ADEB$; and therefore the arcs ab, AB are similar.

Deduction of criteria of similarity.

29. Test (1) follows immediately from the definition.

Test (2) may be deduced as follows.

If $ABCD...$, $abcd...$, be corresponding portions of similar polygons, AB, BC, ... ab, bc, ... being homologous sides, and AS,

$BS, \ldots$ be drawn to any point S, construct the triangle sab equiangular with SAB and join $sb, se, \ldots$ (See fig. p. 45.)

Then $sb : SB :: ab : AB :: bc : BC$,
and $\angle SBC = \angle sbc$;

therefore, SBC, sbc are similar triangles,

and $sc : SC :: sb : SB :: sa : SA$;

and similarly for sd, se, &c.

Hence, if two polygons are similar, and any point be taken in one, another point can be found in the other, such that the radii drawn to corresponding angular points are proportional and include the same angles.

If we now increase the number of sides indefinitely and diminish their magnitude, the same property holds with respect to the curvilinear limit of the polygon.

30. The converse proposition may be thus proved.

If the angles ASB, $BSC \ldots$ be equal to the angles asb, $bsc, \ldots$

and $SA : SB : SC \ldots :: sa : sb : sc \ldots$

the triangles ASB, asb, &c. are similar,

and $AB : ab :: SB : sb :: BC : bc$,

$\therefore AB : BC : CD \ldots :: ab : bc : cd \ldots$

or the part of the polygons are similar which are bounded by corresponding radii.

Hence, proceeding to the ultimate form of the hypothesis, the similarity of the curves which are the curvilinear limits of the corresponding portions of the polygons is proved.

Test (3) can be deduced in a similar manner.

Centers of Similitude.

31. If two similar curves are so situated that a point can be found, such that the radii, drawn from that point, either in the same or opposite directions, are in a constant ratio, such a point is called a *center of similitude*.

LEMMA V.

If the radii are measured in the same direction, the point is a center of *direct* similitude, and of *inverse* similitude if they are in opposite directions.

It is easily shewn that there can only be one center of similitude of one kind.

Properties of similar Curves, and application of tests of Similarity.

1. *Similar conterminous arcs, which have their chords coincident, have a common tangent.*

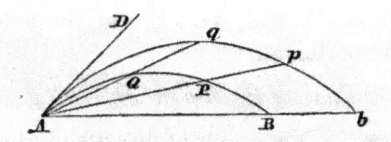

Let APB, Apb be similar conterminous arcs, ABb the line of their chords, AQq, APp any straight lines meeting the curves in Q, q and P, p respectively;

$$\therefore AQ : Aq :: AP : Ap;$$

hence, AP, Ap are similar portions of the curve;

therefore, by Lemma V,

arc AP : arc Ap :: AP : Ap :: AB : Ab;

therefore arcs AP, Ap vanish simultaneously,

or, when AP assumes its limiting position AD for the curve APB, this is also the limiting position for Apb, that is, the curves have a common tangent.

2. *To find the centers of direct and inverse similitude of any two circles.*

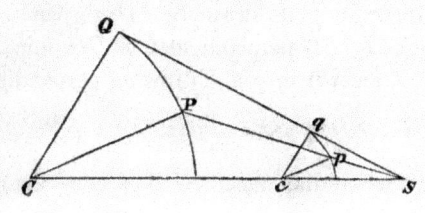

Let S be the intersection of two common tangents to the circles which intersect in the *produced* line Cc joining their centers, and let CQ, cq be radii at the points of contact.

Draw SpP through S cutting the circles in p, P,

Cq is parallel to CQ,

and $CP : cp :: CQ : cq :: CS : cS$;

$\therefore CS : CP :: cS : cp$,

also CPS, cpS are each greater or each less than a right angle, and CSP is common to the triangles CPS, cpS, therefore the triangles are similar (Euclid, VI. 7), and the sides about the angle CSP are proportional,

that is, $SP : Sp :: SC : Sc$;

therefore S is the center of direct similitude.

Similarly, the intersection of two common tangents which cross between the circles is a center of inverse similitude.

3. *To find the condition of similarity of two conic sections.*

Let the conic sections be placed so that their directrices are parallel and foci coincident, and let SpP be any line through the

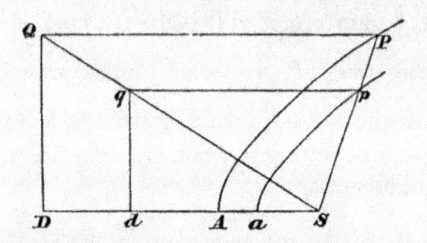

focus meeting them in p, P, draw $SaAD$ perpendicular to the directrix DQ of AP, PQ perpendicular to DQ, join SQ, and let pq, parallel to PQ, meet it in q, and draw qd perpendicular to SD.

Then $\quad Sd : SD :: Sq : SQ :: Sp : SP$;

and, if the curves be similar, $Sp : SP$ is a constant ratio, therefore $Sd : SD$ is a constant ratio,

and dq is a fixed straight line for all positions of p,

also, since $pq : Sp :: PQ : SP$,

$pq : Sp$ is a constant ratio;

therefore qd is the directrix of ap, and the constant ratio being the same in both, the eccentricities are the same.

4. *All parabolas are similar.*

For, using the last figure, if DQ, dq be the parallel directrices and S the focus of the two parabolas AP, ap, draw SpP meeting them in p, P, and let pq, PQ be perpendicular to dq, DQ; then

$$Sp = pq, \text{ and } SP = PQ;$$

$$\therefore Sp : pq :: SP : PQ,$$

and $\angle Spq = \angle SPQ$,

therefore the triangles are similar and SqQ is a straight line,

hence, $Sp : SP :: Sq : SQ$,
$$:: Sd : SD,$$
$$:: Sa : SA;$$

therefore the parabolas ap, AP are similar.

5. *All cycloids are similar.*

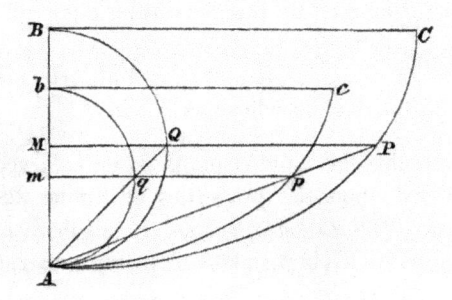

Let two cycloids APC, Apc be placed so that their vertices are the same, and their axes coincident in direction, and describe circles on the axes AB, Ab as diameters. Draw AqQ cutting the circles in q, Q.

Then, since the segments Aq, AQ are similar,
$$\text{arc } Aq : \text{arc } AQ :: Aq : AQ.$$
And, if mqp, MQP be ordinates to the cycloids,
$$\text{arcs } Aq, AQ = qp, QP \text{ respectively};$$
$$\therefore qp : QP :: Aq : AQ,$$
and ApP is a straight line.

Also $Ap : AP :: Aq : AQ$,
$$:: Ab : AB, \text{ a constant ratio};$$
hence, a condition of similarity is satisfied.

OBS. In this position of the cycloids the point A is a center of direct similitude.

6. The properties of similar curves may be employed to construct curves which satisfy given conditions, as in the following problem.

To construct a cycloid which shall have its vertex at a given point, its base parallel to a given straight line, and which shall pass through a given point.

Let A be the given vertex, AB perpendicular to the given line, P the given point.

In AB take any point b, and with the generating circle, whose diameter is Ab, describe a cycloid Apc, join AP intersecting this cycloid in p.

Take AB a fourth proportional to Ap, AP, and Ab; then AB will be the diameter of the generating circle of the required cycloid.

For, since $Ap : AP :: Ab : AB$, and all cycloids are similar, P is a point in the cycloid whose axis is AB.

7. Instruments for copying plans on an enlarged or reduced scale are founded upon the properties of similar figures, as the *Pantagraph* and the *Eidograph*; as are also other methods of copying, such as by dividing plans or pictures into squares.

LEMMA V. 53

The Pantagraph is an instrument for drawing a figure similar to a given figure on a smaller or larger scale; one of its forms is as in the figure; AD, EF, GC and AE, DG, FC are two sets of parallel bars, joined at all the angles by compass-joints; at B is

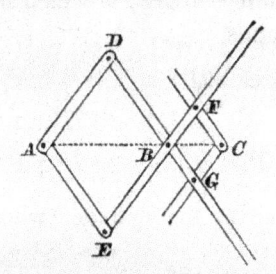

a point, which serves to fix the instrument to the drawing board, at A is a point, which is made to pass round the figure to be reduced or enlarged; at C is a hole for a pencil pressed down by a weight, and the pencil traces the similar figure, altered in dimensions in the ratio of $BC : AB$, or $BF : AD$.

The similarity of the figure traced by the pencil is a consequence of continual similarity of the triangles ABD, BFC.

By changing the positions of the pegs at F and G the figure described by C may be made of the required dimensions.

For a description of the Eidograph, invented by Professor Wallace, see the *Transactions of the Royal Society of Edinburgh*, Vol. XIII.

8. *Volume of a cone whose base is a plane closed figure of any form.*

Let V be the vertex, AB the base, VH perpendicular to the base from V: let VH be divided into n equal portions, of which

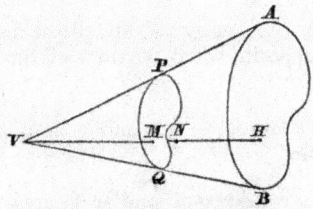

MN is the $\overline{r+1}|^{\text{th}}$; and let PQ be the section through M parallel to AB.

Let A be the area of the base.

Then, if VPA be *any* generating line,

$$PM : AH :: VM : VH;$$

therefore, PQ is similar to AB, in which M, H are similar and similarly situated points,

$$\text{and area } PQ : \text{area } AB :: r^2 : n^2,$$
$$MN : VH :: 1 : n;$$
$$\text{hence area } PQ.MN : A.VH :: r^2 : n^3;$$

therefore the volume of the cylinder whose base is PQ and height MN

$$= \frac{r^2}{n^3} \times A.VH;$$

and the volume of the cone $= A.VH \times$ limit of

$$\frac{1^2 + 2^2 + \ldots\ldots + \overline{n-1}|^2}{n^3}$$

$=$ one-third of the cylinder whose base is AB and height VH.

IV.

1. Apply a criterion of similarity to shew that segments of a circle, which contain equal angles, are similar.

2. From the definition of an ellipse, as the locus of a point the sum of whose distances from two fixed points is constant, shew that the ellipses are similar when the eccentricities are the same.

3. Prove that the center of an ellipse is a center of inverse similitude to two opposite equal portions of the circumference of the ellipse.

4. Employ the properties of similar figures to inscribe a square in a given semicircle.

5. Construct, by means of similar figures, two circles, each of which shall touch two given straight lines and pass through a given point.

LEMMA V.

6. If A be the vertex of a conical surface, G the center of gravity of the base, H that of the volume of the conical figure,

$$AH = \frac{3}{4} AG.$$

7. Find the centers of gravity, the surface and volume of a right cone on a circular base. Explain why the method does not apply to the surface of an oblique cone, while it does to the volume.

8. Deduce the position of the center of gravity of a circular sector from that of a circular arc; shew that the distance from the center is $\frac{2}{3} \cdot \frac{\text{radius} \times \text{chord}}{\text{arc}}$.

9. Shew that all the spirals of Archimedes, in which the radius vector varies as the angle, are similar.

10. Find the condition of similarity of equiangular spirals.

11. Shew that arcs of catenaries are similar, whose horizontal abscissæ from the lowest points are proportional to the tensions at the extremities.

12. All Lemniscates are similar.

LEMMA VI.

If any arc ACB *given in position be subtended by a chord* AB, *and if at any point* A, *in the middle of continued curvature, it be touched by the straight line* AD *produced in both directions, then, if the points* A, B, *approach one another and ultimately coincide; the angle* BAD *contained by the chord and tangent will diminish indefinitely and ultimately vanish.*

For, if that angle does not vanish, the arc ACB will contain with the tangent AD an angle equal to a rectilineal angle,

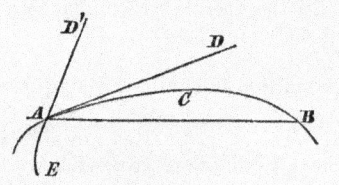

and therefore, the curvature at the point A will not be continuous, which is contrary to the hypothesis, that A was in the middle of continuous curvature.

Definitions of a tangent to a curve.

32. (1) If a straight line meet a curve in two points A, B, and if B move up to A, and ultimately coincide with A, AB in its limiting position is a tangent to the curve at the point A.

If two portions of a curve, EA and AB, cut one another at a finite angle in A, there are two tangents, AD, AD', which are the limiting positions of straight lines AB and AE when B and E move up to A along the different portions AE and AB of the curve respectively. And similarly, if there be a multiple point in A, in which several branches of the curve cut one another at finite angles.

(2) The tangent is the direction of the side of the polygon, of which the curve is the curvilinear limit, when the number of sides are increased indefinitely.

LEMMA VI.

This is founded on the same idea of a tangent as definition (1).

(3) The tangent to a curve at any point is the direction of the curve at that point.

In order to apply geometrical reasoning to the tangent by employing this definition, we are obliged to explain the notion of the direction of a curve, by taking two points very near to one another, and asserting that the direction of the curve is the limiting position of the line joining these points when the distance becomes indefinitely small, which reduces this definition to the preceding.

Observations on the Lemma.

33. "Curvatura Continua," if we consider curves as the curvilinear limits of polygons, requires the curves to be limits of polygons whose angles continually increase as the number of the sides increase, and may be made to differ from two right angles by less than any assignable angle before the assumption of the ultimate form of the hypothesis.

If, however, as we increase the number of sides and diminish their magnitude, one of the angles remains less than two right angles by any finite difference, the curvature of the curvilinear limit is discontinuous, and the form is that of a pointed arch; in which the two portions cut one another at a finite angle.

A curve may be of continued curvature for one portion between two points, while for another its curvature changes "per saltum."

Thus, if ABC be a curve forming at B a pointed arch, it may

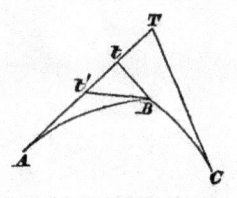

be of continued curvature from B to A and from C to B, though not from C to A.

In this case the tangents in passing from C to A assume all positions intermediate to *CT*, *Bt*, and *Bt'*, *TA*, but at *B* they pass from *Bt* to *Bt'* without assuming the intermediate positions.

34. "In medio curvaturæ continuæ," implies that the point *A* in the enunciation of the Lemma is not such a point as *B* in the last figure, but that, in passing from a point on one side of *A* to another on the other side, the tangents pass through all the intermediate positions.

The curvature is supposed to be in the same direction in the figure of the Lemma, which in all curves of continued curvature is possible, if *B* be taken sufficiently near to *A* at the commencement of the change in the construction.

If the point *A* be not "in medio curvaturæ continuæ," two tangents *AD*, *AD'* may be drawn at *A* to the two parts of the curve, and the curve *BCA* makes a finite angle with one of the tangents *AD'*.

But, even in this case, the angle between the chord and that tangent which belongs to the portion of the curve considered, continually diminishes and ultimately vanishes.

Definition of the subtangent.

35. The part of the line of abscissæ intercepted between the tangent at any point and the foot of the ordinate of that point is called the *subtangent*.

36. The subtangent may be employed as follows, to find a tangent at any point of a curve.

Let *OM*, *MP* be the abscissa and ordinate of a point *P* in

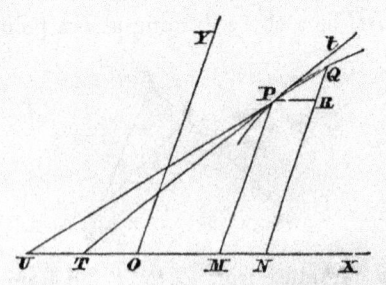

a curve, and let *Q* be a point near *P*, *ON*, *NQ* its abscissa and ordinate.

LEMMA VI.

Let QPU meet OX the line of abscissæ in U; then, if PR parallel to OM meet QN in R;

$$PM : MU :: QR : PR$$
$$:: QN - PM : ON - OM.$$

Now as Q approaches to P, the limiting position of QPU is that of the tangent at P (Lemma VI), viz. tPT,

and $PM : MT$ is the limiting ratio of

$$QN - PM : ON - OM.$$

This ratio determines the position of T, and therefore of the tangent at P, and, if the ordinates be perpendicular to the abscissæ, is the trigonometrical tangent of the angle made by the tangent with the line of abscissæ.

Illustrations.

1. *To find the subtangent in the common parabola.*

Since $\qquad PM^2 : QN^2 :: OM : ON;$

$\therefore QN^2 - PM^2 : PM^2 :: ON - OM : OM,$

and $QN - PM : PM :: ON - OM : MT,$

$QN + PM : PM :: 2 : 1$, ultimately,

$\therefore QN^2 - PM^2 : PM^2 :: 2(ON - OM) : MT,$

$\therefore MT = 2OM.$

2. *Surface of a segment of a sphere.*

Let AKH be the portion of a circle which generates by revolution round AH the spherical segment, O the center of the circle, PQ the chord of a small arc, PM, QN perpendicular to AH.

Let $AOCD$ be the rectangle circumscribing the quadrant, and generating the circumscribing cylinder.

Produce MP, NQ, HK to meet CD in p, q, k. Since PQ is in its limiting position a tangent at P, PQ is ultimately perpendicular to the radius OP, also pq is perpendicular to MP;

$$\therefore PQ : pq :: OP : PM, \text{ ultimately,}$$

and the surface generated by PQ is ultimately $2\pi PM.PQ$ (Art. 17),

$$= 2\pi . OP . pq = \text{the surface generated by } pq.$$

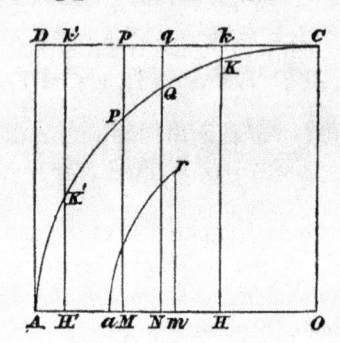

The same is true for each side of the inscribed polygon, when the number is indefinitely increased.

Hence, the surface generated by AK, or the surface of the spherical segment, is equal to the surface of the circumscribed cylinder cut off by the plane of the base of the segment.

COR. Hence also, the surface of any belt of a sphere cut off by two parallel planes is equal to the corresponding belt of the cylindrical surface.

3. *Center of gravity of a belt of the surface of a sphere contained between parallel planes.*

The moment of the belt generated by PQ with respect to the plane through A, perpendicular to AH, is evidently ultimately equal to that of the belt generated by pq; therefore the moment of any belt generated by $K'K$ is equal to that of the corresponding belt by $k'k$.

Hence, the centers of gravity of the two belts are coincident, viz. in the bisection of HH', that is, the distance of the center of gravity of a spherical belt, contained between parallel planes, is half-way between the two planes.

4. *Volume of a spherical sector.*

Let the spherical sector be generated by the revolution of the sector AOP.

LEMMA VI. 61

The volume of the spherical sector is equal to the limit of the sum of a series of pyramids whose vertices are in O, and the sum of whose bases is ultimately the area of the surface of the segment, and the volume of each pyramid is $\frac{1}{3}$ base × altitude.

Hence the volume of the spherical sector is one-third of area of the surface of the spherical segment × radius

$$= \tfrac{1}{3} . 2\pi . AD . Dp . AO$$

$$= \frac{2\pi}{3} . AM . AO^2$$

$$= \frac{2\pi AO^3}{3} \text{ vers } POA.$$

5. *Center of gravity of a spherical sector.*

If we suppose each of the pyramids on equal bases, they may be supposed collected in their centers of gravity, whose distances are $\frac{3}{4} AO$ from O ultimately, and they form a mass which may be distributed uniformly over the surface of a spherical segment whose radius is $\frac{3}{4} AO$, viz. that generated by ar, whose center of gravity is in the bisection of am, rm being perpendicular to AH.

Therefore the distance of the center of gravity of the spherical sector from O

$$= \tfrac{1}{2} (Oa + Om)$$
$$= \tfrac{1}{2} Oa (1 + \cos r Oa)$$
$$= \tfrac{3}{4} OA . \cos^2 \tfrac{1}{2} POA.$$

If the angle POA become a right angle, the distance of the center of gravity of the corresponding sector, which in this case becomes the hemisphere, is $\frac{3}{8} OA$, as in page 30.

6. *If* SY *be the perpendicular on the tangent* PY *at* P *in a curve,* Y *will trace out a curve, and if* YZ *be a tangent to the locus of* Y, SZ *perpendicular to it,*

$$SY^2 = SP . SZ.$$

Let P' be a point near P, SY' perpendicular on $P'P$, SZ perpendicular on $Y'Y$.

Since angles SYP, $SY'P$ are right angles, a semicircle on SP passes through Y, Y'; therefore the angles $SY'Y$, SPY, in the same segment are equal, and the right angles SZY', SYP are equal; therefore the triangles SPY, $SY'Z$ are similar,

and $SZ : SY' :: SY : SP$,

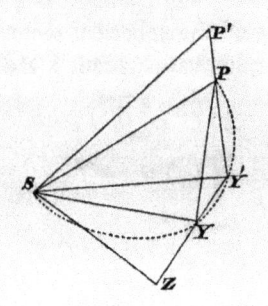

but, ultimately, as P' moves up to P, $P'PY'$ becomes the tangent at P, and $Y'YZ$ that at Y to its locus, also $SY' = SY$;

$$\therefore SZ \cdot SP = SY^2.$$

V.

1. In the curve in which the abscissa varies as the cube of the ordinate, shew that the subtangent is three times the abscissa.

2. If PY a tangent to an ellipse at P meet the auxiliary circle at Y, and ST be perpendicular to the tangent at Y, ST' varies inversely as HP.

3. AB is the diameter of a semicircle AQB, in which AM is taken equal to BN, QN is an ordinate, AQ meets the ordinate corresponding to AM in P, the locus of P is the Cissoid; shew that the subtangent at $P : AM :: 2AN : 2AN + AB$.

4. In the Lemniscate, if SY be perpendicular to the tangent at Q, and SA be the greatest value of SQ, shew that

$$SQ^3 = SY \cdot SA^2.$$

LEMMA VII.

If any arc, given in position, be subtended by the chord AB, *and at the point* A, *in the middle of continued curvature, a tangent* AD *be drawn, and the subtense* BD, *then, when* B *approaches to* A *and ultimately coincides with it, the ultimate ratio of the arc, the chord, and the tangent to one another is a ratio of equality.*

For whilst the point B approaches to the point A, let AB, AD be supposed always to be produced to points b and d at a finite distance, and bd be drawn parallel to the subtense BD, and let the arc Acb be always similar to the arc ACB, and have, therefore, ADd for its tangent at A.

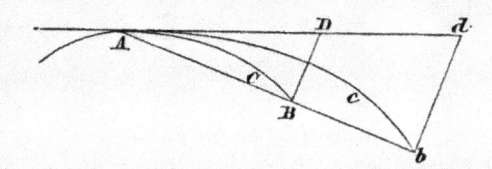

But, when the points B, A coincide, the angle bAd by the preceding Lemma, will vanish, and therefore, the straight lines Ab, Ad, which are always finite, and the arc Acb which lies between them [and is of continuous curvature in one direction, if the change commence when B is near enough to A], will coincide ultimately, and therefore will be equal.

Hence also, the straight lines AB, AD, and the intermediate arc ACB, which are always proportional to them, will vanish together, and have an ultimate ratio of equality to one another.

Cor. 1. Hence, if through B, BF be drawn parallel to the tangent, always cutting any straight line AF passing through A in F, this BF will have ultimately to the vanishing arc ACB a ratio of equality, since, if the paral-

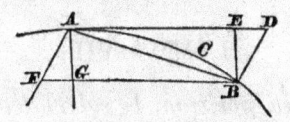

lelogram $AFBD$ be completed, it has always a ratio of equality to AD.

COR. 2. And if, through B and A be drawn many straight lines BE, BD, AF, AG cutting the tangent AD and BF, parallel to it; the ultimate ratio of all the abscissæ AD, AE, BE, BG and of the chord and arc AB to one another will be a ratio of equality.

COR. 3. And, therefore, all these lines in every argument concerning ultimate ratios may be used indifferently one for the other.

Observations on the Lemma.

37. The *subtense* of the *angle of contact* of an arc is a straight line drawn from one extremity of the arc to meet, at a finite angle, the tangent to the arc at the other extremity.

This subtense is the secant which defines the limited line called, in the Lemma, "the tangent."

The chord is called by Newton "the subtense of the arc," see Lemma XI.

38. In the construction for this Lemma, BD must be a subtense, *i.e.* inclined throughout the change of position at a finite angle to the tangent or chord, for, otherwise, the angles BAD and ABD being both small, the ultimate ratio of the chord to the tangent might be any finite ratio instead of being one of equality.

LEMMA VII. 65

This is the only limitation of the motion of *BD*; the following figure represents changes which may take place in the approach towards the ultimate state of the hypothesis.

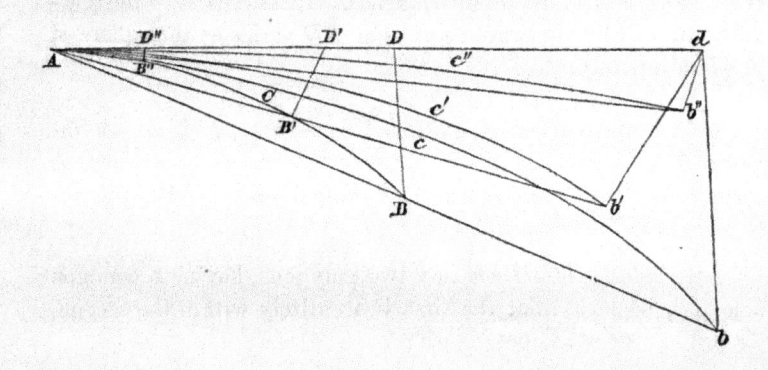

Here *b, d* are the distant points, that is, points at a finite distance from *A*; *BD, B'D', B"D"* are consecutive positions of the subtense, when *B* approaches towards *A*, and *db, db', db"* are parallel to these, *Ac'b', Ac"b"* are the forms of *Acb changed* so as to be always similar to the corresponding portion of *ACB* cut off by the chord.

39. It should be remarked that the curve *Acb* is not intermediate in *magnitude* to the two lines *Ab, Ad*, but only in *position*, for example, *Ab* may be equal to *Ad*, if *BD* make equal angles with the two lines, and the curve line is greater than either *Ab* or *Ad*; but it becomes in all cases less bent, until it is ultimately rectilinear; hence the three *Acb, Ab, Ad* will be ultimately equal, the only alternative being that the curve

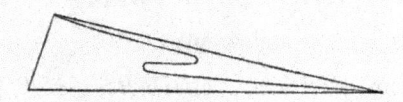

becomes doubled up as in the figure, which is precluded by the supposition that the curvature, near *A*, is continued in the same direction throughout the passage from *B* to *A*.

40. *The subtense ultimately vanishes compared with the arc.*

For $BD : ACB :: bd : Acb$,

and since bd vanishes, and Acb remains finite, in the limit, the ratio $BD : ACB$ ultimately vanishes. In curves of finite curvature it will be afterwards seen that BD varies as the square of ACB ultimately.

41. *If two curves of continued curvature which do not intersect have a common chord, the length of the exterior curve is greater than that of the interior, if the curvature of the interior be always in the same direction.*

Let $AcdeB$, $ACDEFB$ any two polygons, having a common side AB, be such, that the first lies entirely within the second,

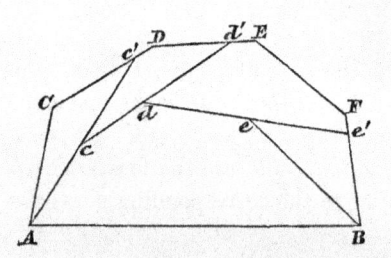

and that neither has internal angles, the perimeter of the first is less than that of the second.

For, produce Ac, cd, de to meet the perimeter of the exterior in c', d', e'.

Then $AC + Cc' > Ac'$;

$$\therefore ACDEFB > Ac'DEFB.$$

Similarly $\quad Ac'DEFB > Acd'EFB$,

and so on;

therefore, a fortiori, $ACDEFB > AcdeB$.

And, since the same is true in the limit when the number of sides is increased indefinitely, the curvilinear limits of the polygons have the same property, and the proposition is proved.

LEMMA VII.

The polar subtangent and the inclination of the tangent to the radius vector, at any point of a spiral.

42. Let S be the pole, PT the tangent to the curve at any point P, and let ST, perpendicular to SP, meet PT in T; then ST is called the *polar subtangent* at the point P.

43. *To find the inclination of the tangent at any point of a curve to the radius vector.*

Let Q be a point near P, QM perpendicular to SP, produced if necessary, QR the circular arc, center S, meeting SP in R.

Let QP meet ST in U, then
$$SU : SP :: QM : PM,$$
and $MR : QM :: QM : SM + SR,$

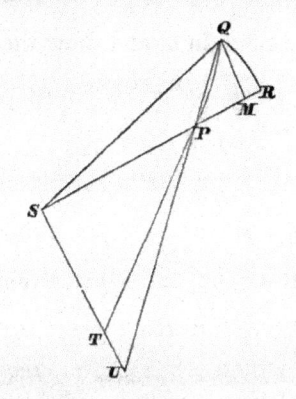

and, when Q approaches indefinitely near to P, QM vanishes compared with $SM + SR$; therefore MR vanishes compared with QM or PM;

$$\therefore SU : SP :: QM : PR, \text{ ultimately};$$

$\therefore ST : SP$ is the limiting ratio of $QR : PR$; or $QR : SQ \sim SP$.

Hence ST, and also the trigonometrical tangent of the angle SPT between the tangent and the radius vector can be found.

44. *To find the inclination of the tangent to the radius vector in the Cardioid.*

If Bqp be a circle whose center is S and diameter BC, pm an ordinate at p, produce Sp to P, making $SP = Bm$, P traces out the *Cardioid APS*.

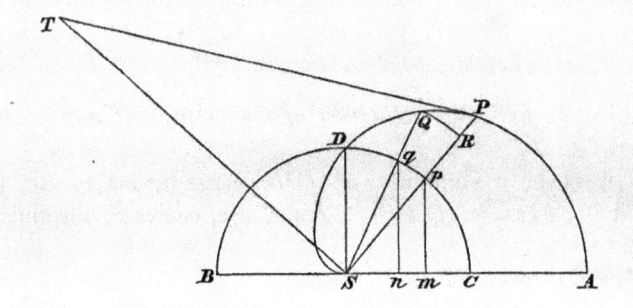

Making the same construction as before, Art. (43),
$$ST : SP :: QR : SQ \sim SP \text{ ultimately.}$$

Let SQ meet the circle in q, and draw the ordinate qn,
$$\text{then, } SP - SQ = mn;$$
$$\text{and } QR : pq :: SQ : Sq$$
$$:: SP : Sp \text{ ultimately;}$$
$$\text{also } pq : mn :: Sp : pm \text{ ultimately;}$$
$$\therefore QR : SP - SQ :: SP : pm \text{ ultimately;}$$
$$\therefore ST : SP :: Bm : pm;$$
$$\therefore \angle PTS = \angle pBm = \tfrac{1}{2} \angle PSA;$$

whence the cardioid cuts SA at right angles at A, touches SB at S, and cuts the circle at an angle equal to half a right angle.

VI.

1. RQq is a common subtense to two curves PQ, Pq, which have a common tangent PR at P. When RQq approaches to P, RQ and Rq ultimately vanish; is the ratio $RQ : Rq$ ultimately a ratio of equality?

2. Prove that the circular measure of an angle which is less than $90°$ lies between the trigonometrical sine and tangent of the angle.

LEMMA VII.

3. AB is a diameter of a circle, P a point contiguous to A, and the tangent at P meets BA produced in T: prove that ultimately the difference of BA, BP is equal to one half of TA.

4. From a point in the circumference of a vertical circle a chord and tangent are drawn, the one terminating at the lowest point, and the other in the vertical diameter produced; compare the velocities acquired by a heavy body in falling down the chord and tangent, when they are indefinitely diminished.

5. In any curve, if Q be the intersection of perpendiculars to two consecutive radii vectores through their extremities, and SY be the perpendicular from the pole S on the tangent at P, prove that ultimately $SP^2 = SY \cdot SQ$.

6. Prove that the extremity of the polar subtangent from the focus of a conic section is always in a fixed straight line.

7. PQ, pq are parallel chords of an ellipse whose center is C; shew that if p move up to P, the areas CPp, CQq are ultimately equal.

8. In the hyperbolic spiral, in which the radius vector varies inversely as the spiral angle, prove that the subtangent is constant.

9. In the spiral of Archimedes, in which the radius vector varies directly as the angle, prove that if a circle be described, of which a radius is the radius vector of the spiral, the polar subtangent will be equal to the arc of the circle subtended by the spiral angle.

LEMMA VIII.

If two straight lines AR, BR, *make with the arc* ACB, *the chord* AB, *and the tangent* AD, *the three triangles* RACB, RAB, *and* RAD, *and the points* A, B *approach one another; then the ultimate form of the vanishing triangles is one of similitude, and the ultimate ratio one of equality.*

For, whilst the point B is approaching the point A, let AB, AD, AR be always produced to points b, d, r at a finite distance, and rbd be always drawn parallel to RD, and let the arc Acb be always similar to the arc ACB, and therefore have Dd for the tangent at A. Then, when the points

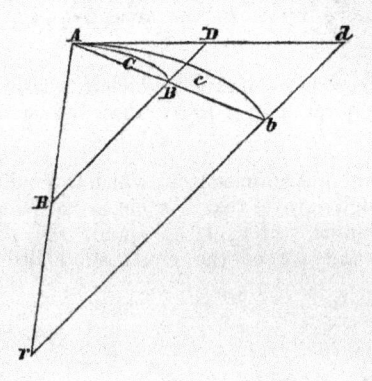

B, A coincide the angle bAd will vanish, and therefore the three triangles rAb, $rAcb$, rAd, will coincide, and are therefore in that case similar and equal. Hence also, RAB, $RACB$, RAD, which are always similar and proportional to these, will be ultimately similar and equal to one another.

COR. And hence, in every argument concerning ultimate ratios, these triangles can be used indifferently for one another.

Observations on the Lemma.

45. If RB throughout the change in the hypothesis make a finite angle with RA, the three triangles rAb, $rAcb$, rAd remain

always finite, and are ultimately identical and equal. But, if the angle ARB is ultimately not finite, for example, if RB revolve round a fixed point R, the three triangles $rAb, \ldots$ become infinite, since r moves to r' and so on to an infinite distance, and there is the same kind of objection to dealing with these infinite triangles, as to reasoning immediately upon the relation of the triangles RAB, RAD in the former case.

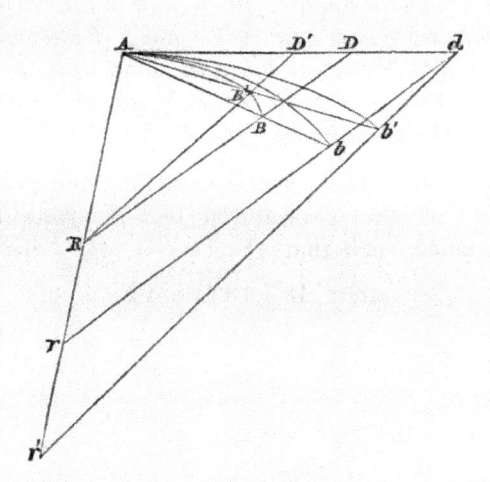

In this case we can at once deduce the equality of the triangles without producing AD to a point d at a finite distance. For, the ratio of the difference of RAD and RAB to RAB is $BD : RB$, which vanishes ultimately, since RD is finite in this case; hence, RAB and RAD and also the curvilinear triangle, which is intermediate in magnitude to them, are ultimately in a ratio of equality.

LEMMA IX.

If a straight line AE *and curve* ABC, *given in position, cut one another in a finite angle* A, *and ordinates* BD, CE *be drawn, inclined at another finite angle to that straight line, and meeting the curve in* B, C; *then, if the points* B, C *move up together to the point* A, *the areas of the curvilinear triangles* ABD, ACE, *will be ultimately to one another in the duplicate ratio of the sides.*

For, as the points B, C are approaching the point A, let AD, AE be always produced to the points d, e at a finite distance, such that

$$Ad : Ae :: AD : AE,$$

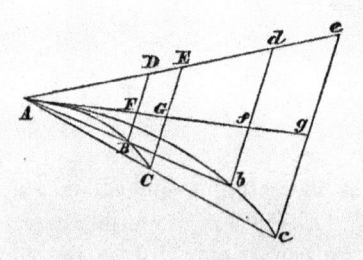

and let the ordinates db, ec be drawn parallel to DB, EC meeting the chords AB, AC produced in b, c.

Then, [since $Ab : AB :: Ad : AD$
$:: Ae : AE :: Ac : AC$,
and therefore $Ab : Ac :: AB : AC$,]

a curve Abc can be supposed to be drawn always similar to ABC, while B and C move up to A.

Let the straight line Ag be drawn touching both curves at A, and cutting the ordinates DB, EC, db, ec in F, G, f, g.

[Now areas ABD, Abd, by Lemma V, are always in the duplicate ratio of AD, Ad, and areas ACE, Ace, in the duplicate ratio of AE, Ae, and $AD : Ad :: AE : Ae$;

therefore $ABD : Abd :: ACE : Ace$.]

LEMMA IX.

If, then, the points B and C move up to A and ultimately coincide with it, the angle cAg will ultimately vanish, and the curvilinear areas Abd, Ace will coincide with the rectilinear triangles Afd, Age, and therefore will be ultimately in the duplicate ratio Ad, Ae.

But ABD, ACE are proportional to Abd, Ace, always, also AD, AE are proportional to Ad, Ae; therefore also areas ABD, ACE are ultimately in the duplicate ratio of AD, AE.

Observations on the Lemma.

46. By a finite angle is to be understood an angle less than two right angles, and neither indefinitely small nor indefinitely near to two right angles.

The angles between AD and the curve and between AD and BD are different finite angles, because otherwise BD would not meet the curve.

47. It is not necessary that d and e be fixed, but only that they remain at a finite distance from A, and that the proportion be retained.

The student, by reference to Arts. 38 and 45, will be able to exhibit the change in the figure which will correspond to a change of the position of B and C in the progress towards the ultimate position.

48. When the angle CAG vanishes, the curvilinear areas Abd, Ace coincide with the rectilinear triangles Afd, Age, and so are in the duplicate ratio of $Ad : Ae$. But if the angle DAF be not finite those triangles will not themselves be finite, and the object aimed at by producing to a finite distance will not be attained.

The fact is, that the triangle Adb is made up of the triangle Adf and the curvilinear triangle Afb, of which the latter is indefinitely small ultimately, and the former is finite; therefore, in the Lemma, Afb vanishes compared with Afd; but this is not the case if Adf be indefinitely small, and the ratio $\triangle AFB : \triangle AGC$ must be found by another process, and it will be found, by referring to Lemma XI, that the ratio is that of cubes of the arcs ultimately, if the curvature of the curve at A be finite.

49. If the angle DAF be greater than a right angle, the figure may assume a form in which AD lies below ABC, in this case, DB, EC, ... must be produced to meet the tangent, and the argument proceeds in the same manner as before.

LEMMA X.

The spaces which a body describes [from rest] under the action of any finite force, whether that force be constant or else continually increase or continually diminish, are in the very beginning of the motion in the duplicate ratio of the times.

[Let the times be represented by lines measured from A, along AK, and the velocities generated at the end of those times, by lines drawn perpendicular to AK. Suppose the time represented by AK to be divided into a number of equal intervals, represented by AB, BC, CD,...

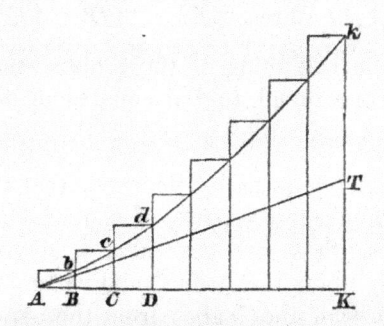

let Bb, Cc, Dd, ... Kk represent the velocities generated in the times AB, AC, ... AK respectively, and let $Abcd$... be the curve line which always passes through the extremities of these ordinates. Complete the parallelograms Ab, Bc, Cd, ...

In the interval of time denoted by CD, the velocity continually changes, from that represented by Cc, to that represented by Dd, and therefore, if CD be taken small enough, the space described in that time is intermediate between the spaces represented by the parallelograms Dc and Cd; therefore the spaces described in the times AD, AK are represented by areas which are intermediate between the sums of the parallelograms inscribed in, and circumscribed about, the curvilinear areas ADd and AKk respectively.

Therefore, by Lemma II, the number of intervals being increased, and their magnitudes diminished indefinitely, the spaces described in the times AD, AK are proportional to the curvilinear areas ADd, AKk.

Now the force being finite, the ratio of the velocity to the time is finite, therefore $Kk : AK$ is a finite ratio, however small the time be taken; hence, if AT be the tangent to the curve line at A, meeting Kk in T, $KT : AK$ is a finite ratio; therefore the angle TAK is finite, or AK meets the curve at a finite angle.

Hence, by Lemma IX, if AD, AK be indefinitely diminished,
$$\text{area } ADd : \text{area } AKk :: AD^2 : AK^2;$$
therefore, in the beginning of the motion, the spaces described are proportional to the squares of the times of describing them. Q.E.D.]

COR. 1. And hence it is easily deduced, that the errors of bodies, describing similar parts of similar figures in proportional times, which are generated by any equal forces acting similarly upon the bodies, and which are measured by the distances of the bodies from those points of the similar figures, to which the same bodies would have arrived in the same proportional times without the action of the disturbing forces, are approximately as the squares of the times in which they are generated.

COR. 2. But the errors which are generated by proportional forces, acting similarly at similar portions of similar figures, are approximately as the forces and the square of the times conjointly.

COR. 3. The same is to be understood of the spaces which bodies describe under the action of different forces. These are, in the beginning of the motion, conjointly, as the forces and the squares of the times.

LEMMA X.

COR. 4. Consequently, in the beginning of the motion the forces are as the spaces described directly, and the squares of the times inversely.

COR. 5. And the squares of the times are as the spaces described directly and the forces inversely.

The proof given in the original Latin is as follows:

Exponantur tempora per lineas AD, AE, et velocitates genitæ per ordinatas DB, EC; et spatia, his velocitatibus descripta, erunt ut areæ ABD, ACE his ordinatis descriptæ, hoc est, ipso motus initio (per Lemma IX) in duplicata ratione temporum AD, AE. Q.E.D.

50. This proof has been amplified in order to exhibit in what manner the description of areas, by the flux of the ordinates, corresponds to that of spaces by the velocities represented by the ordinates; also to shew the propriety of the application of the ninth Lemma, by reference to the definition of finite force, which may be stated as follows:

"A force is finite when the ratio of the velocity generated in any time to the time in which it is generated, is finite, however small the time be taken."

Observations on the Lemma.

51. In the proof of this Lemma, time is represented by the length of a straight line, and a distance traversed by a body is represented by an area.

If the length of a straight line be always proportional to the period of time elapsed, the straight line is a proper representation of the time. Thus n inches has the same ratio to one inch that n seconds has to one second; and on this scale the length n inches is a proper representation of n seconds.

If an area is always in the same ratio to the unit of area that the length of a straight line is to the unit of length, the area is a proper representation of the length of the straight line.

Thus, if Ab be one foot, AB, n feet, Ac an inch, and AC, t inches: complete the parallelograms $ABDC$, $Abdc$, and Bc, $ABCD$ contains nt such areas as $Abdc$.

If now a particle move with a uniform velocity of n feet a second, and AC represent t seconds, on the scale of one inch to a second; the parallelogram Bc represents the space travelled

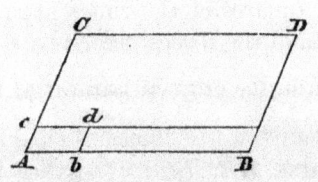

over in the first second, since it contains n times the parallelogram $Abdc$, and $ABDC$ represents the space travelled over in t seconds.

There will be no difficulty in the representation of a period of time by a line, or of a distance by an area, if the student bears in mind that periods of time and lengths of lines, although existing absolutely, are only estimated by their ratios to certain standard periods, and standard lengths, and they are therefore determined whenever these ratios are given, which may be given either directly in numbers or by the comparison of any magnitudes whatever *of the same kind*.

52. COR. 1, 2. If bodies describe orbits under the action of certain forces, and small forces, extraneous to those under the action of which the orbits are described, be supposed to act upon the bodies, the orbits are disturbed slightly, and the errors spoken of are the linear disturbances of the bodies, at any time, from the positions which they would have occupied at that time, if the extraneous forces had not acted.

Thus, in calculating the motion of the Moon considered as moving under the attraction of the Sun and Earth, it is convenient to estimate the motion which she would have, if subjected to the attraction of the Earth alone, and then to calculate what would be the disturbing effect of the Sun upon this orbit.

53. If AB be a portion of an orbit described by a body in any time, AC the portion of the orbit described when a disturbing force is introduced, BC is "quam proxime" the space which would have been described in the same time from rest by the

action of the disturbing force alone. When the time is taken small, but not *indefinitely* small, the expression, in the statement of the corollaries, "approximately," is necessary for two reasons; for, in the first place, the position of the body in space is not the same, at the end of any interval in the lapse of the time, as if the body had moved from rest under the action of the disturbing force alone, and therefore the magnitude of the force is not the same generally either in direction or magnitude; and, in the second place, since the force is not generally uniform, the variation according to the duplicate ratio of the times is not exact, except in the limit.

But, when the times are taken very small, the variation of direction and magnitude of the force may be neglected, as an approximation to the true state of the case.

54. *Application of the method of Lemma X to determine the space described in a finite time from rest by a particle under the action of a* constant *force.*

In this case, since the acceleration is constant, the velocity varies as the time.

Hence, the curve Ak is a straight line, because the ordinates vary as the abscissæ.

Therefore, the space which is described in the time represented by AK is represented by the area of the triangle AKk, and the space, which would be described uniformly in the same time with the velocity acquired at the end of that time, is represented by the rectangle whose diagonal is Ak, or twice the area of the triangle AKk; therefore the space described in the time $t = \frac{1}{2}Vt = \frac{1}{2}ft^2$, where V is the velocity at the end of the time t, and f the acceleration caused by the force in an unit of time.

55. *General geometrical representation of the space described by a body in a finite time when it moves with a variable velocity.*

PROP. If a curve be found, such that the ordinate at each point represents the velocity corresponding to a time represented by the abscissa, then the space described by the body will be represented by the area bounded by the curve, the line of abscissæ, and the ordinates corresponding to the commencement and end of the time of motion.

Let OA, OB represent the times at the commencement and end of the interval during which the motion of the body is to be examined. Let OM be any other time, and let AC, MP, BD

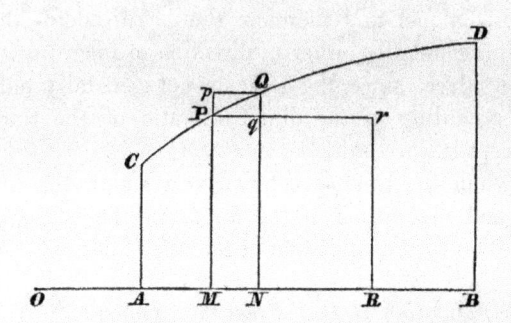

represent the velocity at the end of the times represented by OA, OM, OB; CPD the curve which passes through the extremities of all such ordinates as MP.

Let AB be divided into any number of small portions, such as MN; NQ the ordinate corresponding to ON. Complete the parallelograms $PMNq$, $QNMp$, and suppose corresponding parallelograms to be constructed on all the bases corresponding to MN.

The body during the time represented by MN moves with a velocity, which, if MN is taken small enough, is intermediate in magnitude to the velocities represented by PM and QN, and the space described during that time is intermediate in magnitude to the spaces which would have been described with uniform velocity equal to those represented by PM and QN, or to the spaces represented by the areas PN, QM.

Hence the whole space described in the interval of time represented by AB is greater than that represented by the inscribed series, and less than that by the circumscribed series of parallelograms, which, by the Lemma II, are ultimately equal to the area $ACDB$, when the number of portions into which AB is divided is indefinitely increased, and their magnitudes diminished; therefore the proposition is proved.

LEMMA X.

56. Cor. 1. *The velocity is the limit of the ratio of the space to the time when the time is indefinitely diminished.*

The velocity V at the time OM is represented by MP, therefore, if T be the time represented by MN, VT : space described in time T :: MP . MN : area $PMNQ$, but MP . MN = area $PMNq$ = area $PMNQ$, ultimately; therefore VT = space described in time T, ultimately. Whence the truth of the proposition.

57. Cor. 2. *The velocity is measured by the space which would be described in an unit of time if the velocity remained uniform during this time.*

Let MR represent the unit of time. Complete the parallelogram $PMRr$. Then $PMRr$ represents the space described in an unit of time, with the velocity at time OM continued uniform, and since MR is constant, therefore $PMRr$ varies as PM; therefore the velocity is properly represented by $PMRr$, and the proposition is proved.

58. *Geometrical representation of the velocity generated by a finite and variable force in a given time.*

PROP. If a curve be found such that the ordinate at each point represents the accelerating effect of the force corresponding to a time represented by the abscissa, then the velocity generated in a body in a given time, moving in the direction of the force, will be represented by the area bounded by the curve, the line of abscissæ, and the ordinates corresponding to the commencement and end of the time considered.

The proof proceeds in a manner similar to that given in (55). The student can supply it, employing the same figure, in which the ordinates now represent the accelerating effect of the force at the times represented by the corresponding abscissæ, and observing that the motion of the body is accelerated during the time represented by MN by a force whose accelerating effect is intermediate in magnitude to those represented by PM and QN, if MN is taken small enough, and the velocity generated is intermediate to those which would have been generated by uniform forces equal to those whose accelerating effects are represented by PM, QN, that is, to the velocities represented by the areas PN, QM.

59. And, as before, the force at any time is measured by the limit of the ratio of the velocity generated to the time in which it is generated.

Also, the force at any time is measured by the velocity which would be generated in an unit of time, if the force continued uniform during that time, and equal to the force at the given time.

60. *Geometrical representation of the square of the velocity generated by a force, which acts upon a body moving in the direction of the force's action, when the force is described as depending in any manner upon the* distance *from any fixed point in that direction.*

Let OAB be the line of motion of the body, O a fixed point in this line, and when it arrives at a point M, let MP be taken to represent the accelerating effect of the force acting upon it.

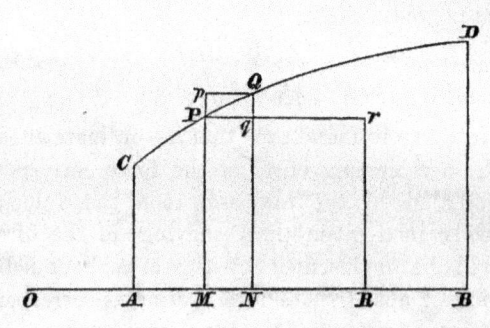

Draw a curve CPD whose ordinates shall represent the accelerating effect of the force, for the different positions of the body at the foot of the ordinates.

Let AB be the space traversed by the body, and let it be divided into any number of small portions, of which suppose MN one, and let QN be the ordinate at N, $PMNq$, $QNMp$ complete parallelograms.

If during the time occupied in describing MN the force remained constant, the difference of the squares of the velocities at M and N would be represented by $2MN \cdot PM$ or $2MN \cdot QN$, or by twice the parallelograms PN or QM, according as the uniform force was that represented by PM or QN.

LEMMA X.

Hence the difference of the squares of the velocities at M and N is represented by an area lying between $2PN$ and $2QM$, if MN be sufficiently diminished; hence it follows by reasoning similar to the above that the difference of the squares of the velocities at A and B is represented by twice the area $ACDB$.

61. Hence we obtain another measure for the force corresponding to the position M. For the increase of (velocity)² in MN is represented by 2 area $PMNQ$,

$$\text{and } PM = \text{limit } \frac{PMNq}{MN} = \text{limit } \frac{PMNQ}{MN};$$

therefore the accelerating effect of the force at M is measured by the limit of $\dfrac{\text{increase of the (velocity)}^2 \text{ in } MN}{2MN}$.

Application to the determination of the motion of a particle, under various circumstances.

1. *To find the space travelled over in a given time t'' by a body moving with a velocity which varies as the square of the time from the beginning of the motion.*

Let AB represent the time, and let BC perpendicular to AB represent the velocity at the end of that time, *i.e.* let BC represent the space which would be described in the next unit of time, if the body, instead of moving with constantly increasing velocity, were to move with uniform velocity for an unit of time from the end of the time represented by AB.

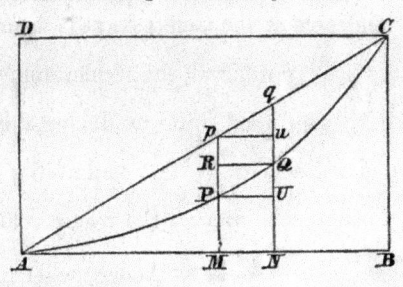

Let AB be divided into any number of equal portions of which MN is one, and let MP, NQ represent the velocities at the end of the times represented by AM, AN.

Then, since $MP : NQ : BC :: AM^2 : AN^2 : AB^2$,

G 2

84   NEWTON.

a parabola, whose vertex is at A can be described, touching AB and passing through P, Q, C and the extremities of all ordinates described on MP.

Hence, the space described in the time represented by AB is represented by the parabolic area ABC or $\frac{1}{3}AB.BC$.

And if p be the velocity at the end of $1''$, pt^2 that at the end of t''; then $\frac{1}{3}pt^2 . t = \frac{1}{3}pt^3$ is the space described in the time t.

Or, we can further illustrate the meaning of Art. 51, by employing another method of representing the space.

Join AC, and let pM, qN be the ordinates, and suppose the figure to revolve round AB, pM generates a circle which $\propto pM^2 \propto AM^2$, therefore this circle may be taken to represent the velocity at the time corresponding to AM, and the solid generated by $pqNM$ represents the space described in time MN. The whole space is therefore represented by the cone generated by ABC, or $\frac{1}{3}AB.\pi BC^2$, which gives the same result as before.

2. *To find the space described from rest at any time by a particle under the action of a force, whose accelerating effect varies as the* mth *power of the time.*

This problem is more simply solved by applying directly the method of summation, since in order to find the area of the curve, constructed as in Lemma X., we should eventually be obliged to have recourse to that method.

Let the time t be divided into n equal intervals, and let the acceleration by the force at the time t be pt^m; hence, at the commencement of the $(r+1)^{\text{th}}$ interval, the acceleration will be $p\left(\dfrac{rt}{n}\right)^m$, and, if the force be continued uniform during this interval, the velocity generated will be $p\left(\dfrac{rt}{n}\right)^m . \dfrac{t}{n}$, and if the same arrangement be made during each interval the whole velocity generated will be $\dfrac{1^m + 2^m + \ldots + \overline{n-1}\,|^m}{n^{m+1}} pt^{m+1}$, hence, when the number of intervals is increased indefinitely, it follows, by the reasoning of Lemma II. that the velocity at the time $t = \dfrac{pt^{m+1}}{m+1}$.

In the same manner, if the velocity at the commencement of each interval, were continued uniform during the interval, the space described could be shewn to be

$$\frac{1^{m+1} + 2^{m+1} + \ldots + \overline{n-1}\,]^{m+1}}{n^{m+2}} \cdot \frac{pt^{m+2}}{m+1};$$

whence, proceeding to the limit, the space described in the time $t = \dfrac{pt^{m+2}}{(m+1)(m+2)}$.

3. *To find the velocity acquired from rest, when a body is acted on by an attractive force whose accelerating effect varies as the distance from a fixed point.*

Let S be the fixed point, A the point from which the motion commences, and let AB, perpendicular to SA, represent the accelerating effect of the force at A.

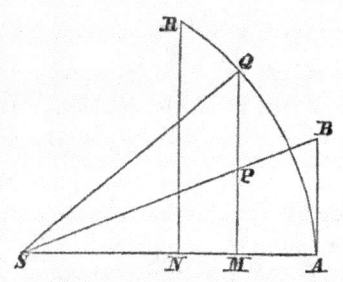

Join SB, and from any point M, let MP, perpendicular to SA, meet SB in P; then, since $PM : BA :: SM : SA$, PM represents the accelerating effect of the force at M, and, by Art. 61, (velocity)^2 at M is represented by $2 \times$ area $BAMP$.

Let V be the velocity which the force, continued uniform from A, would have generated in the space AS; describe the circle AQR with centre S, and produce MP to Q.

$$\begin{aligned}
\text{(velocity)}^2 \text{ at } M : V^2 &:: 2 \text{ area } BAMP : AS.AB \\
&:: \triangle SAB - \triangle SMP : \triangle SAB \\
&:: SA^2 - SM^2 : SA^2 \\
&:: QM^2 : SA^2;
\end{aligned}$$

therefore, velocity at $M : V :: QM : SA$,

or, velocity at $M = V \sin QSA$.

If $\mu \cdot SA$ be the measure of the accelerating effect of the force at A, since V^2 is represented by the rectangle AS, AB, $V^2 = \mu \cdot AS^2$; therefore the velocity at $M = \sqrt{\mu} \cdot QM$.

4. *Time of describing a given space from rest under the action of a force varying as the distance from a fixed point.*

Making the same construction as before, let $t =$ time from M to N; therefore $t \times$ velocity at $M = MN$, ultimately.

Now, $MN : QR :: QM : QS$, ultimately
$$:: QM : SA$$
$$:: \text{velocity at } M : V$$
$$:: t \times \text{velocity at } M : tV;$$
$$\therefore tV = QR,$$
and $V \times$ time from A to $M =$ arc AQ;

hence, time in $AM = \dfrac{\text{arc } AQ}{\sqrt{\mu} \cdot AS} = \dfrac{1}{\sqrt{\mu}} \times$ circular measure of QSA.

5. *Space described by a body moving in a medium, in which the resistance varies as the velocity, when no other force acts on the body, varies as the velocity destroyed.*

Let the time AK be divided into equal portions AB, BC, CD, ...; and let Aa', Bb', ... be the velocities at the beginning of times, the space in time AK is represented by the area $a'AKk'$.

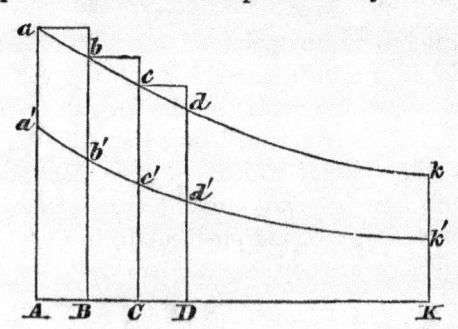

Suppose the force of resistance to be constant throughout the intervals of time AB, BC, ... and equal to the amount at the commencement of each, and let Aa, Bb, ... be the measures of those forces;

LEMMA X.

$$\therefore Aa : Bb : \ldots\ldots :: Aa' : Bb' : \ldots\ldots$$

and the velocity destroyed is represented by the limit of the sum of the parallelograms aB, bC, ... or the area $aAKk$;

therefore, velocity destroyed in time AK : space described

$$:: aAKk : a'AKk' :: Aa : Aa' :: \text{resistance : the velocity,}$$

hence, since the resistance varies as the velocity, the velocity destroyed varies as the space described.

6. *A particle slides down the smooth arc of a cycloid, whose axis is vertical, and vertex downwards, to find the time of an oscillation.*

Let AB be the vertical axis of the cycloidal arc APL, L the point from which the particle begins to move, PQ a small arc of its path, LR, PM, QN perpendicular to AB.

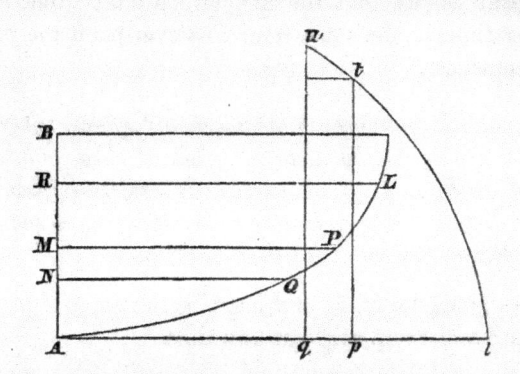

Let $v =$ velocity at P, and $T =$ time in falling from B to A; therefore $\qquad v^2 = 2g \cdot RM$, and $2AB = gT^2$. \hfill (1).

But, by the properties of the cycloid, (see Appendix II.)

$$AL^2 = 4AB \cdot AR,$$
$$AP^2 = 4AB \cdot AM;$$
$$\therefore AL^2 - AP^2 = 4AB \cdot RM. \qquad (2).$$

Take Al, Ap, Aq, on the tangent at A respectively equal to AL, AP, AQ, and let pt, qu perpendicular to Al be ordinates to a circle whose center is A and radius Al;

$$\therefore AL^2 - AP^2 = Al^2 - Ap^2 = pt^2;$$

and, by (1), $v^2 T^2 = 4AB \cdot RM$; $\therefore pt = vT$ by (2);

$$\therefore v^2 T^2 = 2g T^2 RM;$$
$$= 4AB \cdot RM = pt^2, \text{ by (2)},$$

hence, pt would be described with uniform velocity v in time T, and, ultimately, PQ is described with velocity v;

hence, time in $PQ : T :: QP : pt$
$:: pq : pt$
$:: tu : At$ ultimately;

hence, time in $PQ = T \times$ circular measure of $\angle tAu$ ultimately;

and time in $LA = T \times \dfrac{\pi}{2} = \dfrac{\pi}{2} \sqrt{\dfrac{2AB}{g}}$; by (1),

hence, the time of an oscillation $= \pi \sqrt{\dfrac{2AB}{g}}$.

The result shews that the cycloid is a tautochronous curve, that is, the time is the same from whatever point the particle's motion commences.

7. *A particle is subject to the action of a force, whose accelerating effect varies as the distance from a fixed point, in the direction of which it acts, the particle is projected from a given point in a direction perpendicular to the direction of the force at that point, to find the path described by the particle.*

Let the force tend to C, and let A be the point of projection, P the position of the particle at any time.

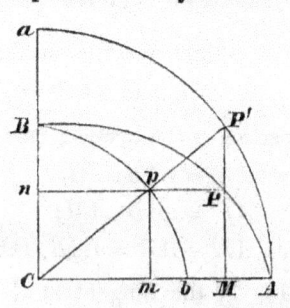

Let CB, perpendicular to CA, be the distance in which a particle would be reduced to rest, if projected from C with the velocity of projection.

LEMMA X.   89

Describe circles Bb, Aa having the common center C, and draw CpP' cutting the circles in p and P', and draw pn perpendicular to CB, and pm, $P'M$ to CA.

Referring to Prob. 4, it will be seen that two particles starting respectively from rest at A, and with the velocity of projection at C, under the action of the same force, would arrive simultaneously at M and n, since the time in both cases is proportional to the angle $P'CA$.

But the particle in the proposed problem is acted on at P by a force which is represented by PC, whose accelerating effect parallel to AC and CB is represented by MC and PM, therefore the acceleration in AC is the same as that of the particle supposed to move in AC from rest, and the retardation parallel to BC the same as that of the particle in CB, projected from C. Therefore P is in the intersection of np and MP',

$$\text{and } PM : P'M :: pm : P'M$$
$$:: Cp : CP'$$
$$:: CB : CA;$$

therefore the required path of the particle is an ellipse whose semiaxes are CA and CB.

Cor. 1. If $\mu \cdot CP$ is the accelerating effect of the force at P, and V the velocity of projection, $V^2 = \mu \cdot CB^2$.

$$\text{Also, area } ACP \propto \text{ area } ACP'$$
$$\propto \text{ angle } ACP'$$
$$\propto \text{ time from } A \text{ to } P,$$

or the area swept out by the radius vector is proportional to the time.

Cor. 2. Also (velocity)^2 at P = sum of the squares of the velocities of the particles at M and n

$$= \mu \cdot P'M^2 + \mu \cdot pn^2 = \mu \cdot CD^2,$$

where CD is the semidiameter conjugate to CP.

VII.

1. If the square of the velocity of a body be proportional to the space described from rest, prove that the accelerating force is constant.

2. At what point of the proof of the Lemma X. is it assumed that the body starts from rest?

3. State the proposition by which Lemma X. is replaced, when the body, instead of starting from rest, commences its motion with a given velocity.

4. How may the acceleration be measured at any time by reference to the velocity curve which is employed in the proof of the Lemma.

5. Two points move from rest, in such a manner that the ratio of the times, in which the same uniform acceleration would generate their respective velocities at those times, is constant. Shew that their respective accelerations, at any times bearing that ratio, are equal.

6. If a body move from rest under the action of a force, which varies as the square of the time from the beginning of the motion, shew that the velocity at any time varies as the cube of the time, and the space described as the fourth power of the time.

7. If the velocity after a time t from rest be equal to $a(2t + t^2)$, what will be the shape of the curve in the figure, and the space described in any time?

8. When a body moves from rest at A under the action of a force which varies as the square of the distance from $S (=\mu.SM^2$ at $M)$, the square of the velocity at $M = \frac{2\mu}{3}(SA^3 - SM^3)$.

9. If the curve employed in the proof of the Lemma be an arc of a parabola, the axis of which is perpendicular to the straight line on which the time is measured, prove that the accelerating effect of the force will vary as the distance from the axis of the parabola.

10. If a body be acted on from rest by a repulsive force which varies as the distance from a fixed point, find the velocity when the body arrives at any position.

11. A particle is placed in the line joining two centers of attracting force, the accelerating effect of which varies as the distance, find the time in which the particle oscillates.

12. Two forces reside at S, one attractive and whose accelerating effect on a particle varies as the distance from S, and the other constant and repulsive; prove that, if a particle be placed at S it will move until it be brought to rest at a point which is double the distance from S, at which it would rest in equilibrium under the action of the forces.

LEMMA XI.

The vanishing subtenses of the angle of contact in all curves which have finite curvature at the point of contact, are ultimately in the duplicate ratio of the chords of the conterminous arcs.

Case 1. Let AB be the arc of a curve, AD its tangent at A, BD the subtense of the angle of contact BAD perpendicular to the tangent, AB the chord of the arc.

Let AG, BG be drawn perpendicular to the tangent AD and the chord AB respectively, meeting in G; then let the

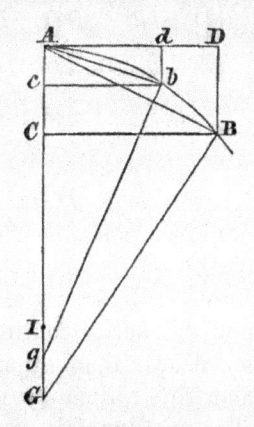

points D, B, G move towards the points d, b, g, and let I be the point of ultimate intersection of the lines BG, AG, when the points B, D move up to A.

It is evident that the distance GI may be made less than any assigned distance by diminishing AB.

But since the angles ABD and GAB are equal, and also the right angles BDA, ABG, the triangles ABD, GAB are similar; therefore $BD : AB :: AB : AG$, or $BD.AG = AB^2$, and similarly, $bd.Ag = Ab^2$;

$$\therefore AB^2 : Ab^2 = BD.AG : bd.Ag;$$

therefore the ratio $AB^2 : Ab^2$ is a ratio compounded of the ratios of $BD : bd$, and $AG : Ag$.

But, since GI may be made less than any assigned length, the ratio $AG : Ag$ may be made to differ from a ratio of equality less than by any assigned difference; therefore the ratio $AB^2 : Ab^2$ may be made to differ from the ratio $BD : bd$ less than by any assigned difference.

Hence, by Lemma I., the ultimate ratio $AB^2 : Ab^2$ is the same as the ultimate ratio of $BD : bd$. Q.E.D.

Case 2. Let now the subtenses BD', bd' be inclined at any given angle to the tangent; then, by similar triangles $D'BD$, $d'bd$,

$$BD' : bd' :: BD : bd,$$
but ultimately, $\quad BD : bd :: AB^2 : Ab^2;$
therefore ultimately, $\quad BD' : bd' :: AB^2 : Ab^2,$

Q.E.D.

Case 3. And although the angle D' be not a given angle, if BD' converges to a given point, or is drawn according to any other [fixed] law, [by which the angle D' remains finite, since BD' is a subtense,] still, the angles D', d', constructed by this law common to both, continually approach to equality and become nearer than by any assigned difference, and will be therefore ultimately equal, by Lemma I., and hence BD', bd', are ultimately in the same ratio as before. Q.E.D.

COR. 1. Hence, since the tangents AD, Ad, the arcs AB, Ab, and their sines BC, bc, become ultimately equal to the chords AB, Ab; their squares also will be ultimately as the subtenses BD, bd.

COR. 2. The squares of the same lines are also ultimately as the sagittæ of the arcs, which bisect the chords, and converge to a given point: for those sagittæ are as the subtenses BD, bd.

COR. 3. And therefore the sagittæ are in the duplicate ratio of the times in which a body describes the arcs with a given velocity.

COR. 4. The rectilinear triangles ADB, Adb are ultimately in the triplicate ratio of the sides AD, Ad, and in the sesquiplicate ratio of the sides DB, db; since these triangles are in the ratio compounded of $AD : DB$ and $Ad : db$. So also the triangles ABC, Abc are ultimately in the triplicate ratio of the sides BC, bc. The sesquiplicate ratio is the subduplicate of the triplicate, which is compounded of the simple and the subduplicate ratios.

COR. 5. And, since DB, db are ultimately parallel and in the duplicate ratio of AD, Ad, [therefore, this being a property of a parabola,] at every point at which a curve has finite curvature an arc of a parabola can be drawn which ultimately coincides with the curve; and the curvilinear areas ADB, Adb will be ultimately two thirds of the rectilinear triangles ADB, Adb: and the segments AB, Ab the third parts of the same triangles. And hence these areas and these segments will be in the triplicate ratio as well of the tangents AD, Ad as of the chords and arcs AB, Ab.

SCHOLIUM.

But, in all these propositions, we suppose the angle of contact to be neither infinitely greater nor infinitely less than the angles of contact which circles have with their tangents; that is, that the curvature at the point A is neither infinitely great nor infinitely small, in other words, that the distance AI is of finite magnitude.

For DB might be taken proportional to AD^3, in which case no circle could be drawn through the point A between the tangent AD and the curve AB, and the angle of contact would be infinitely less than that of any circle.

And, similarly, if different curves be drawn in which DB varies successively as AD^4, AD^5, AD^6, &c., a series of angles of contact will be presented which may be continued to an infinite number, of which each will be infinitely less than the preceding. And if curves be drawn in which DB varies as AD^2, $AD^{\frac{3}{2}}$, $AD^{\frac{4}{3}}$, $AD^{\frac{5}{4}}$, $AD^{\frac{6}{5}}$, &c., another infinite series of angles of contact will be obtained, of which the first is of the same kind as in the circle, the second infinitely greater, and each infinitely greater than the preceding. But, moreover, between any two of these angles, an infinite series of other angles of contact can be inserted, of which each may be infinitely greater or infinitely less than any preceding; for example, if between the limits AD^2 and AD^3 there be inserted $AD^{\frac{13}{6}}$, $AD^{\frac{11}{5}}$, $AD^{\frac{9}{4}}$, $AD^{\frac{7}{3}}$, $AD^{\frac{5}{2}}$, $AD^{\frac{8}{3}}$, $AD^{\frac{11}{4}}$, $AD^{\frac{14}{5}}$, $AD^{\frac{17}{6}}$, &c. And again, between any two angles of this series there can be inserted a new series of intermediate angles differing from one another by infinite intervals. Nor does the nature of the case admit any limit.

The propositions which have been demonstrated concerning curved lines, and the included areas, are easily applied to curved surfaces and solid contents.

These Lemmas have been premised for the sake of escaping from the tedious demonstrations by the method of *reductio ad absurdum*, employed by the old geometers. The demonstrations are certainly rendered more concise, by the method of indivisibles; but, as there is a harshness in the hypothesis of indivisibles, and on that account it is considered to be an imperfect geometrical method; it has been preferred to make the demonstrations of the following propositions depend on the ultimate sums and ratios of vanishing quantities and on the prime sums and ratios of nascent quantities, i. e. on the limits of sums and ratios; and therefore to premise demonstrations of those limits as concise as possible. By these demonstrations the same results are deducible as by the method of indivisibles; and we may employ the principles which have been established with greater safety. Consequently, if, in what follows, quantities should be treated of as if they consisted of particles, [indefinitely small parts,] or small curve lines should be employed as straight lines, it would not be intended to convey the idea of indivisible, but of

LEMMA XI.

vanishing divisible quantities, not that of sums and ratios of determinate parts, but of the limits of sums and ratios: and it must be remembered that the force of such demonstrations rests on the method exhibited in the preceding Lemmas.

An objection is made, that there can be no ultimate proportion of vanishing quantities; inasmuch as before they have vanished the proportion is not ultimate, and when they have vanished, it does not exist. But by the same argument it could be maintained that there could be no ultimate velocity of a body arriving at a certain position at which its motion ceases; for that this velocity, before the body arrives at that position, is not the ultimate velocity; and that, when it arrives there, there is no velocity. And the answer is easy: that, by the ultimate velocity is to be understood that, when the body is moving, neither before it reaches the last position, and the motion ceases, nor after it has reached it, but at the instant at which it arrives; i.e. the very velocity *with which* it arrives at the last position, and *with which* the motion ceases.

And similarly, by the ultimate ratio of vanishing quantities is to be understood the ratio of the quantities, not before they vanish, nor after, but *with which* they vanish. Likewise also, the prime ratio of nascent quantities is the ratio *with which* they begin to exist. And a prime or ultimate sum is that *with which* it begins to be increased or ceases to be diminished.

There is a limit, which the velocity can attain at the end of the motion, but cannot surpass. This is the ultimate velocity. And the like can be stated of the limit of all quantities and proportions commencing or ceasing to exist. And since this limit is certain and definite, to determine it is strictly a geometrical problem. And all geometrical propositions may be legitimately employed in determining and demonstrating other propositions which are themselves geometrical.

It may also be argued, that if the ultimate ratios of vanishing quantities be given, the ultimate magnitudes will also be given, and thus every quantity will consist of indivisibles, contrary to what Euclid has demonstrated of incommensurable quantities, in his tenth book of the Elements.

But this objection rests on a false hypothesis. Those ultimate ratios with which quantities vanish, are not actually ratios of ultimate quantities, but limits to which the ratios of quantities decreasing without limit are continually approaching; and which they can approach nearer than by *any* given difference, but which they can never surpass, nor reach before the quantities are indefinitely diminished.

The argument will be understood more clearly in the case of infinitely great quantities. If two quantities, of which the difference is given, be increased infinitely, their ultimate ratio will be given, namely, a ratio of equality, yet in this case the ultimate or greatest quantities of which that is the ratio will not be given.

In what follows, therefore, if at any time, for the sake of facility of conception, the expressions *indefinitely small*, or *vanishing*, or *ultimate* be used concerning quantities, care must be taken not to understand thereby quantities determinate in magnitude, but to conceive them in all cases quantities to be diminished without limit.

Curvature of Curves.

62. The curvature of a curve at any point is greater or less as the amount of deflection from the tangent at that point, in the immediate neighbourhood of the point, is greater or less.

Two curves have the same curvature at two points, taken one in each, if at equal distances from the points of contact, in the immediate neighbourhood of those points, they have the same deflection from the tangents at those points.

63. An exact geometrical test of equality of curvature may be obtained as follows:

If AB, ab be two curves which have the same curvature at

LEMMA XI. 97

A, a respectively, draw the tangents AC, ac and take $AC = ac$.

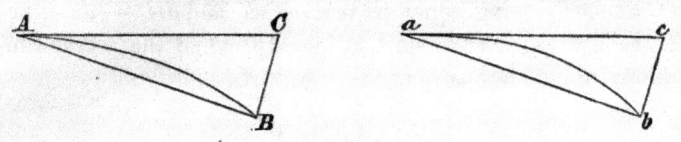

Draw subtenses BC, bc inclined at equal angles to the tangents.

If BC and bc were equal, for all equal values of AC, ac, the curves would be equal and similar. If $BC : bc$ be ultimately a ratio of equality, when AC, ac are taken indefinitely small, the curves will have the same deflection from the tangents in the immediate neighbourhood of A, a, or the curves will have the same curvature at those points.

If the chords AB, ab be drawn, it is an immediate consequence that the ultimate ratio of the angles BAC, bac is a ratio of equality. These angles are called *the angles of contact*.

Hence, curves have the same curvature at two points, taken one in each, if, equal tangents being drawn at those points, and subtenses inclined at any equal angles to the tangents, the limiting ratio of the subtenses is a ratio of equality, or, if the limiting ratio of the angles of contact be a ratio of equality.

64. The curvature of one curve is infinitely greater or infinitely less than that of another if the limiting ratio of the subtense of the first to that of the second be infinitely great or infinitely small.

65. The ratio of the curvature of one curve to that of another at two points, or of the curvature of the same curve at two different points, is the limiting ratio of the subtenses drawn from the extremities of equal tangents and inclined at equal angles to the tangents.

66. The curvature of a curve is said to be finite, at any point, when the ratio of the curvature at that point to that of any circle whose radius is finite, is a finite ratio.

67. *The curvature of a circle is the same at every point.*

Let A, a be any two points on a circle, AC, ac equal tangents at A, a, CB, cb subtenses perpendicular to the tangents,

NEWT. H

OD, Od perpendicular to the subtenses produced; therefore $CD = cd$, each being equal to the radius, and $BD = bd$; hence $BC = bc$ always, and therefore ultimately, when the arcs are indefinitely diminished, $BC : bc$ is a ratio of equality;

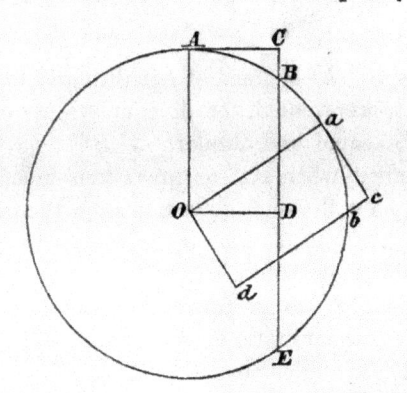

therefore the circle has the same curvature at any two points.

68. *In different circles the curvature varies inversely as the radii.*

In the last figure, produce CB to the circumference in E. Then, $AC^2 = CB \cdot CE$, also, if $A'C'$ be a tangent to another circle, and $A'C'$ be taken equal to AC, and the same construction be made, $A'C'^2 = C'B' \cdot C'E'$;

$$\therefore CB \cdot CE = C'B' \cdot C'E';$$

and $CB : C'B' :: C'E' : CE$;

and, ultimately, when AC, $A'C'$ are indefinitely diminished,

$$CE = 2AO,$$

$\therefore CB : C'B' :: A'O' : AO$, ultimately,

or the curvatures are inversely proportional to the radii.

Measure of Curvature.

69. The curvature of a circle is the same at every point; the curvature of different circles varies inversely as the diameters of the circles; and a circle can be constructed of any degree of finite curvature by varying the magnitude of the diameter.

Hence, a circle can always be found, whose curvature at any point is equal to that of a curve at a fixed point.

The curvature of a curve at any point is therefore completely determined, when the diameter of the circle is found, which has the same curvature as the curve at the given point.

The diameter of the circle, which has the same curvature as the curve at a given point, is called *the diameter of curvature of the curve at that point*.

The chord of the circle, drawn in any direction, is called *the chord of curvature in that direction*.

The circle itself is called *the circle of curvature*, and is the circle which has the same tangent as the curve at any point, and also the same curvature.

70. Any other curve might have been chosen to establish a standard measure of finite curvature; but, since no curve but the circle has the same curvature at every point, it would then have been necessary, after selecting the curve, to specify the point at which the curvature might form the measure of curvature.

Thus, if the standard curve were a parabola, we must choose the curvature of the parabola at the vertex or at the extremity of the latus rectum or at some determinate point, by which to obtain the measure.

The inconvenience is obvious.

General Properties of the Circle of Curvature.

71. If a circle be drawn touching a curve at a given point, and cutting it at a second point, as the second point approaches indefinitely near the point of contact, the circle assumes a limiting magnitude, and evidently satisfies the condition that it has the same curvature as the curve at that point.

72. Since a tangent at any point is the limiting position of a side of a polygon terminated in that point, and inscribed in the curve, when the number of sides is increased indefinitely: so the circle of curvature at any point is the limiting circle which passes through the extremities of two consecutive sides of the polygon either terminated in that point or commencing from that point.

73. *No circle can be drawn whose circumference lies between a curve and its circle of curvature, in the neighbourhood of the point at which the circle of curvature is drawn.*

For, let AQ be the arc of the curve, Aq of the circle of curvature; and let, if possible, another circle be drawn, of which the arc AS lies between the curve and circle, and having therefore the same tangent AR at A, and let RQ, the subtense perpendicular to the tangent, cut the circles in S, q.

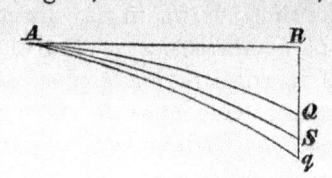

Then $SR : qR$ is ultimately in the inverse ratio of the diameters of the circles; therefore SR is ultimately unequal to qR; but, since qR and QR are ultimately in a ratio of equality, SR which is intermediate in magnitude is ultimately equal to either, which is absurd; therefore no circle, &c.

This proposition corresponds to Euclid, III, Prop. XVI.

74. *The circle of curvature generally cuts the curve.*

For the curvature of the curve at different points taken along the curve continually increases or continually diminishes, until it arrives at a maximum or minimum value.

If therefore the circle of curvature be drawn at any point, on the side on which the curvature is increasing, as we proceed from the point, the curve lies within the circle, and on the other side, on which the curvature is diminishing, the curve lies without the circle; which proves the proposition in the general position of the point.

For the particular case, in which the point is at a position of maximum or minimum curvature, as at the extremities of the axes of an ellipse, if the curvature be a maximum the curvature at adjacent points on either side is less than that of the circle of curvature at the point under consideration, therefore the circle lies entirely within the curve on both sides near the point of maximum curvature; and similarly, it lies without the curve at points of minimum curvature.

LEMMA XI.

We can illustrate this by reference to the polygon inscribed in the curve; see the figure in the following page.

If, in a curve, equal chords AB, BC, CD, DE, ... be placed in order, generally the angles ABC, BCD, CDE, ... increase or decrease, commencing from any point, which property of the polygon has in the curvilinear limit, when the chords are diminished indefinitely, the corresponding property, that the curvature decreases or increases continually.

Suppose the angles are increasing from B, in the circle described about BCD, let BA', DE' be placed equal to BC or CD.

Then, BA' and DE' lie on opposite sides of the perimeter of the polygon, whence, if we proceed to the limit, the circle of curvature at a point in the middle of increasing curvature cuts the curve.

If the angles ABC and DEF be each less than the angles BCD, CDE, supposed equal, the curvature decreases and then increases, and the circle about BCD passes through E, and BA, EF lie within the circle, and proceeding to the limit, the circle of curvature lies without the curve, near the point of minimum curvature.

Evolute of a Curve.

75. If the circles of curvature be drawn at every point of a curve, the centers of those circles lie in a curve which is called the *evolute* of the proposed curve.

Properties of the Evolute.

76. *The extremity of a string unwrapped from the evolute of a curve traces out the curve.*

Let $ABCDE$ be any equilateral polygon, and let $a'a$, $b'b$, $c'c$, $d'd$ be drawn perpendicular to the sides from the middle points a', b', &c., these intersect in the angular points $abcd$ ... of another polygon.

If a string were wrapped round $a'abcd$ ... the extremity a' would as the string was unwrapped pass through the points $a'b'c'd'$.

Let now the number of sides of the polygon be increased and the magnitude diminished indefinitely.

The points $a'b'c'\ldots$ are ultimately in the curve which is the limit of the polygon, and since $a, b, c, \ldots$ are the centers of the circles described about $ABC, BCD, \ldots a, b, c, \ldots$ are ultimately the centers of the circles of curvature at $a'b'c'\ldots$, and the curve

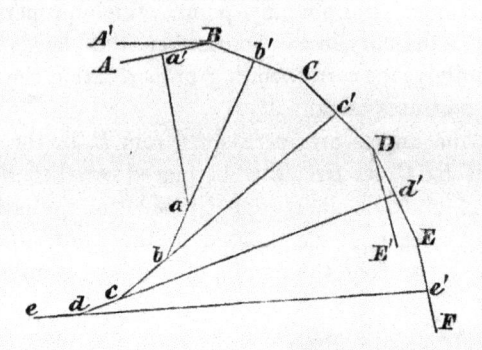

which is the limit of the polygon $abcd\ldots$ is the evolute of the curve $a'b'c'\ldots$, and the property proved for the polygons is true for the limits of the polygons, therefore the extremity of the string unwrapped from the evolute traces the curve of which it is the evolute. This property gives rise to the name of evolute.

The curves formed by the unwrapping of the string from the evolute are called *involutes*.

77. *The tangent to the evolute of a curve is a normal to the curve.*

Since $b'b$ is ultimately the tangent to the evolute and is perpendicular to BC which is ultimately the tangent to the curve $a'b'c'\ldots$, therefore the tangent to the evolute is a normal to the curve.

Propositions on Diameters and Chords of Curvature.

78. *If a subtense be drawn from the extremity of an arc of finite curvature, in any direction, the chord of curvature parallel to that direction is the limit of the third proportional to the subtense and the arc.*

Let PQ, Pq be arcs of a curve and its circle of curvature at P, PR the common tangent, RQq the direction of a common subtense, meeting the circle in U.

LEMMA XI. 103

Draw the chord PV parallel to RQ. Therefore, since $Rq \cdot RU = PR^2$, RU is the third proportional to Rq and PR.

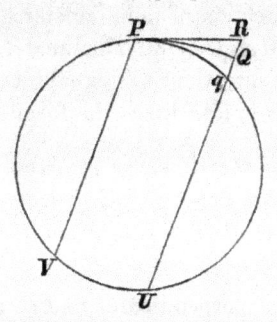

But, ultimately, when PQ is indefinitely diminished, $RU = PV$, and $PR = PQ$, by Lemma VII. also, $Rq = RQ$ by the property of the circle of curvature.

Therefore PV is the limit of the third proportional to RQ and PQ.

COR. *The diameter of curvature is the limit of the third proportional to the subtense perpendicular to the tangent and the arc.*

79. *The chord of curvature at any point of a parabola drawn through the focus, and in the direction of a diameter, is equal to four times the focal distance of that point.*

Let AP be a parabola, P any point, RQ a subtense parallel to the diameter PMx, QM the ordinate at Q, S the focus. Then, by a property of the parabola, $QM^2 = 4SP \cdot PM$; therefore $4SP$ is a third proportional to PM and QM, i.e. to RQ and PR;

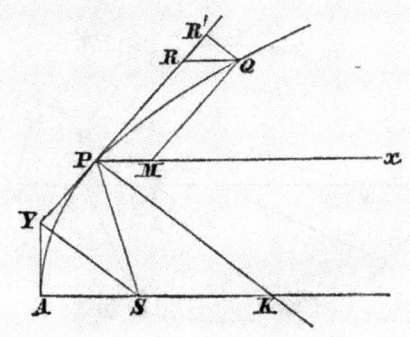

Hence, $4SP$ is the limit of the third proportional to the subtense QR and the arc PQ, and is therefore equal to the chord of curvature at P in direction of the diameter.

And, since PS, PM are equally inclined to the tangents at P, the chords in those directions are equal; therefore, the chord of curvature through S is four times the focal distance SP.

80. *One fourth of the diameter of curvature at any point of a parabola is a third proportional to the perpendicular from the focus on the tangent at that point, and the focal distance of that point.*

For, draw SY, QR' perpendicular to PR, and let PI be the diameter of curvature at P.

Then $PI : PQ :: PQ : QR'$ ultimately;

∴ $PI : PR :: PR : QR'$ ultimately.

But, $PR : 4SP :: QR : PR$;

∴ $PI : 4SP :: QR : QR'$ ultimately,

:: $SP : SY$,

since the triangles SYP, $QR'R$ are similar;

∴ $4SP^2 = PI \cdot SY$;

therefore $\frac{1}{4}PI$ is a third proportional to SY and SP.

81. *The chord of curvature at any point of an ellipse drawn through the center of the ellipse, is a third proportional to the diameter through that point and the diameter conjugate to it.*

Let P be any point in an ellipse, PCG the diameter, DCD' conjugate to it, Q any point near P, QR a subtense parallel

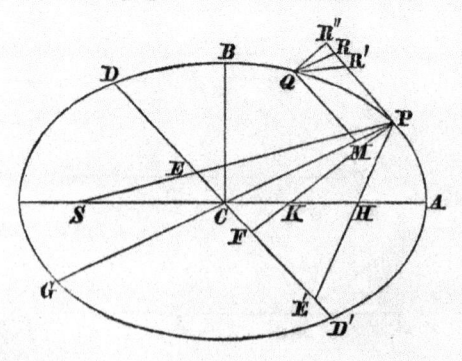

LEMMA XI.

to CP, QM an ordinate parallel to DC, PV the chord of curvature drawn through C.

Then, $PV \cdot QR = PQ^2 = QM^2$, ultimately,

and $QM^2 : PM \cdot MG :: CD^2 : CP^2$;

$\therefore PV \cdot QR : QR \cdot MG :: CD^2 : CP^2$, ultimately.

$\therefore PV : 2CP :: CD^2 : CP^2$, ultimately:

$\therefore PV \cdot CP : CP^2 :: 2CD^2 : CP^2$,

and $PV \cdot CP = 2CD^2$;

or $2CP : 2CD :: 2CD : PV$;

or PV is a third proportional to PG and DCD'.

82. *The chord of curvature at any point through the focus is a third proportional to the major axis, and the diameter parallel to the tangent at that point.*

Draw the focal distance SP cutting the diameter DCD' in E, let PV' be the chord of curvature through S, and draw the subtense QR' parallel to SP.

Then $PV' : PV :: QR : QR'$, ultimately,

$:: CP : PE$, by similar triangles;

$\therefore PV' \cdot PE = PV \cdot CP = 2CD^2$;

$\therefore PV'$ is a third proportional to $2PE$ and DCD', and $2PE$ is equal to the major axis.

Similarly for the other focus H.

83. *The diameter of curvature at any point, is a third proportional to twice the perpendicular from the point on the diameter parallel to the tangent and that diameter.*

Draw QR'' perpendicular to the tangent, and PF perpendicular to DCD', and let PI be the diameter of curvature.

$PI : PV :: QR : QR''$,

$:: CP : PF$;

$\therefore PI \cdot PF = PV \cdot CP = 2CD^2$;

$\therefore PI$ is a third proportional to $2PF$ and DCD'.

84. Since the chord of curvature in any direction varies inversely as the subtense QR, drawn in that direction, it is easily seen that, if PL be the portion of the chord intercepted between

106   NEWTON.

P and DCD', the chord of curvature at P in the direction PL is the third proportional to $2PL$ and DCD'.

85. The propositions concerning the chords and diameter of curvature of an ellipse may be proved in the same words for the hyperbola, employing the following figure.

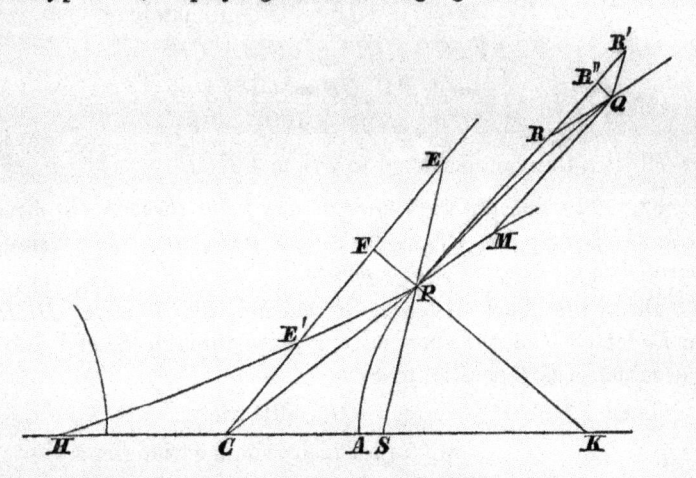

86. *The radius of curvature at any point of a conic section is to the normal in the duplicate ratio of the normal to the semi-latus rectum.*

Let PK be the normal, PO the radius of curvature, L the semi-latus rectum.

I. For the parabola,
$$PO : 2SP :: SP : SY,$$
$$:: SY : SA,$$
$$\therefore PO : 2SY :: SP : SA,$$
$$:: 4SP.SA : L^2;$$
and $PK = 2SY$, or $PK^2 = 4SP.SA$;
$$\therefore PO : PK :: PK^2 : L^2.$$

II. For the ellipse or hyperbola,
$$PO.PF = CD^2, \text{ and } PK.PF = BC^2;$$
$$\therefore PO : PK :: CD^2 : BC^2,$$
$$:: AC^2 : PF^2;$$

and $AC : PF :: AC.PK : PF.PK = BC^2 = L.AC$,
$$:: PK : L;$$
$$\therefore PO : PK :: PK^2 : L^2.$$

87. *To find the chord common to a conic section and the circle of curvature at any point.*

If a circle intersect a conic section in four points, as $PQUR$, and these points be joined in pairs by two lines, these lines will be equally inclined to the axis of the conic section. Thus, in the conic section, PQ, RU are equally inclined to the axis.

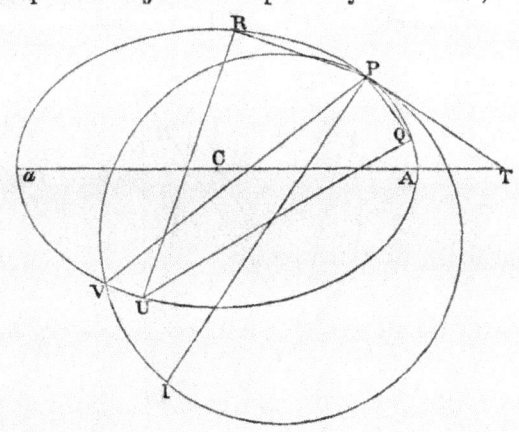

For, if UR, QP intersect in O, $OR.OU = OP.OQ$, hence the diameters of the ellipse parallel to UR, QP are equal, and therefore equally inclined to the axis.

Let Q and R move up to and ultimately coincide with P, then the intersecting circle becomes the circle of curvature at P, and PQ is in the direction PT of the tangent, ultimately, and RU assumes the position of the chord common to the conic section and the circle of curvature at P. Hence, if PV be drawn at an equal inclination with PT to the axis, PV will be the common chord required.

And if VI be drawn perpendicular to PV meeting the normal at P in I, PI is the diameter of curvature at P.

88. *To find the radius of curvature of a curve defined by the relation between the radius vector and the perpendicular from the pole on the tangent.*

Let PY, $PP'Y'$ be consecutive sides of a polygon inscribed in a curve, SY, SY' perpendicular on these sides; PO, $P'O$ perpendicular to the same sides intersecting in O, $P'U$ perpendicular SP, and SY, PY' intersect in W.

Describing a semicircle $PYY'S$ on SP
$$\angle YPW = \angle YSY' = \angle POP',$$
$$\text{and } \angle WYP = \angle OP'P;$$
therefore the triangles POP', WPY are similar.

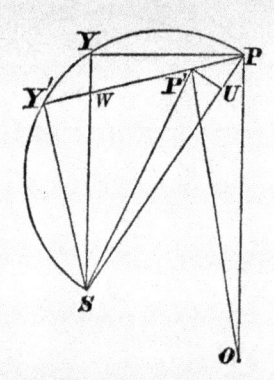

$$\therefore PO : PP' :: PW : YW;$$
also $PP' : SP :: PU : PY'$, by similar triangles $P'UP$, $SY'P$; therefore, since $PW = PY'$ ultimately,
$$PO : SP :: PU : YW$$
$$:: SP \sim SP' : SY \sim SY', \text{ ultimately.}$$

Also, if PV be the chord of curvature through S,
$$PV : 2PO :: SY : SP;$$
$$\therefore PV : 2SY :: SP \sim SP' : SY \sim SY', \text{ ultimately.}$$

89. *Two tangents* AT, BT *are drawn at the extremities of an arc* AB, *to prove that* AT *is ultimately equal to* BT, *when* AB *is indefinitely diminished.*

Draw $TCUV$ in any direction making a finite angle with the tangents, and meeting the circles of curvature at A and B in UV. Then since the circle of curvature at A is the limit of the circle which passes through C and has the tangent AT, and similarly for that at B, we have ultimately,

LEMMA XI.   109

$$TA^2 : TB^2 :: TC.TU : TC.TV,$$
and $TU = TV$, ultimately; $\therefore TA = TB$, ultimately.

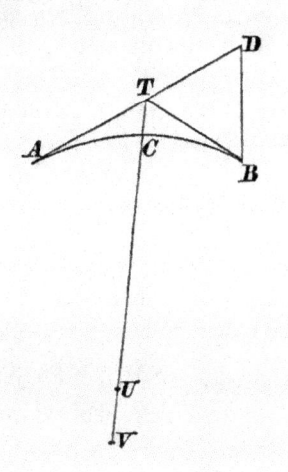

COR. If the subtense BD be drawn
$$AT + TB = AB = AD, \text{ ultimately};$$
therefore, T is ultimately the point of bisection of AD.

90. *To find the radius and chord of curvature through the pole, at any point of an equiangular spiral.*

Let SP, SQ be radii drawn to two points P and Q, near to

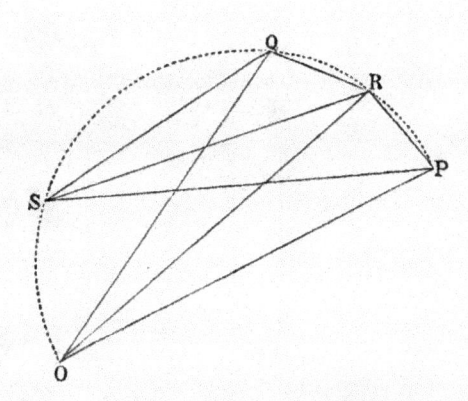

one another, let the tangents PR, QR at P and Q intersect in R, and let the normals PO, QO intersect in O; join OR, SR.

Then, since angles SQR, SPR are equal to two right angles, and each of the angles OQR, OPR is a right angle, the circle which passes through P, R, and Q will also pass through S and O, and OR will be its diameter; therefore $\angle OSR$ is a right angle.

Hence, proceeding to the limit, O is the center of the circle of curvature at P, and OSP is a right angle.

Therefore OP is the radius of curvature, and $2SP$ is the chord of curvature through the pole.

If α be the angle of the spiral, $OP = SP \operatorname{cosec} \alpha$.

91. The following is an illustration of Art. 88.

Since $SY : SY' :: SP : SP'$,
$SY : SP :: SY \sim SY' : SP \sim SP'$,
$:: 2SY :$ chord of curvature at P, by Art. 88;

therefore the chord of curvature at P through $S = 2SP$.

92. *To find the radius and vertical chord of curvature of a catenary.*

Let PQ be a small arc of a catenary, $RSPT$, QS tangents at P and Q, PM, QN ordinates, TOM the directrix.

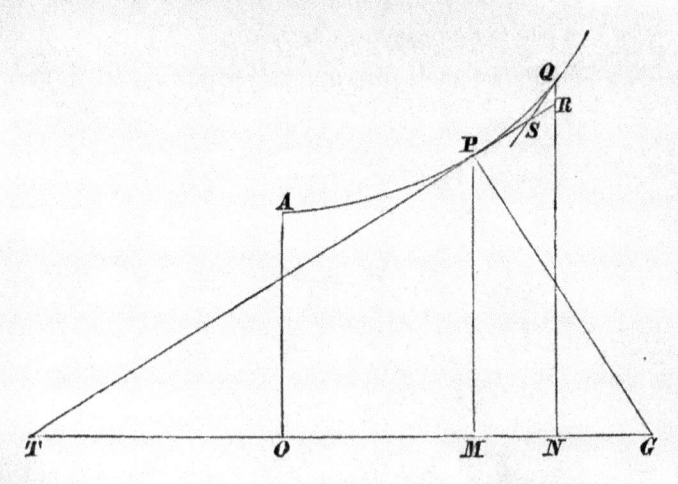

By the triangle of forces QSR (see Appendix II).

Tension at P : weight of $PQ :: SR : QR$;

LEMMA XI. 111

$$\therefore PM : PQ :: SR : QR,$$
$$:: \tfrac{1}{2}PQ : QR \text{ ultimately};$$

therefore $2PM$ is the limit of the third proportional to QR and PQ, and is, therefore, the vertical chord of curvature.

Hence, the normal PG is equal to the radius of curvature.

Also, $PG : PM :: PT : TM$,
$$:: \text{tension at } P : \text{tension at } A,$$
$$:: PM : AO;$$

hence the radius of curvature at P is a third proportional to AO and PM.

93. *To find the chord of curvature at any point of the cardioid, through the focus.*

Reverting to the construction used in Art. 44, it is easily seen that SY being perpendicular to PT, the triangles PSY, pBm, and CBp are similar;

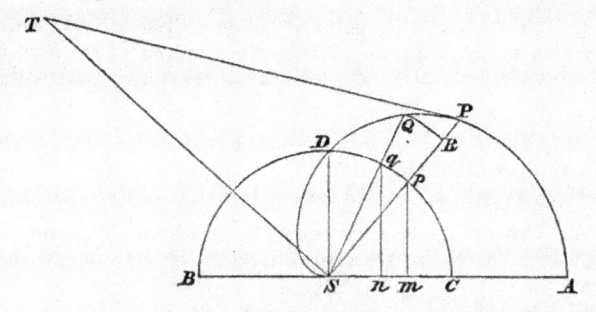

$$\therefore SY : SP :: Bm : Bp,$$
$$:: Bp : BC;$$
$$\therefore SY^2 : SP^2 :: SP : BC,$$

and by Article 88, we have, ultimately,

chord of curvature $: 2SY :: SP \sim SP' : SY \sim SY'$,

and $(SY^2 - SY'^2) BC = SP^3 - SP'^3$;

$\therefore$ ultimately $SP \sim SP' : SY \sim SY' :: 2SY.BC : 3SP^2$,
$$:: 2SP : 3SY;$$

therefore the chord of curvature through $S = \dfrac{4}{3}. SP$.

VIII.

1. Prove that the focal distance of the point in the parabola at which the curvature is one-eighth of that at the vertex is equal to the latus rectum.

2. Prove that the diameter of curvature at the vertex of the major axis of an ellipse is equal to the latus rectum: and shew that the ratio of the curvatures at the extremities of the axes is that of the cubes of the axes.

3. Apply the property that the radius of curvature at any point of an ellipse is to the normal in the duplicate ratio of the normal to the semi-latus rectum, to shew that the radius of curvature at the extremity of the major axis is equal to the semi-latus rectum.

4. Find for what point of an ellipse the circle of curvature passes through the other extremity of the diameter at that point, shew that the distance of this point from the center is the side of the square of which AB is the diagonal.

5. In a rectangular hyperbola, the diameter of curvature at any point, and the chords of curvature through the focus and center are in geometrical progression.

6. Prove that at a point P in an ellipse for which the minor axis is a mean proportional between the radius of curvature and the normal, $PC = AC - BC$. Shew that this is impossible unless $AC \geq 2BC$.

7. If the radius of curvature for an ellipse at P is twice the normal, prove that $CP = CS$.
If moreover $AC = 2BC$, prove that $CP = 3PM$.

8. Prove that the distance of the center of curvature, at any point of a parabola, from the directrix is three times that of the point.

9. SK drawn parallel to the tangent at a point P of a parabola meets any chord of curvature PV in K, prove that $PV \cdot PK = 4SP^2$.

10. Prove that the chord of curvature through the vertex A of a parabola : $2PY :: 2PY : AP$, Y being the intersection of the tangents at P and A.

11. If the circle of curvature at a point P of a parabola passes through the other extremity of the focal chord through P, and the tangent at P meet the axis in T, prove that the triangle PST will be equilateral.

12. If Pp be any chord of an ellipse, PT, pT tangents at P and p, shew that the curvatures at P and p are as the cubes of pT and PT.

13. Shew that the sum of the chords of curvature through a focus of an ellipse at the extremities of conjugate diameters is con-

stant. Also, if ρ, σ be the radii of curvature at those points, prove that $\rho^{\frac{2}{3}} + \sigma^{\frac{2}{3}}$ is constant.

14. Prove that the portion of the diameter of curvature, intercepted between the line joining the extremities of the two chords of curvature through the foci of an ellipse, and the point of contact P, is $\dfrac{2BC^2}{PF}$.

15. A hyperbola touches an ellipse, having a pair of conjugate diameters of the ellipse for its asymptotes. Prove that the curves have the same curvature at the point of contact.

16. Prove that the rectangle, contained by the chords of curvature parallel to the asymptotes at any point of a hyperbola, varies as the fourth power of the conjugate diameter.

17. EF is a chord of a given circle passing through a given point S; construct the ellipse of which E is one point, S one focus, and the given circle the circle of curvature to the ellipse at E.

18. A circle is a circle of curvature, at a fixed point in the circumference, to an ellipse, one focus of which lies on the circle, shew that the locus of the other focus is also a circle.

19. AB is the chord of a conic, and also the diameter of curvature at A, prove that the locus of the center of the conic is a rectangular hyperbola, whose transverse axis is coincident in direction with AB, and equal in length to $\frac{1}{4}AB$.

20. If x, y be the co-ordinates of a point P of a curve OP passing through the origin O, the diameters of curvature at O is $\dfrac{x^2 + y^2}{x \sin a - y \cos a}$ ultimately, a being the inclination of the tangent at O to the line of abscissæ.

Hence shew that, if the equation of a curve be
$$y^2 + 2ay - 2ax = 0,$$
the radius of curvature at the origin is $2\sqrt{2}.a$.

21. Shew that the evolute of an equiangular spiral is a similar spiral, and also that the extremities of the diameters of curvature lie in a similar spiral.

22. Prove that the chord of curvature at any point of the Lemniscate drawn through the focus is two-thirds of the radius vector.

Observations on the Lemma.

94. In the proof of Lemma XI, AI is the limit of the third proportional to BD and AB, hence it is the diameter of curvature to the curve at A.

NEWT. I

114   NEWTON.

95. For an example of a law according to which in Case 3, the directions of the subtenses may be determined, we may suppose that they always pass through a point given in position, at a finite distance from A, or, that they always touch a given curve; but it must be observed that the case, in which they touch a curve which has the same tangent AD at A, is excluded, since in this case the angles D', d' do not in the limit remain finite, a property required in the name subtense.

96. Cor. 2. If a line be drawn from the middle point of an arc of a curve, making a finite angle with the chord, the part intercepted between the chord and the arc is called the *sagitta* of the arc.

97. Cor. 5. The parabola mentioned in this corollary is a parabola of curvature at that point; for, since DB is taken in any given direction, the proportion $BD : bd :: AD^2 : Ad^2$ proves that the curve is ultimately in the form of a parabola, and that, therefore, the line through A drawn in the given direction is the corresponding diameter of the parabola of curvature.

Hence, the axis of the parabola may be taken in any assigned direction.

If the subtenses be perpendicular to the tangent, the parabola of curvature is the parabola whose curvature at the vertex determines the curvature of the curve, since the axis is perpendicular to the tangent, and if $4AU$ (fig. page 117) be the third proportional to the subtense and arc, the limiting position of U is the focus of the parabola.

By means of this corollary, the proposition alluded to under Lemma IX. Art. 48, is established; viz. that the ratio of the areas which takes place of the duplicate ratio, obtained in that Lemma, is the triplicate ratio of the same lines, when the line AE, instead of cutting the tangent at a finite angle, coincides with the tangent.

98. In order to shew the danger of falling into an error by a careless employment of the propositions proved in the first section, the following fallacious proof may be noticed of the proposition, that if, in figure Art. 101, BT be a tangent to

a curve BC of finite curvature at the point B, and BT be taken equal to the arc BC and CT be joined, CT is ultimately parallel to the normal at B. Join BC, then $BT : CB$ is ultimately a ratio of equality, by Lemma VII; therefore CBT being an isosceles triangle ultimately, CT is perpendicular to the line bisecting the angle CBT, and therefore to the tangent BT, since BT and BC ultimately coincide with the bisecting line.

The fact is that Lemma VII. only allows us to assert that BT and the chord BC differ by a quantity Tt which vanishes compared with either of them, and therefore Tt may $\propto BC^2$; but, by Lemma XI, $CT \propto BC^2$; hence $Tt : CT$ may possibly be a finite ratio, or CT may be ultimately inclined at any finite angle to BT, at least as far as the reasoning given in the above proof is concerned.

99. The following is a rigid proof of the proposition stated in the preceding article.

Let the tangent at C meet BT in D, and produce BT to F, making $DF = DC$, in BT take $BE =$ the chord BC, and join EC, TC, FC.

Since the arc BC is intermediate in magnitude between $BD + DC$ and BC, therefore, BT being equal to arc BC, the point T lies always between E and F. But the triangles BCE, BCF being both isosceles, each of the angles BEC, BFC is ultimately a right angle, therefore the angle BTC, which is less than BEC and greater than BFC, is also ultimately a right angle.

Hence CT is ultimately parallel to the normal at B.

100. *The sagitta of an arc is ultimately one quarter of the subtense drawn at the extremity of the arc parallel to the sagitta.*

Let the sagitta FE bisect the arc AB in E, and be produced to the tangent at A in G, and BD be a subtense parallel to FE.

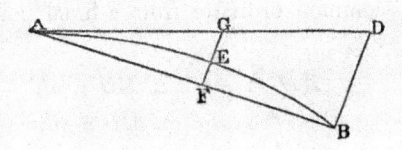

Then, $EG : BD :: AE^2 : AB^2$, ultimately; $\therefore BD = 4EG$,
also $BD : FG :: AD : AG :: AB : AE$, ultimately;
$\therefore BD = 2FG = 4EG$; hence $FE = EG = \frac{1}{4}BD$, ultimately.

101. *If* BT *be a tangent at* B, AB, BC, *equal chords of a curve of finite curvature, drawn from* B, *and* AB *be produced to* c, *making* Bc = AB, *and* Cc *be joined meeting* BT *in* T, cT *is ultimately* = CT, *when the arcs* AB, CB *are diminished indefinitely.*

For, if AU be drawn parallel to CT, meeting the tangent in U, $\quad CT : AU :: AB^2 : BC^2$ ultimately,

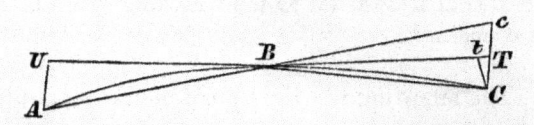

therefore $CT = AU$ ultimately; hence, if BV be drawn parallel to AC meeting Cc in V, TV vanishes compared with CT, also, $CV = cV$, therefore $2TV$ is the difference between CT and cT, which vanishes compared with either of them, therefore $CT = cT$ ultimately.

102. Scholium. Let AB, AC be two curves, having a common tangent AD at A, and let subtenses DB, DBC of the

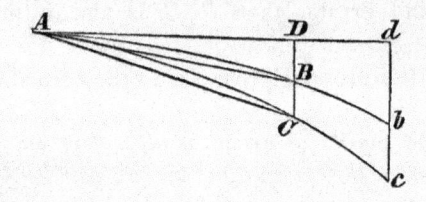

angles of contact be drawn from D at any point in the tangent in the same direction, and let $BD \propto AD^m$, $CD \propto AD^n$ in the curves AB, AC respectively.

Draw dbc a common ordinate from a fixed point d, parallel to DBC.

Then $\qquad AD^m : Ad^m :: BD : bd$,
and $\qquad AD^n : Ad^n :: CD : cd$,

LEMMA XI. 117

and if m be greater than n, $= n + r$ suppose,
$$AD^n . AD^r : Ad^n . Ad^r :: BD : bd;$$
$$\therefore CD . AD^r : cd . Ad^r :: BD : bd$$
$$:: BD . AD^r : bd . AD^r;$$
$$\therefore CD : BD :: cd . Ad^r :: bd . AD^r,$$

and since b, c, d are fixed, and AD vanishes in the limit, therefore CD is infinitely greater than BD; also, since the angles of contact, BAD, CAD, are ultimately proportional to BD, CD, it follows that, if in two curves the subtenses vary according to different powers of the arcs or tangents, the angle of contact of that curve in which the index of the power is the least is infinitely greater than the angle of contact of the other.

Illustrations.

1. *To construct for the axis and focus of the parabola of curvature for any direction of the parallel subtenses.*

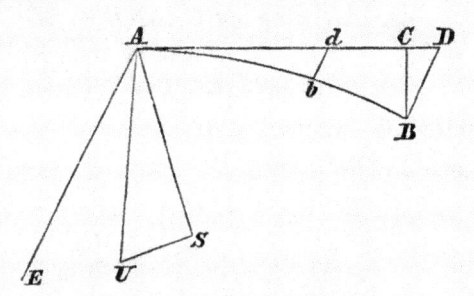

Let AB be the curve of finite curvature, BD, bd parallel subtenses, draw AE parallel to either.

Draw AU perpendicular to AD, and AS making angle $UAS = UAE$; then since AE is a diameter of the parabola, AS is in the direction of the focus.

Also, if $4AS$ be taken a third proportional to BD and AD, the limiting position of S will be the focus of the parabola.

2. *To find the locus of* S *when* BD *is inclined at different angles to* AD.

Let BC be perpendicular to AD, and AU be chosen so that
$$4AU : AC :: AC : BC,$$

the limiting position of U is the focus of the parabola whose curvature at the vertex is the same as that of the curve at A,

and $AD : 4AS :: BD : AD$ ultimately:

therefore, since $AD = AC$ ultimately,

$AU : AS :: BD : BC$,

and $\angle SAU = \angle DBC$;

hence, if we join SU, the triangles SAU, CBD are similar,

and $\angle ASU = \angle BCD = $ a right angle;

therefore the locus of S is a circle on AU as diameter.

3. ABC *is an arc of finite curvature, and is divided so that* AB : BC :: m : n, *a constant ratio.*

Join AB, AC, BC, *and shew that, ultimately,*

$$\triangle ABC : segment\ ABC :: 3 : \left(\sqrt{\frac{m}{n}} + \sqrt{\frac{n}{m}}\right)^2.$$

For by Cor. 5. Lemma XI.

$\quad$ seg AB : seg ABC :: $AB^3 : ABC^3$
$\quad\quad\quad\quad\quad\quad\quad\quad\quad :: m^3 : (m+n)^3$

$\quad$ seg BC : seg ABC :: $n^3 : (m+n)^3$;

$\therefore$ seg $AB +$ seg BC : seg ABC :: $m^3 + n^3 : (m+n)^3$,

and $\triangle ABC = $ seg $ABC -$ seg $AB -$ seg BC;

$\therefore \triangle ABC$: seg ABC :: $3(m^2n + mn^2) : (m+n)^3$

$$:: 3 : \frac{(m+n)^2}{mn},$$

$$:: 3 : \left(\sqrt{\frac{m}{n}} + \sqrt{\frac{n}{m}}\right)^2.$$

IX.

1. Shew that the directrices of all parabolas touching a curve of finite curvature at any given point, and having the same curvature at that point as the curve, pass through a fixed point.

2. Determine a parabola of curvature in magnitude and position for any point in a circle, when the subtenses are inclined at 45° to the tangent.

3. Find the focus of the parabola of curvature, whose vertex is at that of a cycloid, and the locus of the foci of all parabolas which have the same tangent and curvature at that point.

4. If AEB be the chord, AD the tangent, and BD the subtense, for an arc ACB of finite curvature at A, find the limit of the ratio area $ACBE$: area $ACBD$, as B approaches A.

5. An arc of continuous curvature PQR is bisected in Q, PT is the tangent at P; prove that, ultimately, as R approaches P, the angle RPT is bisected by PQ.

6. If BC be the chord of an arc BAC of continued curvature, A, D the middle points of the arc and chord, does AD pass through the center of curvature ultimately, when the arc is indefinitely diminished?

7. A, B, C are three points in a curve of finite curvature: when A and C move up to B, and ultimately coincide with it, the circle circumscribing the triangle formed by the tangents at A, B, and C will ultimately cut the normal at B in a point which is at a distance from B equal to half the radius of curvature there, and the triangle formed by those tangents is ultimately half of the triangle ABC.

8. Two curves of finite curvature touch each other at the point P, and from T, a fixed point in the common tangent, a secant is drawn cutting one curve in the points A, B, and the other in A', B', and the lines PA, PA', PB, PB' are drawn; prove that, if the secant move up to and ultimately coincide with the tangent, the angles APA', BPB' will be ultimately in a ratio of equality.

9. In a segment of an arc of finite curvature a pentagon is inscribed, one side of which is the chord of the arc, and the remaining sides are equal. Shew that the limiting ratio of the areas of the pentagon and segment, when the chord moves up towards the tangent at one extremity, is $15 : 16$.

10. APQ is a curve of continued and finite curvature, P and Q are two points in it, whose abscissæ along the normal at A are always in the ratio $m : 1$, and from B, C two points in the normal, straight lines BPb, CPc, BQb', CQc' are drawn to meet the tangent at A. Shew that when P and Q move up to A, the areas of the triangles bPc, $b'Qc'$ are ultimately in the ratio $m^{\frac{5}{2}} : 1$.

11. AB is an arc of finite curvature at A, and a point P is taken such that $AP : PB$ is in the constant ratio of $m : n$. Tangents at A and B intersect the tangent at P in T and R, and AB is joined. Prove that the ultimate ratio of the area $ATRB$ to the segment APB, as B moves up to A, is $3(m^2 + mn + n^2) : 2(m+n)^2$.

12. PQ is the chord of a closed curve cutting off an arc of constant length, the tangents at P and Q meet in T, a line bisecting the angle PTQ meets PQ in R; if R' be taken in PQ the same distance from P and Q that R is from Q and P, prove that R' is the intersection of the chord PQ with the consecutive chord $P'Q'$.

SECTION II.

Centripetal Forces.

PROP. I. THEOREM I.

When a body revolves in an orbit, subject to the action of forces tending to a fixed point, the areas, which it describes by radii drawn to the fixed center of force, are in one fixed plane, and are proportional to the times of describing them.

Let the time be divided into equal parts, and in the first interval let the body describe the straight line AB with uniform velocity, being acted on by no force. In the second interval it would, if no force acted, proceed to c in AB produced, describing Bc equal to AB: so that the equal areas ASB, BSc described by radii AS, BS, cS drawn to the center S, would be completed in equal intervals.

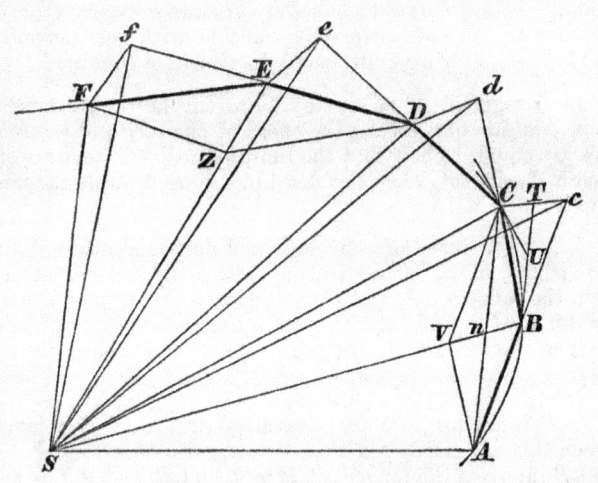

But, when the body arrives at B, let a centripetal force tending to S act upon it by a single instantaneous impulse, and cause the body to deviate from the direction Bc, and to proceed in the direction BC.

Let cC be drawn parallel to BS, meeting BC in C, then, at the end of the second interval, the body will be found at C, in the same plane with the triangle ASB, in which Bc and cC are drawn. Join SC; and the triangle SBC, between parallels SB, Cc, will be equal to the triangle SBc, and therefore also to the triangle SAB.

In like manner, if the centripetal force act upon the body successively at C, D, E, &c. causing the body to describe in the successive intervals of time the straight lines CD, DE, EF, &c. these will all lie in the same plane; and the triangle SCD will be equal to the triangle SBC, and SDE to SCD, and SEF to SDE.

Therefore equal areas are described in the same fixed plane in equal intervals; and, componendo, the sums of any number of areas $SADS$, $SAFS$, are to each other as the times of describing them.

Let now the number of these triangles be increased, and their breadth diminished indefinitely; then their perimeter ADF will be ultimately a curved line; and the instantaneous forces will become ultimately a centripetal force, by the action of which the body is continually deflected from the tangent to this curve, and which will act continuously; and the areas $SADS$, $SAFS$, being always proportional to the times of describing them, will be so in this case. Q.E.D.

Cor. 1. The velocity of a body attracted towards a fixed center in a non-resisting medium, is reciprocally proportional to the perpendicular dropped from that center upon the tangent to the orbit.

For the velocity at the points A, B, C, D, E are as the bases AB, BC, CD, DE, EF of equal triangles, and since the triangles are equal these bases are reciprocally proportional to the perpendiculars from S let fall upon them. [And the same is true in the limit, in which case the bases are in the direction of tangents to the curvilinear limit, therefore the velocity, &c.]

COR. 2. If on chords AB, BC of two arcs described in equal successive times in a non-resisting medium by the same body the parallelogram $ABCV$ be completed, and the diagonal BV of this parallelogram be produced in both directions in that position which it assumes ultimately when those arcs are diminished indefinitely, it will pass through the center of force.

COR. 3. If, on AB, BC and on DE, EF chords of arcs described in a non-resisting medium in equal times, the parallelograms $ABCV$, $DEFZ$ be completed; the forces at B and E are to one another in the ultimate ratio of the diagonals BV, EZ, when the arcs are indefinitely diminished.

For the velocities of the body represented by BC, EF in the polygon, are compounded of the velocities represented by Bc, BV and Ef, EZ; and those represented by BV, EZ, which are equal to cC, fF, in the demonstration of the proposition were generated by the impulses of the centripetal force at B and E, and are thus proportional to those impulses. [And the same is true in the limit, in which case the ultimate ratio of the impulses at any two points is the ratio of the continuous forces at those points.]

COR. 4. The forces by which any bodies moving in non-resisting media are deflected from rectilinear motion into curved orbits, are to one another as those sagittæ of arcs described in equal times, which converge to the center of force and bisect the chords, when those arcs are indefinitely diminished.

For the diagonals of the parallelograms $ABCV$, $DEFZ$ bisect each other, and these sagittæ are halves of the diagonals BV, EZ when the arcs are indefinitely diminished. [And the same is true whether ABC and DEF be parts of the same or of different orbits described by bodies of equal mass, if the arcs be described in equal times.]

Cor. 5. And therefore the accelerating effects of the same forces are to that of the force of gravity as those sagittæ are to vertical sagittæ of the parabolic arcs which projectiles describe in the same time.

Cor. 6. All the same conclusions obtain, by the Second Law of Motion, when the planes, in which the bodies move together with the centers of force which are situated in those planes, are not at rest, but are moving uniformly and parallel to themselves.

The statement of the proposition in the original Latin is,

"Areas, quas corpora in gyros acta radiis ad immobile centrum virium ductis describunt, et in planis immobilibus consistere, et esse temporibus proportionales."

Observations on the Proposition.

103. In all cases of motion of bodies, it is of great importance for the student to distinguish between the forces themselves under the action of which the bodies may be moving, and the effects which these forces produce.

It is only by an examination of the motion of a body that we are able to infer that it is, or is not, acted on by any force; if we find that the body is moving with uniform velocity in a straight line, we infer that it is, during such motion, acted upon by no force, or that the forces which are acting upon it are in equilibrium; if we find that there is any change of direction or velocity, gradual or abrupt, we infer that the body is moving under the action of some force or forces; if the change be gradual, we infer that such forces are *finite*, by which we mean that the forces require a finite time to produce a finite change whether of direction or velocity; if, on the contrary, the change be abrupt, we infer that the forces are what are called *impulsive*, that is, such as produce a finite change in an instant.

Since then, in order to make any inference with respect to the forces supposed to act, a clear conception of the motion of a body must be first attained, it becomes necessary for the student to be able to describe the motion of a particle of matter as he would that of a point, independently of the causes of such motion.

In doing this he must give a geometrical description of the line traced by the point either in a plane or in space, and then he must describe the rate, uniform or variable, with which this line is traversed.

He may then proceed to attribute any change of direction or velocity to the action of forces upon the particle, whose motion he has been examining.

104. In accordance with this method of separating the geometry of the motion from the causes of the deviations, the first proposition would be stated in such a manner as the following:

"When a point moves in a curve, in such a manner that the accelerations at every point are in the direction of a fixed point, the areas, which it describes by radii drawn to the fixed point to which the accelerations tend, are in one fixed plane, and are proportional to the times of describing them."

And, generally, if the words *force* and *body*, employed by Newton, be replaced by *acceleration* and *point*, the resulting statements will be in accordance with this geometrical method of description. It will then be easy to use such terms in the proofs, as will not imply, in the manner of expression, the action of force; thus, instead of saying "let a centripetal force tending to S act upon the body by a single instantaneous impulse," we may use the words, "let a finite velocity be communicated to the point in the direction of S."

105. It should be carefully observed, that, before proceeding to the limit, it is proved that *any* polygonal areas $SADS$, $SAFS$, are proportional to the times of description of their perimeters; so that ultimately these areas become *finite* curvilinear areas, described in *finite* times.

106. In proceeding to the ultimate state of the hypothesis, it is concluded readily from Lemmas II, and III, that the curvilinear areas are the limits of the polygons; but a greater difficulty arises in the transition from the *discontinuous* motion

PROP. I. THEOREM I.   125

under the action of instantaneous impulsive forces to the *continuous* motion under the action of a continuous force tending to S. For, in the curvilinear path of the body which is the limit of the perimeter of the polygon, the direction of the motion at the angular points of the polygon is different, and also the deflection from the direction of motion is twice as great in the polygon as it is in the curve.

Now, although we may assume that the curvilinear limit of the perimeter of the polygon may be described under the action of some force, is that force the same which is the limit of the series of impulses?

The centripetal force supposed to act with a simple instantaneous impulse, "impulsu unico et magno," is supposed to generate a finite velocity at once, which effect a finite force cannot produce.

If, instead of this imaginary impulse, we suppose a force finite, but very great, and acting for a very short time, the effect upon the figure would be to round off the angular points of the polygon.

The transition from the impulses to the continuous force, in the ultimate form of the hypothesis, must be considered as axiomatic, like the ultimate equality of the ratio of the finite arc to the perimeter of the inscribed polygon.

107. We can, however, shew that if the curvilinear limit of the polygon be described under the action of some continuous force tending to S, the effect of this force, estimated by the quantity of motion generated in the interval between the impulses, is ultimately the same as that generated by the impulse.

Consider first the geometrical properties of the limit of the polygonal perimeter.

Let BT, CU be tangents at B, C, to the curvilinear limit, and let Cc intersect BT in T (fig. page 120).

Now, since Cc ultimately vanishes compared with Bc, BC and Bc or AB and BC are ultimately in a ratio of equality, and Cc is ultimately bisected by BT (Art. 101); also, $CU = BU = UT$, ultimately (Art. 89).

Consider next, the effects produced by the different kinds of force which act in the two cases.

In the polygonal path, the impulsive force at B generates a velocity with which the body describes Cc in the time t, in which AB or BC is described, the measure of the effect of the force is therefore the velocity $\dfrac{Cc}{t}$.

In the curvilinear path, the deflection from the direction BT at B, in the same time t, is TC, by means of the continuous action of finite forces, and if we suppose the force ultimately uniform in magnitude and direction, the measure of the accelerating effect of the force is $\dfrac{2TC}{t^2}$, and the velocity generated in that time is $\dfrac{2TC}{t^2} \cdot t = \dfrac{Cc}{t}$.

Hence the effects of the finite and impulsive forces measured by the quantity of motion produced are the same.

108. We can also shew that a continuous force, which generates the same quantity of motion as the impulse at B in the time from B to C, would cause the body on arriving at C to move in the direction of the tangent to the curvilinear limit of the perimeter.

For the velocity due to the action of the finite force at the end of time t being ultimately $\dfrac{2TC}{t}$ in the direction TC, and that in the direction BT being $\dfrac{BT}{t} = \dfrac{2TU}{t}$; therefore TC, UT represent the velocities in those directions; therefore UC is the direction of motion at C, that is, the body moves in the direction of the tangent at C.

109. COR. 1. The corollary may be proved directly from the proposition, for the proportionality of the areas to the times of describing them is true if the force suddenly cease to act, in which case the body proceeds in the direction of the tangent.

Let V be the velocity at the point A, ASB the curvilinear area described in any time T, $AT = V \cdot T$ the space described if the force cease to act.

Join ST and draw SY perpendicular to AT, then area $ASB =$ triangle $SAT = \tfrac{1}{2} V \cdot T \times SY$, also area $ASB \varpropto T$;

$$\therefore V \varpropto \frac{1}{SY}.$$

Again, if h be twice the area described in the unit of time employed in estimating the accelerating effect of the force tending to S and the velocity V of the body,

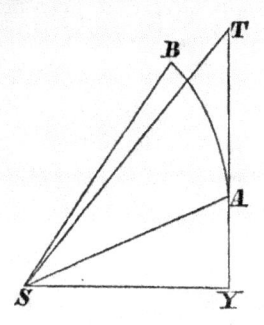

$$2 \cdot \text{area } SAB = hT;$$
$$\therefore h = V \cdot SY.$$

By the use of this area the proportions employed by Newton may be converted into equations, for the convenience of calculation.

If bodies move in curves for which the areas, described in the same time, are not equal,

$$V \propto \frac{h}{SY}.$$

110. COR. 4. The statement in this corollary requires modification, for, unless the forces be considered only with reference to their accelerating effects, or unless the bodies be supposed of equal mass, they will not be proportional to the sagittæ.

111. COR. 5. The object of this corollary is to determine the numerical measure of the central force which governs the motion of a body, when the circumstances of the motion are known: for it supplies us with the ratio of this force to the force of gravity on the same body at any place, the measure of which can be determined by experiment.

Application of the Proposition.

112. PROP. *When the force, instead of tending to a fixed point, acts in parallel lines, the property of the motion enunciated*

in the proposition may be replaced by the property that the resolved part of the space described perpendicular to the direction of the force is proportional to the times.

This is immediately deducible from the second law of motion, since there is no force in the direction perpendicular to that of the forces, and the velocity in that direction is uniform.

That this is the result of the properties in the proposition may be shewn by removing the center of force to an infinite distance.

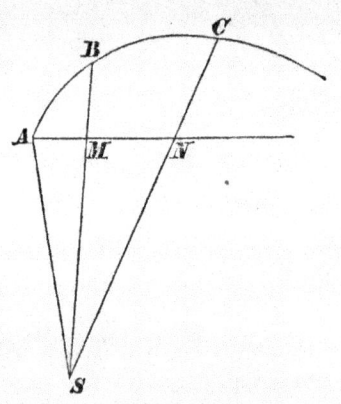

If S be the center of force, AMN perpendicular to SB, the area $ABCS$ is proportional to the time of describing AC, and the areas $AMNS$ and $ABCS$ are ultimately equal when S is removed to an infinite distance in BMS, hence the triangle ASN is proportional to the time, and therefore the base AN, which varies as the triangle ASN, is also proportional to the time, which therefore, since CN is ultimately perpendicular to AN, proves the proposition.

113. PROP. *If a body describe a curvilinear orbit about a force tending constantly to a fixed point, the area described in a given time will be unaltered, if the force be suddenly increased or diminished, or if the body be acted on at any moment by an impulsive force tending to that point.*

For, if in the polygon the impulse at any point B be increased or diminished by any force tending to or from S, the only effect is to remove the vertex C of the triangle SBC to some other point in the line cC parallel to BS, hence the area will be unaltered, and the argument which establishes the equality of polygonal areas in a given time proceeds as before.

In the limit the curvilinear areas in a given time are unaltered.

If at B the new force introduced be impulsive, the angle ABC remains less than two right angles when we proceed to the limit, and the parts of the curve cut one another at a finite angle.

Hence, in any calculation made upon supposition of such changes of force, the value of h (Art. 109), will be the same before and after the change of the force.

Apses.

114. DEF. In any orbit described under the action of a force tending to a fixed center, a point at which the direction of the motion is perpendicular to the central distance is called an *apse*, the distance from the center is called an *apsidal distance*, and the angle between consecutive apsidal distances is called an *apsidal angle*.

Thus, in the ellipse about the center, the four extremities of the axes are apses, there are two different apsidal distances, and every apsidal angle is a right angle.

In the ellipse about a focus, the apses are at the greatest and least distances, and the apsidal angle is two right angles.

115. *In a central orbit described under the action of forces tending to a fixed point, each apsidal distance divides the orbit symmetrically, if the forces be always equal at equal distances.*

It is easily shewn that, in any orbit described by a body under the action of forces tending to a fixed point, the forces depending only upon the distance, if a second body be projected at any point with the velocity of the first in the opposite direction, it will proceed to describe the same orbit in the reverse direction, under the action of the same forces.

For, let ABC be a portion of the polygon whose limit is the curvilinear path of the body, and produce AB to c, and CB to a, making $Bc = AB$, and $Ba = CB$.

The impulse at B is measured by cC when the body describes ABC, and if the motion be reversed, the same impulse at B would cause the body to move in BA, with the velocity which it had in AB, since $aA = cC$. And the same is true throughout the polygonal path, hence the assertion is true for the whole path, described under the action of impulses which are always the same at the same points, and therefore proceeding to the limit, the statement made for any orbit is proved.

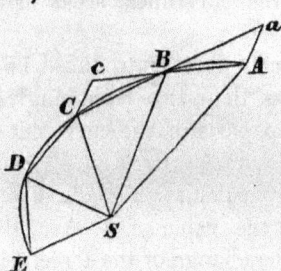

Hence, since the forces are equal at equal distances on both sides of the apse, the path of the body from an apse being similar and equal to the path which would be described if the velocity were reversed at the apse, is similar to the path described in approaching the apse; whence the proposition is established.

116. *There are only two different apsidal distances, and all apsidal angles are equal.*

For, after passing a second apse, the curve being symmetrical on both sides, a third apse will be in such a position that the apsidal distance is the same as for the first apse, and all the apsidal angles are shewn similarly to be equal.

117. COR. Hence a central orbit can never re-enter unless the ratio of the apsidal angle to a right angle be commensurable, and if it be so the curve will always re-enter.

Illustrations.

1. *If a body describe an ellipse under the action of a force tending to one of the foci, the square of the velocity varies inversely as the distance from that focus, and directly as the distance from the other.*

PROP. I. THEOREM I. 131

The square of the velocity $\propto \dfrac{1}{SY^2} \propto HZ^2$,

and $HZ : SY :: HP : SP$;

$\therefore HZ.SY : SY^2 :: HP : SP$,

and $HZ.SY = BC^2$; $\therefore SY^2 \propto \dfrac{SP}{HP}$,

and the (velocity)$^2 \propto \dfrac{HP}{SP}$.

2. *The velocity is greatest when the body is at the extremity of the major axis which is nearest to the focus to which the force tends, and least at the other extremity.*

For SY is the least in the first and greatest in the second position.

3. *The velocity at the extremities of the minor axis is a geometric mean between the greatest and least velocities.*

For at this point $HZ = BC$, and at the extremities of the major axis the values of HZ are Sa and SA,

and $BC^2 = SA.Sa$.

4. *In the equiangular spiral described under the action of a force tending to the focus, the velocity* $\propto \dfrac{1}{SP}$.

For, $SY \propto SP$.

5. *If the force tends to the center of the elliptic orbit described by a body, the time between the extremities of conjugate diameters is constant.*

For the area PCD is constant.

X.

1. If different bodies be projected with the same velocity from a given point, all being attracted by forces tending to one fixed point, shew that the areas described by the lines drawn from the fixed points to the bodies are proportional to the sines of the angles of projection.

2. When a body describes a curvilinear orbit under the action of a force tending to a fixed point, will the direction of motion or the curvature of the orbit at any point be changed, if the force at the point receive a finite change?

3. From the center of a planet, a perpendicular is let fall upon the plane of the ecliptic; prove that the foot of this perpendicular will move as if it were acted on by a force tending to the sun's center.

4. A body moves in a parabola about a center of force in the vertex, shew that the time of moving from any point to the vertex varies as the cube of the distance of the point from the axis of the parabola.

5. In a parabolic orbit described round a force tending to the focus, shew that the velocity varies inversely as the normal at any point. Shew also that the sum of the squares of the velocities at the extremities of a focal chord is constant.

6. A body describes a parabola about a center of force in the focus; shew that its velocity at any point may be resolved into two equal constant velocities, respectively perpendicular to the axis and to the focal distance of the point.

7. If the velocity at any point of an ellipse described about the center can be equal to the difference of the greatest and least velocities the major axis must not be less than double of the minor.

8. If an ellipse be described under the action of a force tending to the center, shew that the velocity varies directly as the diameter conjugate to that which passes through the body; also that the sum of the squares of the velocities at the extremities of conjugate diameters is constant.

9. In an ellipse described round a force tending to the focus, compare the intervals of time between the extremities of the same latus rectum, when $AC = 2CS$.

10. In the ellipse described about the focus S, $ASHA'$ being the major axis, time in AB : time in BA' :: $\pi - 2e : \pi + 2e$.

11. A body describes a parabola about the focus; if the segments PS, Sp of the focal chord PSp be in the ratio $n : 1$, prove that the time of describing pA : time of describing AP

$$:: 3n + 1 : n^2(n+3).$$

12. In an ellipse described about a focus, the time of moving from the nearest focal distance to the extremity of the minor axis

is m times that from the extremity of the minor axis to the greatest focal distance; find the eccentricity, and shew that, if there be a small error in m, the corresponding error in the eccentricity varies inversely as $(1+m)^2$.

13. If a body move in an ellipse under the action of a force tending to the center, shew that the velocity at any point perpendicular to either focal distance is constant; and that the sum of the squares of the velocities at the extremities of any pair of semi-conjugate diameters resolved in any given direction is constant.

14. If a body move in an ellipse about the center, having given any point P in the ellipse, determine geometrically the points p_1, p_2, p_3, &c... so that the time in $Pp_1, p_1p_2, p_2p_3,...$ may each be equal to $\frac{1}{n}$-th of the periodic time. Also, shew that if the times in $AP_1, P_1P_2, P_2P_3, P_3B$ be equal, and v, v_1, v_2, v_3, v' be the velocities at A, P_1, P_2, P_3, B respectively,

$$2(v_1^2 + v_2^2 + v_3^2) = 3(v^2 + v'^2).$$

15. If a body describe an ellipse under the action of a central force tending to one of the foci, shew that the sum of the velocities at the extremities of any chord parallel to the major axis varies inversely as the diameter parallel to the direction of motion at those points.

16. If the velocities at three points in an ellipse described by a particle, the acceleration of which tends to the focus, be in arithmetical progression, prove that the velocities at the opposite extremities of the diameters, passing through these points, are in harmonical progression.

17. A particle describes an ellipse about a center of force in one of the foci; if lines be drawn always parallel to the direction of motion at a distance from the center of force proportional to the velocity of the particle, these lines will touch a similar ellipse.

18. A hyperbola is described under the action of a repulsive force tending from the center, and at any point P of the curve, PQ is taken along the tangent at P, proportional to the velocity at P; prove that the locus of Q is a similar hyperbola.

19. Prove that, in an equiangular spiral described by a body about a force tending to the pole, the time in any arc varies as the difference of the squares of the focal distance of the extremities.

20. Two particles revolve in the same direction in an oval orbit round a centre of force S, which divides the axis unequally, starting simultaneously from the extremities of a chord PQ, drawn

through S. Prove that, when they first arrive in positions R, T respectively, such that the angle RST is a minimum, the time from R to the next apse will be an arithmetic mean between the times from P to the next apse, and to Q from the last apse.

21. Two equal particles are attached to the extremities of a string of length $2l$, and lie in a smooth horizontal plane with the string stretched, if the middle point of the string be drawn with uniform velocity v in a direction perpendicular to the initial direction of the string, shew that the path of each particle will be a cycloid, and that the particles will meet after a time $\dfrac{l\pi}{2v}$.

22. The velocity in a cardioid described about a force tending to the pole varies in the inverse sesquiplicate ratio of the distance.

23. The velocity in the Lemniscate varies inversely as the cube of the central distance, when a particle moves in the curve round a force tending to the center.

Prop. II. Theorem II.

Every body, which moves in any curve line described in a plane, and describes areas proportional to the times of describing them about a point either fixed or moving uniformly in a straight line, by radii drawn to that point, is acted on by a centripetal force tending to the same point.

Case 1. Let the time be divided into equal intervals, and, in the first interval, let the body describe *AB* with uniform velocity, being acted on by no force; in the second interval it would, if no force acted, proceed to *c* in *AB* produced, describing *Bc* equal to *AB*; and the triangles *ASB*, *BSc* would be equal. But, when the body arrives at *B*, let a force, acting upon it by a single impulse, cause the body to describe *BC* in the second interval of time, so that the triangle *BSC* is equal to the triangle *ASB*, and therefore also to the triangle *BSc*; therefore *BSC* and *BSc* are between the same parallels, hence *BS*

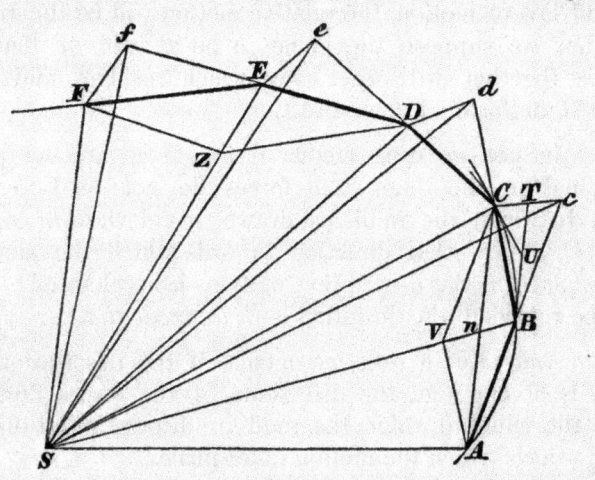

is parallel to cC, and therefore BS was the direction of the impulse at B.

Similarly, if at $C, D,...$ the body be acted on by impulses causing it to move in the sides $CD, DE,...$ of a polygon, in the successive intervals, making the triangles $CSD, DSE,...$ equal to ASB and BSC, the impulses can be shewn to have been in the directions $CS, DS...$ Hence, if *any* polygonal areas be described proportional to the times of describing them, the impulses at the angular points all tend to S.

The same is true if the number of intervals be increased and their length diminished indefinitely, in which case the series of impulses approximates to a continuous force tending to S, and the polygons to curvilinear areas, as their limits. Hence the proposition is true for a *fixed* center.

Case 2. The proposition will also be true, if S be a point which moves uniformly in a straight line, for, by the second law of motion, the relative motion will be the same, whether we suppose the plane to be at rest, or that it moves together with the body which revolves and the point S, uniformly in one direction.

Cor. 1. In non-resisting media, if the areas are not proportional to the times, the forces do not tend to the point to which the radii are drawn, but deviate *in consequentiâ*, i.e. in that direction towards which the motion takes place, if the description of areas is accelerated; but if it be retarded, the deviation is *in antecedentiâ*.

Cor. 2. And also in resisting media, if the description of areas is accelerated, the directions of the forces deviate from the point to which the radii are drawn in that direction towards which the motion takes place.

SCHOLIUM.

A body may be acted on by a centripetal force compounded of several forces. In this case, the meaning of the proposition is, that that force, which is the resultant of all,

PROP. II. THEOREM II. 137

tends to S. Moreover, if any force act continually in a line perpendicular to the plane of the areas described, this force will cause the body to deviate from the plane of its motion, but will neither increase nor diminish the amount of area described, and therefore must be neglected in the composition of the forces.

Observations on the Proposition.

118. The description of an area round a point in motion may be explained by the following construction for the relative orbit, in the case of motion about a point which is itself moving uniformly in a straight line.

Let SS' be the line in which S moves uniformly and let the body move from A to B in the same time as S moves from S to S', and let P, σ be simultaneous positions of the body and of S.

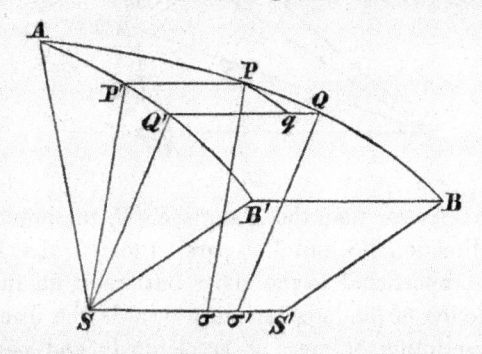

If PP' be drawn equal and parallel to σS, and the same construction be made for every point in the path of the body, the curve $AP'B'$, which is the locus of P', is the orbit which the body would appear to describe to an observer at S, who refers all the motion to the body.

This is clear, since SP' is equal and parallel to σP, and therefore the distance of the body, and the direction in which it is seen, is the same in the two cases.

If QQ' be corresponding points near P and P', and the force at σ be supposed to act impulsively, the relative motion round σ will be unaltered if we apply to both P and σ velocities equal to that of σ and in a contrary direction, but in this case σ will be reduced to rest and the velocity of P will be the velocity relative to σ. Take PQ and $\sigma\sigma'$, which are described in the same time, to represent the velocities of P and σ, and let Qq be equal and parallel to $\sigma'\sigma$, then Pq represents the velocity of P relative to σ: and, since $Q'q = S\sigma' - \sigma'\sigma = P'P$, $P'Q'$ is equal and parallel to Pq, and therefore the velocity in the orbit AB' about S at rest, is equal to the relative velocity about S in motion.

119. COR. 1. Reverting to the polygonal area, if the triangle SBC' be greater than the triangle SAB, the impulse at B is not in the direction BS, but BU, parallel to cC', that is, if the areas are not proportional to the times but are in an increasing ratio, the direction of the force deviates towards the direction in which the description of areas is accelerated: and *vice versâ*, when the description is retarded.

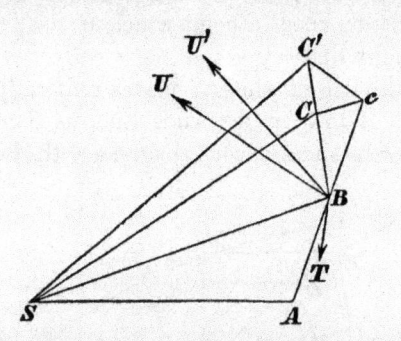

120. COR. 2. The effect of a resisting medium is to retard the motion, or, supposing it the limit of a series of impulses, we must conceive an impulse at B, in the case of the polygon, in the direction BA; if therefore the description of areas be accelerated, the impulse applied at B in the direction BU' must act still further *in consequentiâ* than that in BU, in order that, with the impulse corresponding to the resistance of the medium, it may produce a resultant impulse in the direction of BU.

The effect of the resistance alone is to retard the description of areas.

If the force act *in consequentiâ*, the resistance of this force

PROP. II. THEOREM II.

and the resistance of the medium may act in the direction BS, and the proportionality of the areas to the time be preserved.

121. Prop. *Let* ABCDE *be any plane curve,* S *any point in the plane, to shew that,* generally, *the curve can be described under the action of a force tending to or from* S, *with finite velocity, the velocity at any given point being any given velocity.*

For arcs AB, BC, ... can be measured from any point A, along the curve, such that the areas SAB, SBC, ... are all equal,

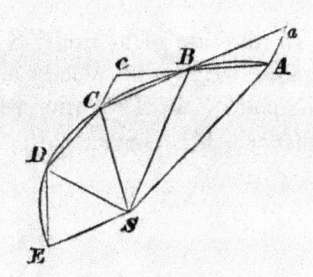

and of any magnitude. Also a body can be made, by some force, to move along the curve with finite velocity, so as to describe the arcs AB, BC, ... in equal times, unless the tangent to one of the arcs, as DE, pass through S, in which case, if the arcs be indefinitely diminished, $DE : AB$ is not finite ultimately.

Hence by Prop. II. a body *can* move with finite velocity under the action of some force tending to or from S, *generally.*

122. Cor. 1. Since in making the motion of the body such that it shall describe equal areas in equal times we are only concerned with the ratio of the velocities, the velocity at any point A may be any given velocity.

123. Cor. 2. Or if we please we may suppose the force at any point any given force; for, in the case of the polygon, the velocity generated by the impulse at B is to the velocity in AB as cC to Bc, hence the impulse at B may be of any magnitude if we choose the velocity in AB properly.

124. COR. 3. The ratio of the velocities is the same at two given points, for all forces tending to a given center, under the action of which the curve can be described.

125. COR. 4. Hence a body can move throughout any ellipse under the action of a centripetal force tending to the center or focus, the force depending only on the distance, since in these cases the curve is symmetrical on opposite sides of any apse; or about any point within the ellipse, if the forces do not depend only on the distance, since no point within an ellipse lies on any tangent.

126. COR. 5. In the case of a circle, S being an external point, a body can move with finite velocity under the action of a force tending to the point S, in the portion which is concave to S, and from S, in that which is convex to S; but not from one portion to the other.

Prop. III. Theorem III.

Every body, which describes areas proportional to the times of describing them by radii drawn to the center of another body which is moving in any manner whatever, is acted on by a force compounded of a centripetal force tending to that other body, and of the whole accelerating force which acts upon that other body.

Let the first body be L, the second T, T moves under the action of some force P, L under the action of another

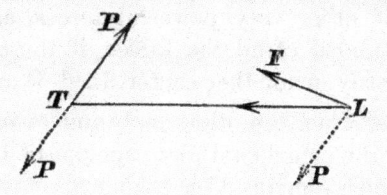

force F. At every instant apply to both bodies the force P in the contrary direction to that in which it acts, as represented by the dotted arrows.

L will continue to describe about T, as before, areas proportional to the times of describing them, and since there is now no force acting on T, T is at rest or moves uniformly in a straight line.

Therefore, (by Theor. 2) the resultant of the force F and the force P applied to L tends to T.

Hence F is compounded of a centripetal force tending to T, and of a force equal to that which acts on T. Q.E.D.

Cor. 1. Hence, if a body L describes areas proportional to the times of describing them by radii drawn to another body T; and from the whole force which acts upon L, whether a single force or compounded of several forces, be taken away the whole accelerating force which acts upon the other body T; the whole remaining force, which acts upon L, will tend to the other body T as a center.

COR. 2. And, if these areas are very nearly proportional to the times of describing them, the remaining force will tend to the other body very nearly.

COR. 3. And conversely, if the remaining force tends very nearly to the other body T, the areas will be very nearly proportional to the times.

COR. 4. If the body L describes areas which are very far from being proportional to the times of describing them, by radii drawn to another body T; and that other body T is at rest, or moves uniformly in a straight line: then, either there is no centripetal force tending to that other body T, or such centripetal force is compounded with the action of other very powerful forces, and the whole force, compounded of all the forces, if there be many, is directed towards some other center fixed or moving.

The same holds, when the other body moves in any manner whatever, if the centripetal force spoken of be understood to be that which remains after taking away the whole force acting upon the other body T.

SCHOLIUM.

Since the equable description of areas is a guide to the center to which that force tends, by which a body is principally acted on, and by which it is deflected from rectilinear motion, and retained in its orbit, we may, in what follows, employ the equable description of areas as a guide to the center, about which all curvilinear motion in free space takes place.

Illustration.

127. As an illustration of the last propositions and their corollaries, we may state some of the observed facts in the motion

PROP. III. THEOREM III. 143

of the Moon, Earth, and Sun, and make the deductions corresponding to them.

Suppose the Moon's orbit relative to the Earth to be nearly circular, and let $ABCD$ be this orbit, E the Earth.

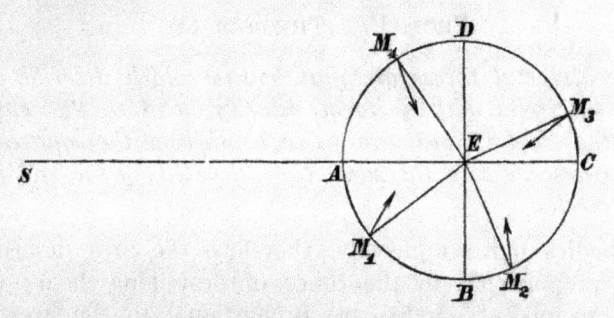

1. The areas described by the radii drawn from the Moon to the Earth are nearly proportional to the times of describing; hence the resultant force on the Moon tends nearly to E.

2. If ES the line joining the centers of the Earth and Sun meets the Moon's relative orbit about the Earth in A, C, and DEB be perpendicular to ES, the description of areas is accelerated as the Moon moves from D to A and from B to C, and retarded from A to B and from C to D; hence the direction of the resultant force on the Moon in the positions M_1, M_2, M_3, M_4, is in the directions of the arrows slightly inclined to the radii drawn to E.

From these observed facts, we see that when the force, under the action of which E moves, is applied to the Moon in the contrary direction, the remaining force tends in the directions of the arrows.

By the supposition that the Earth and Moon are acted on by forces tending to the Sun, whose distance compared with EM is very great, and that the differences of the forces on these bodies are not very great, the circumstances of the description of areas in the motion of the Moon are accounted for.

Prop. IV. Theorem IV.

The centripetal forces of equal bodies, which describe different circles with uniform velocity, tend to the centers of the circles, and are to each other as the squares of arcs described in the same time, divided by the radii of the circles.

The bodies move uniformly, therefore the arcs described are proportional to the times of describing them; and the sectors of circles are proportional to the arcs on which they stand, therefore the areas described by radii drawn to the centers are proportional to the times of describing them; hence, by Prop. II, the forces tend to the centers of the circles.

Again, let AB, ab be small arcs described in equal times,

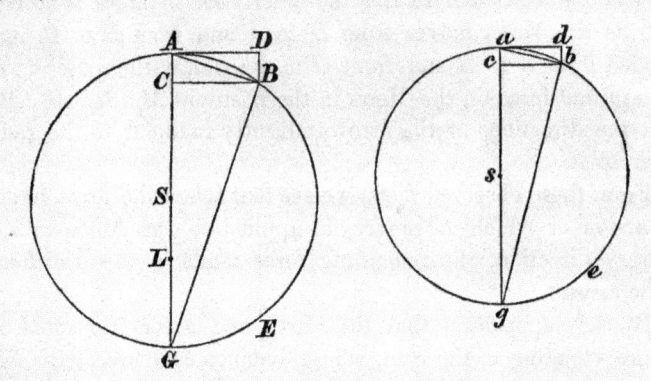

AD, ad tangents at A, a, $ACSG$, $acsg$ diameters through A, a. Join AB, ab, and draw BC, bc perpendicular to AG, ag.

By similar triangles, $AC : AB :: AB : AG$,

$$\therefore AC \cdot AG = (\text{chord } AB)^2;$$

$$\therefore AC : ac :: \frac{(\text{chord } AB)^2}{AG} : \frac{(\text{chord } ab)^2}{ag}.$$

PROP. IV. THEOREM IV.

But, ultimately, when the arcs AB, ab are indefinitely diminished, since AC, ac are sagittæ of the double of arcs AB, ab, and are therefore, by Prop. I. Cor. 4, ultimately as the forces at A and a, therefore ultimately,

$$\text{force at } A : \text{force at } a :: \frac{(\text{chord } AB)^2}{AG} : \frac{(\text{chord } ab)^2}{ag}$$

$$:: \frac{(\text{arc } AB)^2}{AG} : \frac{(\text{arc } ab)^2}{ag}, \text{ by Lemma VII.}$$

Take AE, ae two arcs described in *any* equal finite times, then $AE : ae :: AB : ab$, since the bodies move uniformly, and this is also true in the limit;

$$\text{therefore, force at } A : \text{force at } a :: \frac{AE^2}{AS} : \frac{ae^2}{as}.$$

Q. E. D.

COR. 1. Since these arcs are proportional to the velocities of the bodies, the centripetal forces will be in the ratio compounded of the duplicate ratio of the velocities directly, and the simple ratio of the radii inversely.

That is, if V, v be the velocities in the two circles, R, r the radii, F, f the centripetal forces,

$$AE : ae :: V : v;$$

$$\therefore F : f :: \frac{V^2}{R} : \frac{v^2}{r}.$$

COR. 2. And since the circumferences of the circles are described in their periodic times, the velocities are in the ratio compounded of the ratio of the radii directly and the ratio of the periodic times inversely; hence the centripetal forces are in the ratio compounded of the ratio of the radii directly, and of the ratio of the squares of the periodic times inversely.

If P, p be the periodic times in the two circles respectively,

$$V : v :: \frac{2\pi R}{P} : \frac{2\pi r}{p} :: \frac{R}{P} : \frac{r}{p};$$

$$\therefore F : f :: \frac{V^2}{R} : \frac{v^2}{r} :: \frac{R}{P^2} : \frac{r}{p^2}.$$

COR. 3. Hence, if the periodic times be equal, and therefore the velocities proportional to the radii, the centripetal forces will be as the radii; and conversely.

If $P = p$, then $V : v :: R : r$;

$$\therefore F : f :: \frac{V^2}{R} : \frac{v^2}{r} :: R : r.$$

COR. 4. Also if the periodic times are in the subduplicate ratio of the radii, the centripetal forces are equal.

That is, if $P^2 : p^2 :: R : r$, then $F = f$, by Cor. 2.

COR. 5. If the periodic times are as the radii, and therefore the velocities equal, the centripetal forces are reciprocally as the radii; and conversely.

COR. 6. If the periodic times are in the sesquiplicate ratio of the radii, and therefore the velocities reciprocally in the subduplicate ratio of the radii, the centripetal forces are reciprocally as the squares of the radii; and conversely.

That is, if $P^2 : p^2 :: R^3 : r^3$,

$$\text{then } V^2 : v^2 :: \frac{R^2}{P^2} : \frac{r^2}{p^2} :: \frac{1}{R} : \frac{1}{r};$$

$$\therefore F : f :: \frac{V^2}{R} : \frac{v^2}{r} :: \frac{1}{R^2} : \frac{1}{r^2}.$$

COR. 7. And, generally, if the periodic times vary as any power R^n of the radius R, and, therefore, the velocity vary inversely as the power R^{n-1}; the centripetal force will vary inversely as R^{2n-1}; and conversely.

COR. 8. All the same proportions can be proved concerning the times, velocities, and forces, by which bodies describe similar parts of any figures whatever, which are similar and have centers of force similarly situated, if the demonstrations be applied to those cases, *uniform description of areas* being substituted for *uniform velocity*, and *distances of the bodies from the centers of force* for *radii of the circles*.

PROP. IV. THEOREM IV. 147

Let AE, ae be similar arcs of similar curves described by bodies about forces tending to similarly situated points S, s; and let AB, ab be small arcs described in equal times;

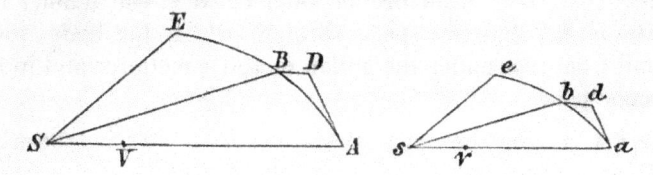

BD, bd subtenses parallel to SA, sa; AV, av chords of curvature at A, a, so that, by similar figures, we have

$$AV : av :: AS : as.$$

Then, force at A : force at a :: $DB : db$, ultimately,

$$:: \frac{AB^2}{AV} : \frac{ab^2}{av} :: \frac{AB^2}{SA} : \frac{ab^2}{sa}, \text{ ultimately};$$

and if V, v be the velocities at A, a, since AB, ab are described in equal times,

$$AB : ab :: V : v, \text{ ultimately};$$

$\therefore$ force at A : force at a $:: \dfrac{V^2}{SA} : \dfrac{v^2}{sa}$,

corresponding to Cor. 1.

Again, if AB, ab be small similar arcs described in times T, t, instead of being arcs described in equal times, and P, p be the times of describing similar finite arcs AE, ae,

$$T : P :: \text{area } ASB : \text{area } ASE$$
$$:: \text{area } asb : \text{area } ase :: t : p;$$
$$\therefore T : t :: P : p;$$

and this, being true always, is true when AB, ab are indefinitely diminished.

Hence, $F : f :: \dfrac{BD}{T^2} : \dfrac{bd}{t^2}$, ultimately,

$$:: \frac{SA}{P^2} : \frac{sa}{p^2},$$

corresponding to Cor. 2.

L 2

Cor. 9. It follows also from the same proposition, that the arc, which a body, moving with uniform velocity in a circle under the action of a given centripetal force, describes in any time, is a mean proportional between the diameter of the circle, and the space through which the body would fall from rest under the action of the same force and in the same time.

For, let AL be the space described from rest in the same time as the arc AE, then since, if BD be perpendicular to the tangent at A, BD is ultimately the space described by the body, under the action of the force at A, in the time in which the body describes the arc AB, and the times are proportional to the arcs;

$$\therefore AL : BD :: AE^2 : AB^2;$$

$$\therefore AL.AG : BD.AG :: AE^2 : AB^2;$$

and $BD.AG = (\text{chord } AB)^2 = (\text{arc } AB)^2$, ultimately;

therefore $AL.AG = AE^2$,

that is, $AL : AE :: AE : AG$.

Q. E. D.

SCHOLIUM.

The case of the sixth Corollary holds for the heavenly bodies, and on that account the motion of bodies acted upon by a centripetal force, which decreases in the duplicate ratio of the distance from the center of force, is treated of more fully in the following section.

Moreover, by the aid of the preceding proposition and its corollaries, the proportion of a centripetal force to any known force, such as gravity, can be obtained. For, if a body revolve in a circle concentric with the earth by the action of its own gravity, this gravity is its centripetal force.

But, from the falling of heavy bodies, by Cor. 9, both the time of one revolution and the arcs described in any given time are determined.

PROP. IV. THEOREM IV.

And by propositions of this kind Huygens in his excellent tract, *De Horologio Oscillatorio*, compared the force of gravity with the centrifugal force of revolving bodies.

The preceding results may be proved in this manner. In any circle let a regular polygon be supposed to be described of any number of sides. And if a body moving with a given velocity along the sides of the polygon be reflected by the circle at each of its angular points, the force with which it impinges on the circle at each of the reflections, will be proportional to the velocity; and therefore the sum of the forces, in a given time, will vary as the velocity and the number of the reflections conjointly. But if the number of sides of the polygon be given, the velocity varies as the space described in a given time, and the number of reflections in a given time varies, in different circles, inversely as the radii of the circles, and, in the same circle, directly as the velocity. Hence, the sum of the forces exerted in a given time varies as the space described in that time increased or diminished in the ratio of that space to the radius of the circle; that is, as the square of that space divided by the radius, and therefore, if the number of sides be diminished indefinitely so that the polygon coincides with the circle, the sum of the forces varies as the squares of the arc described in the given time divided by the radius.

This is the *centrifugal force* by which the body presses against the circle, and to this the opposite force is equal, by which the circle continually repels the body towards the center.

Symbolical representation of Areas, Lines, &c.

128. In the statement of the proposition the words " arcuum quadrata applicata ad radios" in the text of Newton, is rendered the squares of arcs divided by the radii. Such expressions as $\dfrac{AB^2}{AG}$ may be regarded as representations of lines, (*e.g.* this

expression denotes AC,) whose lengths are determined by such constructions as the following:

To AG apply a rectangle whose area is that of the square on AB, and let AC be the side adjacent to AG; AC is thus obtained by applying the square on AB to AG. The propriety of the symbol $\dfrac{AB^2}{AG}$ employed to represent a line AC, assumed from algebra, is obvious, since the number of units of area in the square on AB and in the rectangle whose sides are AG, AC are the same, hence if m, n, r be the number of units of length in these lines $m^2 = n \times r$, and $r = \dfrac{m^2}{n}$.

129. If symbols of this kind, viz. $\dfrac{AB^2}{AG}$, be used in the same manner as a fraction, we may either treat them numerically, considering AB^2 to represent the number of units of area contained in the square on AB, and AG as the number of units of length in AG, and thus apply the rules of Arithmetical Algebra; or, we may look upon AB^2 as the absolute representation of an area, and AG as that of a line, in which case $\dfrac{AB^2}{AG}$ has no meaning except by interpretation. In this interpretation we are guided by the principles upon which Symbolical Algebra is applied to any science, the laws of operation by symbols being the same in Arithmetical and Symbolical Algebra, and the symbols being interpreted so that these laws are not contradicted. Thus if, in the application to Geometry, the symbol A be supposed to denote an area equal to that of a rectangle whose sides are represented by a and b, the assumption that $A = ab$ or ba supposes that $ab = ba$; hence, the laws remain the same as in Arithmetical Algebra, and $\dfrac{A}{a} = b$; so that the interpretation is legitimate, that, if a rectangle be applied to a, whose area is A, $\dfrac{A}{a}$ denotes the other side of the rectangle.

Observations on the Proposition.

130. In the statement of the proposition the word 'equal' has been inserted before 'bodies,' in order to make the theorem correct, whether we suppose the centripetal force to be estimated with reference to the momentum or the velocity generated.

It would, perhaps, be better to state the proposition as follows; "the forces, under the action of which bodies describe different circles with uniform velocity, are centripetal and tend to the centers of the circles, and their accelerating effects are to each other, &c.," for it is not known, prior to the proof, that the forces are centripetal.

131. Cors. 1 and 9. The first corollary asserts that the centripetal forces or bodies moving in different circles vary as $\frac{V^2}{R}$, but the ninth shews that the accelerating effects of the centripetal forces are in each circle equal to $\frac{V^2}{R}$.

For, if V be the velocity, F the accelerating effect of the force in any circle, T the time of describing any arc, VT is the length of the arc, $\frac{1}{2}FT^2$ is the space through which the body would move under the action of the same force continued constant, in the same time in which the arc is described, therefore

$$\tfrac{1}{2}FT^2 : VT :: VT : 2R;$$

$$\therefore V^2 = FR.$$

132. Scholium. In uniform circular motion the centripetal force is employed in counteracting the tendency of the body to move in a straight line, which it would do, according to the first law of motion, with the uniform velocity which it has at any point of the circle, if the centripetal force were suddenly to cease to act. This tendency to recede is improperly called a *centrifugal force;* for the effect of a force being to accelerate or retard the motion of a body, or to alter its direction, if the tendency could properly be termed a force and the centripetal force which counteracts it were removed, it would accelerate or retard the motion of the body, or alter its direction, which it does not.

The only sense in which the term centrifugal force can be used with propriety as a force, is obtained by the consideration of relative equilibrium, in which case, if the same centripetal force acted on the body, the centrifugal force would keep it in equilibrium, if the body were at rest, as it would appear to be to an observer moving with it.

Thus, if a body be supported on the surface of the earth supposed spherical, since the body describes a circle about the axis of the earth with uniform velocity, the pressure of the support, the attraction tending to the center of the earth, and the centrifugal force will be in statical equilibrium, the centrifugal force being equal to that force which would cause the body to describe the circle which it actually does describe.

133. In this case of circular motion the force is exerted not in accelerating or retarding the motion, but in changing its direction.

Thus, referring to the figure of Prop. I., if the direction of the impulse at B bisect the angle ABC, the triangle CBc is isosceles, and $BC = Bc = AB$: therefore, the velocities in BC and AB are equal, and the effect of the impulse has been to change the direction without altering the velocity of the body.

Hence, the regular polygon inscribed in a circle center S, can be described with uniform velocity under the action of impulses tending to the center; and, by similar triangles SBC, CBc,

$$Cc : BC :: BC : BS.$$

And, if V be the uniform velocity in the polygon, T the time in a side BC, $BC = V \cdot T$;

$$\therefore Cc = \frac{V^2 T^2}{BS}.$$

If now the number of sides be indefinitely increased, Cc will be ultimately twice the space through which the body will be drawn from the tangent by the continuous force, see Art. 107; therefore $\dfrac{Cc}{T^2} = \dfrac{V^2}{BS}$ will be the measure of the accelerating effect of the centripetal force tending to the center of the circle.

Illustrations of Circular Motion.

134. *A small body is attached by an inelastic string to a point on a smooth horizontal table, to determine the tension of the string when the body describes a circle.*

If the body be set in motion by a blow perpendicular to the string, the string will remain constantly stretched, and the only force which acts on the body in the horizontal plane being in the direction of the fixed point, the areas described round this point will be proportional to the time, and the body will move in a circle with uniform velocity.

Let v be the velocity of projection, and l the length of the string, then the accelerating effect of the tension of the string is $\frac{v^2}{l}$; that is, $\frac{v^2}{l}$ is the velocity which would be generated from rest by the action of this tension continued constant, therefore the tension of the string : the weight of the body :: $\frac{v^2}{l}$: g.

Ex. If a velocity of two feet a second be communicated perpendicular to a string whose length is a yard,

$$v^2 : lg :: 4 : 3 \times 32 :: 1 : 24,$$

hence the tension is $\frac{1}{24}$th of the weight, and the time of revolution is evidently $\frac{2\pi l}{v}$ seconds $= \frac{6\pi''}{2} = 3 \times \frac{22''}{7}$, nearly,

$$= \frac{66''}{7} = 9''.4, \text{ nearly}.$$

2. *If a particle be attached by a string of given length to a point in a rough horizontal plane, and a given velocity be communicated to it, perpendicular to the string supposed tight, find the tension of the string at any time, the time in which it will be reduced to rest, and the whole arc described.*

Let V be the velocity of projection, l the length of the string in feet, v the velocity at any time t.

In any short time τ reckoned from the time t if the velocity change from v to v', the accelerating effect of the tension changes from $\dfrac{v^2}{l}$ to $\dfrac{v'^2}{l}$, therefore, when τ is indefinitely diminished, since these accelerations are ultimately equal, $\dfrac{v^2}{l}$ is the accelerating effect of the tension at the time t.

Again, if μ be the coefficient of friction, the retarding effect of friction is μg, which is constant, hence the velocity destroyed in the time t, since friction is the only force acting in the direction of the tangent, is $\mu g t$, and $v = V - \mu g t$.

Therefore the particle comes to rest in $\dfrac{V}{\mu g}$ seconds after describing the arc $\dfrac{V^2}{2\mu g}$ feet.

The tension of the string at the time t : the weight of the particle :: $\dfrac{v^2}{l} : g :: \dfrac{(V - \mu g t)^2}{l} : g$; and $\dfrac{V}{mg}$ is the time in which the particle is reduced to rest, therefore the tension $\propto \left(\dfrac{V}{\mu g} - t\right)^2$ $\propto$ the square of the time which elapses before the particle comes to rest.

3. *Supposing that the Moon describes a circle with uniform velocity about the center of the Earth as its center, to find the ratio of the centripetal acceleration of the Moon to gravity at the Earth's surface.*

Let $n = $ number of seconds in the Moon's periodic time, $R = $ the radius of the Moon's orbit in feet; therefore the velocity of the Moon is $\dfrac{2\pi R}{n}$ and $\dfrac{1}{R} \cdot \left(\dfrac{2\pi R}{n}\right)^2$ is the measure of the accelerating effect of the force exerted on the Moon, and the measure of the same for gravity at the Earth's surface $= 32.2$; hence, the ratio required is $\dfrac{4\pi^2 R}{n^2} : 32.2$.

4. *A body is suspended by a string from a fixed point, and being drawn out of the vertical is projected horizontally so as to describe a horizontal circle with uniform velocity. Find the velocity and tension.*

Let A be the point of suspension, BC the radius of the circle described; therefore, the circle being described uniformly, the

PROP. IV. THEOREM IV. 155

resultant force on the body tends to the center B, and the measure of the accelerating effect of this resultant force is $\dfrac{V^2}{BC}$, in the direction CB.

Let T, W be the tension of the string, and the weight of the body, acting in CA, and parallel to AB, respectively,

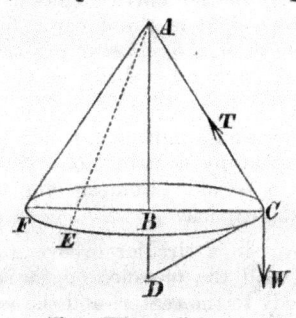

$$\therefore T : W :: CA : AB,$$

also, $\dfrac{V^2}{BC} : g :: CB : AB;$

$$\therefore V^2 = \dfrac{g \cdot BC^2}{AB},$$

and, if CD be perpendicular to AC, $BC^2 = AB \cdot BD$;

therefore the velocity is that due to the space $\tfrac{1}{2}BD$.

XI.

1. If the sixth power of the velocity, in circles uniformly described, be inversely proportional to the square of the periodic time, shew that the law of force varies inversely as the square of the radii.

2. Given the Earth's radius, the force of gravity at the Earth's surface, and the periodic time of the Moon, supposed to describe a circular orbit about the Earth, find her distance from the Earth's center.

3. Compare the areas described in the same time by the planets, supposed to move in circular orbits about the Sun in the center, exerting a force which varies inversely as the square of the distance.

4. If F be the measure of the acceleration of a force which tends to a given center, and a body be projected, from a point at

a distance R from the center, at right angles to this distance, with velocity V, such that $V^2 = F.R$, shew that the body will describe a circle.

5. If the forces by which particles describe circles with uniform velocity vary as the distance, shew that the times of revolution are the same for all.

6. If the velocity of the Earth's motion were so altered that bodies would have no weight at the equator, find approximately the alteration in the length of a day, assuming that, before the alteration, the centrifugal force on a body at the equator was to its weight :: 1 : 288.

7. A particle moves uniformly on a smooth horizontal table, being attached to a fixed point by a string, one yard long, and it makes three revolutions in a second. Compare the tension of the string with the weight of the particle.

8. A body moves in a circular groove under the action of a force to the center, and the pressure on the groove is double the given force on the body to the center, find the velocity of the body.

9. If a locomotive be passing a curve at the rate of twenty-four miles an hour, and the radius of the curve be $\frac{11}{15}$ of a mile; prove that the resultant of the forces which retain it on the line, viz. of the action of the rails on the flanges of the wheels, and the horizontal part of the forces which act perpendicular to the inclined road-way, is $\frac{1}{100}$ of the weight of the locomotive, nearly.

10. If a body be attached by an extensible string to a fixed point in a smooth horizontal table, to find the velocity with which the body must move in order to keep the string constantly stretched to double its length.

If W be the weight of the body, and nW be the weight which if suspended at the extremity of the string would just double its length, l the length of the string, shew that the square of the required velocity $= 2nlg$.

11. Two equal bodies lie on a rough horizontal table, and are connected by a string, which passes through a small ring on the table; if the string be stretched, find the greatest velocity with which one of the bodies can be projected in a direction perpendicular to its portion of the string without moving the other body.

12. One end of a string is attached to the vertex of a smooth cone, which stands with its axis vertical, and the other to a particle, which revolves in a circle on the surface of the cone. If $2a$ be the length of the string, 2α the vertical angle of the cone, and the velocity be that which would be acquired in dropping from rest through a height a vers α, prove that the tension of the string will be equal to the weight of the particle.

Prop. V. Problem I.

Having given the velocity with which a body is moving at any three points of a given orbit, described by it under the action of forces tending to a common center, to find that center.

Let the three straight lines PT, TQV, VR, touch the given orbit in the points P, Q, R respectively; and let them meet in T and V.

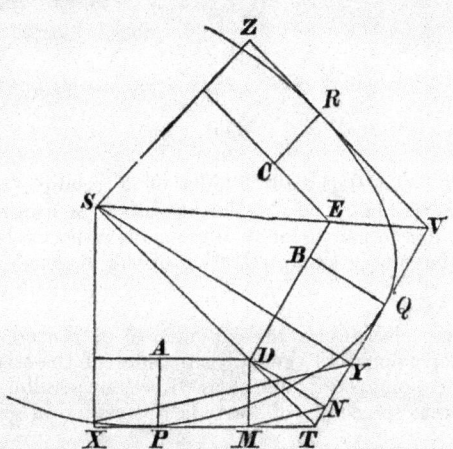

Draw PA, QB, RC perpendicular to the tangents, and inversely proportional to the velocities of the body at the points P, Q, R, i.e. such that

$$PA : QB :: \text{vel}^y. \text{ at } Q : \text{vel}^y. \text{ at } P,$$
$$QB : RC :: \text{vel}^y. \text{ at } R : \text{vel}^y. \text{ at } Q.$$

Through A, B, C draw AD, DBE, CE at right angles to PA, QB, RC meeting in D and E. Join TD, VE; TD and VE produced, if necessary, shall meet in S the required center of force.

For, the perpendiculars SX, SY, let fall from S on the tangents PT, TQV, are inversely proportional to the velocities at P, Q (Prop. I. Cor. 1), and are therefore directly as the perpendiculars AP, BQ, or as the perpendiculars DM, DN on the tangents. Join XY, MN, then, since $SX : SY :: DM : DN$ and the angles XSY, MDN are equal, therefore, the triangles SXY, DMN are similar;

$$\therefore SX : DM :: XY : MN,$$
$$:: XT : MT,$$

and the angles SXT, DMT are right angles; therefore, S, D, T are in the same straight line.

Similarly S, E, V are in the same straight line, and therefore, the center S is in the point of intersection of TD, VE.

Q. E. D.

XII.

1. If AB, BC, CD the three sides of a rectangle be the directions of the motion of a body at three points of a central orbit, and the velocities are proportional to these sides respectively, prove that the center of force is in the intersection of the diagonals of the rectangle.

2. If the velocities at three points of a central orbit be respectively proportional to the opposite sides of the triangle formed by joining the points, and have their directions parallel to the same sides; prove that the center of force is the center of gravity of the triangle.

3. Three tangents are drawn to a given orbit, described by a particle under the action of a central force, one of them being parallel to the external bisector of the angle between the other two. If the velocity at the point of contact of this tangent be a mean proportional between those at the points of contact of the other two, prove that the center of the force will lie on the circumference of a certain circle.

Prop. VI. Theorem V.

If a body revolve about a fixed center of force, in any orbit whatever, in a non-resisting medium, and if, at the extremity of a very small arc, commencing from any point in the orbit, a subtense of the angle of contact at that point be drawn parallel to the radius from that point to the center of force, then the force at that point tending to the center is ultimately as the subtense directly and the square of the time of describing the arc inversely.

Let PQ be the small arc, PS the radius drawn from P to S, the center of force. RQ the subtense of the angle of contact at P, parallel to PS. T the time of describing PQ. F the accelerating effect of the force at P.

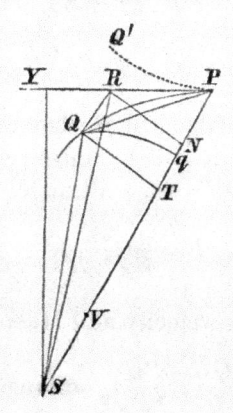

Then, when the body leaves P, it would, if not acted on by the central force, move in the direction PR, and if the force F continued constant in magnitude and direction throughout the time T, QR would be ultimately the space through which it would have been drawn by F in that time; therefore ultimately, $F = \dfrac{2QR}{T^2} \varpropto \dfrac{QR}{T^2}$.

COR. 1. Draw QT perpendicular to SP, and let $h =$ twice the area described in an unit of time.

$$\text{Then, } F = \frac{2h^2}{SP^2} \cdot \frac{QR}{QT^2}, \text{ ultimately.}$$

For area $PSQ = \frac{1}{2}hT$, (Prop. I.), also, since triangle $PSQ = \frac{1}{2}SP \cdot QT$, and area $PSQ =$ triangle PSQ, ultimately, (Lemma VIII.); therefore $hT = SP \cdot QT$, ultimately;

$$\text{hence, ultimately, } F = 2\frac{QR}{T^2} = \frac{2h^2}{SP^2} \cdot \frac{QR}{QT^2}.$$

COR. 2. Draw SY perpendicular on PR.

$$\text{Then } F = \frac{2h^2}{SY^2} \cdot \frac{QR}{PQ^2}, \text{ ultimately.}$$

For triangle $PSQ =$ triangle $PSR = \frac{1}{2}SY \cdot PR$;

therefore $hT = SY \cdot PR = SY \cdot PQ$, ultimately;

$$\text{hence, ultimately, } F = 2\frac{QR}{T^2} = \frac{2h^2}{SY^2} \cdot \frac{QR}{PQ^2}.$$

COR. 3. If the orbit have finite curvature at P, and PV be the chord of the circle of curvature whose direction passes through S, $PV \cdot QR = PQ^2$, ultimately;

$$\therefore F = \frac{2h^2}{SY^2 \cdot PV}.$$

COR. 4. If V be the velocity at P, then $V = \dfrac{PQ}{T}$, ultimately,

and $F = \dfrac{2QR}{T^2} = \dfrac{2QR}{PQ^2} \cdot \left(\dfrac{PQ}{T}\right)^2$, ultimately,

$$\therefore F = \frac{2V^2}{PV}, \text{ or } V^2 = 2F \cdot \frac{PV}{4};$$

that is, the velocity at any point of a central orbit at which the curvature is finite, is that which would be acquired by a body moving from rest under the action of the central force at that point continued constant, after passing through

PROP. VI. THEOREM V.

a space equal to a quarter of the chord of curvature at that point drawn in the direction of the center of force.

COR. 5. Hence, if the form of any curve be given, and the position of any point S, towards which a centripetal force is continually directed, the law of the centripetal force can be found, by which a body will be deflected from its direction of motion, so as to remain in the curve. Examples of this investigation will be given in the following problems.

Observations on the Proposition.

135. In Newton's enunciation of the proposition, the sagitta of the arc, which bisects the chord and is drawn in the direction of the center of force, is employed instead of the subtense used in the text, but it is easily seen that these are ultimately proportional, by reference to Art. 100.

The variations by which Newton expresses the results of the first three corollaries, are replaced by equations, in order to facilitate the comparison of the motion of bodies in different orbits and the forces acting upon them.

136. The figure employed in proof of the proposition is drawn upon supposition that the force is attractive, the orbit being concave to the center of force; the same proof applies also to the case of a repulsive force, if the curve be drawn in the direction of the dotted line PQ' and the same construction be made.

The exception however should be made, that the method fails in the particular positions, in which the body is at the points of contact of tangents drawn from the center of force to the curve; in such cases QR does not ultimately meet the tangent at a finite angle or is not a subtense, the result of the proposition is therefore not demonstrated for these particular positions. For a further description of the case see the note, Arts. 147 and 148, on the next proposition.

137. In the proof it is assumed that the body moves ultimately in the same manner as if the force P remained constant in magnitude and direction, in which case the body would

describe a parabola, whose axis is parallel to PS, and which is evidently the parabola which has at P the same curvature as the curve.

By this consideration the proposition contained in Cor. 4 can be readily proved.

For, since the body moves in a parabola under the action of a constant force in parallel lines, the velocity at P is that acquired by falling from the directrix under the action of the force at P, continued constant, i. e. through a space equal to the distance of the focus of the parabola, which is equal to a quarter of the chord of curvature at P, drawn through S.

138. The supposition that the force at P continued constant in magnitude and direction, causes the body to move in a curve which is ultimately coincident with the path of the body, may be justified by considering that, if PQ' be the arc of the parabola described on this supposition in the same time as the arc PQ actually described, the error $Q'Q$ is due to the change in the magnitude of the forces and the direction of their action in the two cases; now, the greatest difference of magnitude varies as the difference of SP and SQ ultimately, and the ratio of the error from this cause to $Q'R$ vanishes ultimately; also, since $\angle PSQ$ vanishes ultimately, the ratio of the error, arising from the change of direction, to $Q'R$ vanishes; therefore, $Q'Q : Q'R$ vanishes, and the curves may be considered ultimately coincident.

139. It is evident that the results of the Proposition and of the fourth corollary are true of the resultant of any forces, under the action of which any plane orbit is described, for this resultant may be supposed ultimately constant in direction and magnitude, in which case the curve described is a parabola; and the velocity at P is that acquired by falling from the directrix, whose distance is a quarter of the chord of curvature at P, drawn in the direction of that resultant force. Hence, in this case also, if F be the accelerating effect of the resultant of the forces, QR the subtense parallel to the direction of the resultant,

$$V^2 = 2F \cdot \frac{PV}{4}, \text{ and } F = 2 \text{ limit } \frac{QR}{T^2}$$

Homogeneity.

140. COR. 1, 2. In the expressions for F obtained in these corollaries, it is of great importance to observe the dimensions of the symbols.

Thus h, being a measure of the rate of description of areas, is of two dimensions in linear space and of -1 in time; therefore h^2. QR is of five in space, and of -2 in time, and SP^2. QT^2 of four dimensions in space; hence, $\dfrac{2h^2 \cdot QR}{SP^2 \cdot QT^2}$ is of one dimension in space and of -2 in time, and represents either twice the space through which a force would draw a body in an unit of time, or the velocity generated by the force in an unit of time, either of which may be taken as the measure of the accelerating effect of the force; moreover this unit is the same by which the magnitude of h is determined.

Hence, if the actual areas, lines, &c. be represented by the symbols, and not the *number* of units, as mentioned in Art. 128, every term of an equation or of a sum or difference must be homogeneous, or of the same number of dimensions, both in space and time; for example, $PQ + V.T$ representing a line, V must be of -1 dimensions in time.

Tangential and Normal Forces.

141. *To find the accelerating effect of the components of the forces, under the action of which a body describes any plane curve, taken in the directions of the normal and tangent at any point.*

Let PQ be a small arc of the curve described under the action of any forces, F, G the measures of the accelerating effect of these forces, in the direction of the tangent and perpendicular to it. Then, if V be the velocity at P, T the time of describing PQ, the forces may be supposed ultimately to remain the same in magnitude and direction, and if QR be perpendicular to PR, we have ultimately $PR = V.T + \frac{1}{2} F.T^2$, and $QR = \frac{1}{2} G.T^2$, and the ratio of $F.T^2 : V.T$ vanishes ultimately; hence, if ρ be the radius of curvature at P,

$$2\rho = \frac{PR^2}{QR} = \frac{2V^2}{G}, \text{ ultimately; and } G = \frac{V^2}{\rho};$$

therefore, $\dfrac{V^2}{\rho}$ is the measure of the normal acceleration estimated towards the center of curvature.

Also, if $PU = V.T$ be measured in PR, UR is ultimately the space described under the action of the tangential component;

$$\therefore F = \frac{2\,UR}{T^2} = \frac{2\,(PR - V.T)}{T^2}, \text{ ultimately,}$$

$$= \frac{2\,(PQ - V.T)}{T^2}, \text{ ultimately.} \qquad (1).$$

Again, if V' be the velocity at Q, since this velocity is ultimately the component of the velocities whose squares are

$V^2 + 2F.PR$ parallel to PR, and $2G.QR$ in RQ;

$\therefore V'^2 = V^2 + 2F.PR + 2G.QR$, ultimately,

and $QR : PR$ or PQ vanishes ultimately;

$$\therefore F = \frac{V'^2 - V^2}{2PQ}, \text{ ultimately.} \qquad (2).$$

Or, again, by Art. 59, since $V' - V$ is ultimately the velocity generated in the direction of the tangent, by the tangential force continued constant,

$$F = \frac{V' - V}{T}, \text{ ultimately.} \qquad (3).$$

142. *To find the velocity at any point of an orbit described under the action of any forces in one plane.*

Let AB be any arc of an orbit, V, v the velocities at A and B, and suppose the arc AB divided into a large number of small portions of which PQ is one, v_r, v_{r+1} velocities at P and Q, F the accelerating effect of the tangential component of the forces at P,

$$v_{r+1}^2 - v_r^2 = 2F.PQ, \text{ ultimately,}$$

and $v^2 - V^2$ is obtained by taking the limit of the sum of the magnitudes $2F.PQ$ corresponding to the different arcs when their number is indefinitely increased.

That this is rigidly correct may be shewn by considering that $v_{r+1}^2 - v_r^2 : 2F.PQ$ is ultimately a ratio of equality; therefore, by

PROP. VI. THEOREM V. 165

Cor. Lemma IV, or Art. 24, the limiting ratio of the sums is also a ratio of equality.

Radial and Transversal Forces.

143. *To find the accelerating effect of the components of forces, under the action of which a body describes any plane curve, taken in the direction of a radius vector drawn from a fixed point, and perpendicular to it.*

Let PQ be a small arc described in the time T; QRU, PU parallel and perpendicular to SP, P, Q the measures of the accelerating effects of the components in PS and PU, PR a tangent at P.

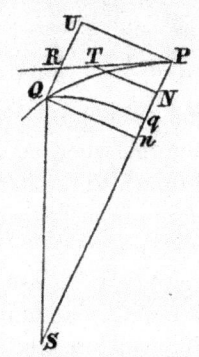

If V be the velocity at P, make $PT = V \cdot T$, draw TN perpendicular to SP, and let Qq be the arc of a circle, center S.

Since the forces may be considered ultimately constant in magnitude and direction,

$$\tfrac{1}{2} P \cdot T^2 = Nn = Nq + \frac{Qn^2}{2Sq}, \text{ ultimately.}$$

Let h be twice the area which would be described in an unit of time by radii from S, if the transverse force at P ceased to act,

then $Qn \cdot SP = TN \cdot SP = h \cdot T$, ultimately,

and if P' be the measure of the accelerating effect of a force, under the action of which the body would move in PS, so that its distance from S would be always equal to that of the body in PQ at the same time, $\frac{1}{2}P'.T^2 = Nq$, ultimately;

also, $\dfrac{Qn^2}{2Sq} = \dfrac{h^2 T^2}{2 SP^3}$, ultimately;

$$\therefore P = P' + \frac{h^2}{SP^3}.$$

Again, if, at Q, h' corresponds to h, $h' - h$, the increase of h, is due to the increase of velocity in direction PU, which is equal to $Q.T$, ultimately;

$$(h' - h)\, T = Q.T^2.SP, \text{ ultimately};$$

and $Q = \dfrac{h' - h}{SP.T}$, ultimately.

Angular Velocity.

144. DEF. *Angular velocity* of a point, moving about another fixed point, is uniform, when equal angles are described in equal times, by radii drawn to the fixed point.

Uniform angular velocity is measured by the angle described in an unit of time.

Variable angular velocity is measured by the angle which would be described by a radius in an unit of time, if moving with uniform angular velocity equal to the angular velocity at the time under consideration; this is the limit of the angle, described in a time T, divided by T, when T is indefinitely diminished; for, let PSQ be the angle described about S in a time T, then, since this may be ultimately supposed to be described uniformly with the angular velocity at P, the angular velocity at $P \times T = \angle PSQ$, ultimately.

145. *To find the angular velocity in a central orbit.*

Let PQ be a small arc described in the time T, draw QN perpendicular to SP, and let $h =$ twice the area described in an unit of time.

$h.T =$ twice the area $PSQ = QN.SP$ ultimately; if the angles be supposed estimated in circular measure,

$$\angle PSQ = \frac{QN}{SQ}, \text{ ultimately};$$

$$\therefore h \cdot T = SP \cdot SQ \times \angle PSQ, \text{ ultimately};$$

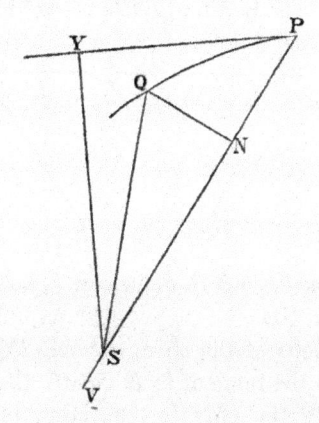

therefore the angular velocity $= \angle \dfrac{PSQ}{T}$, ultimately,

$$= \frac{h}{SP^2}.$$

146. *To find the angular velocity of the perpendicular on the tangent from the center of force.*

Draw SY perpendicular on the tangent PY, and let PV be the chord of curvature through S.

The angle described by SY in the time T is equal to the angle between the tangents at P and Q, or to the angle PVQ,

$\therefore$ angular vel. of SY : angular vel. of SP :: $2 \angle PVQ : \angle PSQ$
:: $2SQ : VQ$, ultimately;

therefore the angular velocity of $SY = \dfrac{2h}{PV \cdot SP}.$

Illustrations.

1. *Two equal rings* P, Q *slide on a string which passes round two fixed pegs* A, B *in a smooth horizontal plane; the rings are brought together, and then projected with equal velocities, so as to keep the string stretched symmetrically. Shew that the tension of the string varies inversely as the distance* AP.

Let the figure represent the position of the system at any time.

Let CR bisect AB and PQ, and let DE be drawn parallel to CR, so that $EP = PA$, then $EPR = AP + PR$ is constant;

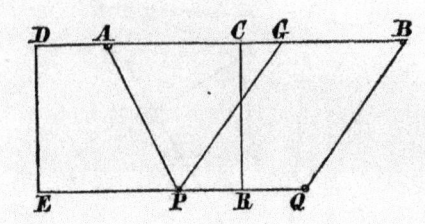

therefore DE is fixed, and P moves in a parabola whose focus is A, and directrix DE.

Also, the tensions of the string in PA, PQ being equal and equally inclined to the tangent to P's path, the resultant of these tensions, which are the only forces acting in the plane of the curve, acts in the normal, hence the rings move with uniform velocity equal to the velocity of projection V, and, if T be the measure of the accelerating effect of the tension, PG the normal, ρ the radius of curvature,

$$2T \cos APG = \frac{V^2}{\rho}, \text{ see Art. 141,}$$

and $2\rho \cos APG =$ chord of curvature through $A = 4PA$;

therefore, $T = \dfrac{V^2}{4PA} \propto \dfrac{1}{PA}$, that is, the tension varies inversely as PA.

2. *A body revolves in a smooth circular tube under the action of a force tending to any point in the circumference, and varying as the distance from that point. Find the pressure on the tube, and the point where there is no pressure, the motion commencing from a given point.*

Take A the center of force, C that of the circle, let B be the point of starting, PQ a small arc, BD, PM, QN ordinates to the diameter through the center of force, Am, Qn perpendicular on CP; let $\mu \cdot PA$ be the measure of the accelerating effect of the force at P, therefore $\mu \cdot mA$, $\mu \cdot Pm$ are those of the tangential and normal forces, $= \mu \cdot PM$ and $\mu \cdot AM$ respectively.

(vel.)² at $Q -$ (vel.)² at $P = 2\mu . PM . PQ = 2\mu . CP . MN$, ultimately, see Art. 141, (2), whence, taking the limit of the summation for all the small arcs in BP, (vel.)² at $P = 2\mu . CP . DM$.

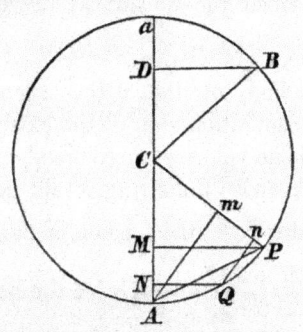

Also, $\dfrac{(\text{vel.})^2 \text{ at } P}{CP} = \mu . AM \mp$ the accelerating effect of the pressure on the tube, the upper or lower sign being taken according as the pressure is from or towards C; therefore the pressure on the tube has for the measure of its accelerating effect

$$\pm \mu (AM - 2DM) = \pm \mu (3AM - 2AD);$$

hence the pressure is outwards from B until $AM = \tfrac{2}{3} AD$, at which point there is no pressure, and inwards from that point to the corresponding one on the opposite side, having its greatest value at A, and the outward pressure at B is half the inward pressure at A.

3. *To find the tension of a string by which a body is attached to the center of a vertical circle in which it revolves.*

Let P be the position of the body at any time, u the velocity at A the lowest point, CP the radius of the circle,

$$(\text{vel.})^2 \text{ at } P = u^2 - 2g . AM,$$

and the accelerating effect of the tension of the string is measured by

$$\dfrac{u^2 - 2g . AM}{CA} + \dfrac{g . CM}{CP};$$

therefore the tension of the string : weight of the body

$$:: u^2 - 2g . CA + 3g . CM : g . CA.$$

COR. 1. In order that the complete circle may be described, since the string must be stretched at the highest point where $-CA$ must be written for CM, $u^2 =$ or $> 5g \cdot CA$, and if the circle be just described the tension at the lowest point is six times the weight.

COR. 2. If the body oscillates, the extent of the oscillation is given by the consideration that at the extremity P' of the arc of oscillation there is no velocity, therefore $u^2 = 2g \cdot AM'$, and AM' is less than AC, otherwise the string would not be stretched;

therefore in this case, the tension of the string at A

$$= \frac{2AM' + AC}{AC} \times \text{weight of the body.}$$

4. *Find the force under the action of which a body may describe the equiangular spiral uniformly.*

The velocity being constant there is only a normal force measured by $(\text{vel.})^2 \div \text{radius of curvature} = \frac{V^2 \sin \alpha}{SP}$. Art. 90.

5. *Find the force tending to the pole of the cardioid, under the action of which the curve is described.*

Since $PV = \frac{4}{3} SP$, and $(\text{vel.})^2 = \frac{h^2}{SY^2} = \frac{h^2 \cdot BC}{SP^3}$, see Art. 93;

therefore the accelerating effect of the force is $\frac{3h^2 \cdot BC}{2SP^4} \propto \frac{1}{SP^4}$.

6. *If in a smooth elliptic tube a particle be placed at any point, and be acted on by two forces which tend to the foci, and vary inversely as the square of the distances from those points; shew that the pressure at any point varies inversely as the radius of curvature.*

Let O be the point of starting, PQ a small arc described by the body, QT, QU perpendiculars on SP, HP.

Take $\frac{\mu}{SP^2}$, $\frac{\mu'}{HP^2}$, R, as the measures of the accelerating effects of the forces, and of the pressure of tube.

Then, employing the usual letters for the lines of the figure, the accelerating effect of the tangential component of force to S is

$$\frac{\mu}{SP^2}\cdot\frac{PT}{PQ}=\frac{\mu(SP-SQ)}{SP.SQ.PQ}=\frac{\mu}{PQ.SQ}-\frac{\mu}{PQ.SP}, \text{ ultimately};$$

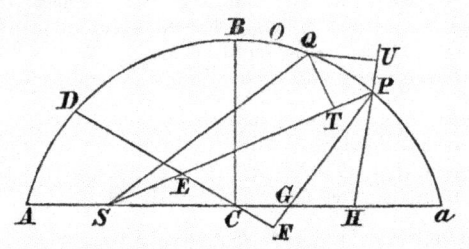

and similarly for the force tending to H;

$$\therefore (\text{vel.})^2 \text{ at } P - (\text{vel.})^2 \text{ at } Q = \left(\frac{2\mu'}{HP}-\frac{2\mu'}{HQ}\right)-\left(\frac{2\mu}{SQ}-\frac{2\mu}{SP}\right),$$

$$\therefore (\text{vel.})^2 \text{ at } P = \frac{2\mu'}{HP}-\frac{2\mu'}{HO}-\frac{2\mu}{SO}+\frac{2\mu}{SP}.$$

Also, $\dfrac{(\text{vel.})^2 \text{ at } P}{\rho}=\dfrac{PF}{PE}\left(\dfrac{\mu'}{HP^2}+\dfrac{\mu}{SP^2}\right)HP^2 - R$, if ρ be the radius of curvature at P,

and $2\rho\cdot\dfrac{PF}{PE}=PV=\dfrac{2CD^2}{AC}=\dfrac{2SP.HP}{AC}$;

$$\therefore R.\rho=\frac{\mu'.SP}{AC.HP}+\frac{\mu.HP}{AC.SP}-\frac{2\mu'}{HP}-\frac{2\mu}{SP}+\frac{2\mu'}{HO}+\frac{2\mu}{SO}$$

$$=\frac{2\mu'}{HO}+\frac{2\mu}{SO}-\frac{\mu'}{AC}-\frac{\mu}{AC}=\frac{\mu'SO}{HO}+\frac{\mu HO}{SO};$$

which is constant;

$$\therefore R \propto \frac{1}{\rho}.$$

XIII.

1. A body is attached to a point by a thread, and is projected so as to describe a vertical circle, prove that, if T_1, T_2 be the tensions of the string at the extremities of any diameter, the arithmetic mean between T_1, T_2 is independent of the position of the diameter, and that $T_2 \sim T_1$ is six times the component of the weight in the direction of the diameter.

2. A string of given length l is capable of sustaining a weight W. One end is fixed, and a given weight W' less than W, attached to the other end, oscillates in a vertical plane, find the greatest arc through which the body can oscillate without breaking the string.

3. A ring slides on a string hanging over two pegs in the same horizontal line, find the tension of the string at the lowest point, if the ring begin to fall from the point in the horizontal line through the pegs, the string being stretched.

4. A body slides down a smooth cycloidal arc, whose axis is vertical and vertex downwards, find the pressure at any point of the cycloid, and shew that, if it fall from the highest point, the pressure at the lowest point is twice the weight of the body.

5. A particle moves in a circular tube, under the action of a force which tends to a point in the tube, and whose accelerating effect varies as the distance, shew that, if the particle begin to move from a point at a distance from the center of force equal to the radius, there is no pressure on the tube at an angular distance from the center of force equal to $\cos^{-1}\frac{2}{3}$.

6. In a central orbit, shew that the centripetal force is to the force, which would cause it to approach directly with its paracentric velocity in the orbit, as $2SP^3 : 2SP^3 - SY^2 . PV$.

7. A curve is described by a body under the action of a central force, the measure of whose accelerating effect is $\frac{\mu}{SP}$, prove that the angular velocity of the perpendicular on the tangent is to that of the radius vector $:: \mu : V^2$.

8. Orbits, having a common point, are described about the same center of force, and the (velocities)^2 at the common point vary as the sine of the angle between the radius vector and the tangent; prove that the centers of curvature of the orbits at this point lie in a circle.

9. A particle, constrained to move on an equiangular spiral, is attracted to the pole by a force proportional to the distance, prove that, at whatever point the particle be placed at rest, the times of describing a given angle about the centre of force will be the same.

10. Given the Sun's motion in longitude at apogee and perigee to be $57'\ 10''$ and $61'\ 10''$; find the eccentricity of the Earth's orbit, supposed to be an ellipse about the Sun in one of the foci.

11. A body is describing an ellipse round a center of force in one of the foci; prove that the velocity of the point of intersection of the perpendicular from that focus upon the tangent at any point of the orbit is inversely proportional to the square upon the diameter conjugate to the diameter through that point.

12. If a particle begin to move from any point of a smooth parabolic tube, being attracted to the focus by a force which varies inversely as the square of the distance, prove that, on arriving at the vertex, the pressure on the tube is equal to the attraction on the particle placed at the point of intersection of the tangent at the vertex with that at the starting-point.

13. A particle moves in a smooth elliptic groove, under the action of two forces tending to the foci and varying inversely as the squares of the distances, the forces being equal at equal distances. Prove that, if the velocity at the extremity of the axis major be to that at the extremity of the axis minor as AC to BC, then the velocity at any point varies inversely as the normal; and find the pressure on the tube.

14. A particle is attached to a point C by a string, and is attracted by a force which tends to a point S, and varies inversely as the square of the distance from S. Find the least velocity with which the particle can be projected from a point in CS, or CS produced, so as to describe a complete circle. If CS be less than the length of the string, prove that the tension is a maximum at a point D, where SD is perpendicular to CS, and that if CS is half the length of the string, the two minimum and the maximum tensions are in the ratio, 0, 4 and $3\sqrt{3}$.

Prop. VII. Problem II.

A body moves in the circumference of a circle, to find the law of the centripetal force, tending to any given point in the plane of the circle.

Let APV be the circumference of the circle, S the given point to which the centripetal force tends, PV the chord

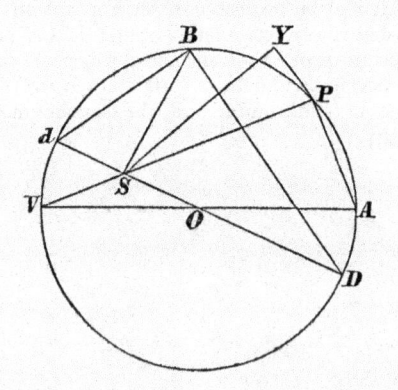

of the circle drawn through S from P, the position of the body at any time. And let SY be drawn perpendicular to PY, the tangent to the curve at P.

By Prop. VI. Cor. 3, if F be the measure of the accelerating effect of the centripetal force,

$$F = \frac{2h^2}{SY^2 . PV},$$

and, since the angles SPY, VAP are equal, and also the right angles PYS, APV, the triangles SPY, VAP are similar;

$$\therefore SY : SP :: PV : VA ;$$

PROP. VII.   PROB. II.   175

$$\therefore F = \frac{2h^2 \cdot VA^2}{SP^2 \cdot PV^3};$$

therefore, since h and VA are given, F varies inversely as $SP^2 \cdot PV^3$.

COR. 1. Hence, if the given point S to which the centripetal force tends, be situated on the circumference of the circle, V coincides with S, and F varies inversely as SP^5.

COR. 2. The force, under the action of which a body P revolves in a circle $APTV$, is to the force, under the action of which the same body P can revolve in the same circle in the same periodic time about any other center of force R, as $RP^2 \cdot SP$ to SG^3, SG being a straight line drawn from the first center S, parallel to the distance RP of the body from the second center of force R, to meet PG, a tangent to the circle.

For, by the construction of this proposition, since the periodic times are the same, the areas described in a given time are the same; therefore, h is the same for both centers, hence, if PRT be the chord through R, the force tending to S : the force tending to R

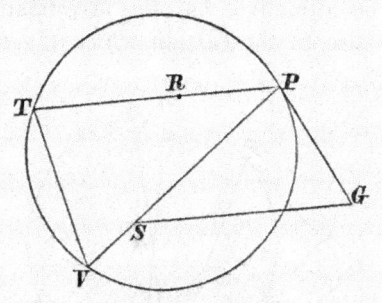

$$:: RP^2 \cdot PT^3 : SP^2 \cdot PV^3;$$

but, by similar triangles TPV, GSP,

$$PT : PV :: SP : SG;$$

$\therefore$ force tending to S : force tending to R

$$:: RP^2 \cdot SP^3 : SP^2 \cdot SG^3$$
$$:: RP^2 SP : SG^3.$$

176   NEWTON.

Cor. 3. The force, under the action of which a body P revolves in any orbit about a center of force S, is to the force, under the action of which the same body P can revolve in the same orbit in the same periodic time about any other center of force R, as $RP^2.SP$ to SG^3, SG being the straight line drawn from the first center of force S, parallel to RP the distance of P from the second center of force R, to meet SG the tangent to the orbit.

For, in each case, the body may be supposed for a short time to be moving in the circle of curvature, and the forces are the same as those which would retain the body in the circular orbit; therefore, since the areas described in a given time are equal, the ratio of the forces is $RP^2.SP : SG^3$.

Observations on the Proposition.

147. In the figure employed in the proposition, the force is supposed to be attractive, but the investigation of the law of force applies also to the case in which the center of force

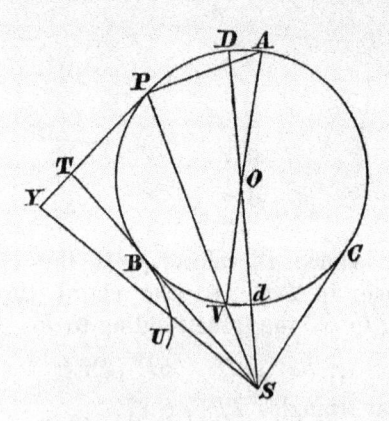

S is exterior to the circle, in which case the force is repulsive through the arc BC, which is convex to the center of force, and contained between the tangents drawn from S to the circle.

It is important, however, to observe that this problem is to

PROP. VII. PROBLEM II.

find what would be the law of force tending to S, under the action of which a body would be moving, supposing that it could move in the circle, or any portion of the circle, under the action of such a force, but it does not assert the possibility of such a motion, which is considered in Art. 126.

In fact, the *complete* description of a circle ABC, under the sole action of a central force tending to an external point S, is impossible, because, as the body approaches the point B, the component of the velocity perpendicular to SB remains finite however near the body approaches B, and since there is no force to generate a velocity in the opposite direction, the body must proceed to describe an arc BU on the opposite side. SB would be a tangent to both curves, because the velocity in direction BS becomes larger than any finite quantity, as the body approaches B, and therefore the angle between BS and the direction of motion is indefinitely small at B.

That a finite velocity in the direction perpendicular to SB could remain up to B, may be shewn by producing SB to T in the tangent PY at P; then the component of the velocity at P perpendicular to SB is $\dfrac{h}{SY} \cdot \dfrac{SY}{ST} = \dfrac{h}{ST} = \dfrac{h}{SB}$, when the body arrives at a point very near to B.

148. The force at a point indefinitely near to B cannot be properly determined by the method of Prop vi., because the

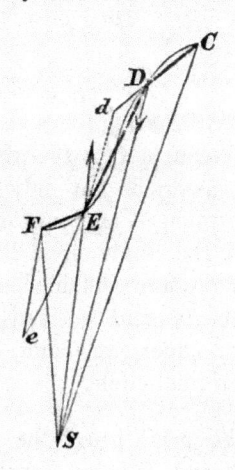

lines parallel to the direction of the force from which the measures of the force are obtained are not subtenses, or sagittæ, being not inclined in this case at a finite angle to the tangent.

But it can be seen in another manner from the polygon of Prop. I, that the force is infinitely great, when the distance from B becomes infinitely small.

Thus, if $CDEF$ be a portion of the polygon whose limit touches the radius from S between D and E, the angle between DE and DS or ES may be made as small as we please, hence the velocity generated by the impulse in the directions DS and SE becomes infinitely great compared with the velocities in CD and EF.

In the figure, the impulses at D and E, whose directions are denoted by the arrows, have corresponding to them, in the limit, the forces on opposite sides of the tangent, which are attractive and repulsive respectively.

149. *If a circle be described by a body under the action of a force tending to a point in the circumference, the force varies inversely as the fifth power of the distance from that point, at all points at a finite distance from* S.

For, in this case, $PV = SP$, and $SY : SP :: SP : SA$;

$$\therefore F = \frac{2h^2}{SY^2 \cdot PV} = \frac{2h^2}{SP^3} \cdot \frac{SP^2}{SY^2} = \frac{2h^2 SA^2}{SP^5};$$

$$\therefore F \propto \frac{1}{SP^5}.$$

We may also observe here that the possibility of a description of a circle is not asserted, but only the law of force required in case of description of any portion of the circle. The complete description of the single circle is, in fact, impossible, for, under the action of the force obtained, the body would pass to the other side of the tangent on arriving at S, then proceed to describe another equal circle, and, on arriving again at S, again describe the original circle.

150. COR. 3. The orbit being the same, and also the periodic times about S and R being equal, the value of h, in

the two cases, is the same; also, the force tending to S for the orbit being of the same magnitude at P as that under the action of which the circle of curvature would be described, and SY, PV being the same in the orbit and the circle, h is also the same (Prop. VI. Cor. 3); and similarly h is the same in the circle and orbit described about R; therefore it is the same in the circle described about S and R as centers of force, and hence Cor. 2 applies.

Velocity in the Circular Orbit.

151. *To find the velocity in the circular orbit described under the action of a force tending to any point in the plane of the orbit.*

The velocity at $P = \dfrac{h}{SY} = \dfrac{h}{SP} \cdot \dfrac{SP}{SY} = \dfrac{h}{SP} \cdot \dfrac{VA}{PV}$

$$\propto \dfrac{1}{SP \cdot PV}.$$

COR. If S be in the circumference of the circle, and $\dfrac{\mu}{SP^5}$ be the measure of the accelerating effect of the force,

$$\mu = 2h^2 SA^2;$$

hence, the velocity at $P = \dfrac{h \cdot VA}{SP^2} = \left(\dfrac{\mu}{2}\right)^{\frac{1}{2}} \cdot \dfrac{1}{SP^2}.$

Or, we may employ the result of Prop. VI, Cor. 4,

$$V^2 = F \cdot \dfrac{PV}{2} = \dfrac{\mu}{SP^5} \cdot \dfrac{SP}{2};$$

$$\therefore V = \left(\dfrac{\mu}{2}\right)^{\frac{1}{2}} \cdot \dfrac{1}{SP^2} \propto \dfrac{1}{SP^2}.$$

Absolute Force.

152. If the force upon a body placed at any distance from the point S varies inversely as the nth power of that distance, the magnitude of the force is determined, or its ratio

to any given force, as that of gravity, when the distance SP is given. The measure of the accelerating effect of the force is written $\frac{\mu}{SP^n}$, where μ the constant part of this measure is an algebraical symbol of $n+1$ dimensions, $\frac{\mu}{SP^n}$ is the space which represents the velocity generated in a body in an unit of time by a constant force equal to the force acting on the body at P. If the unit of space $= a$, $\frac{\mu}{a^n}$ is the measure of the accelerating effect of the force on a body at an unit of distance, and μ is called the *Absolute Force*, being the measure of the accelerating effect of the force at an unit of distance × the nth power of that unit. The absolute force is not the measure of the accelerating effect of any force, unless the symbols be treated numerically, in which case μ is twice the number of units of space through which a constant force, equal to the force at an unit of distance, would draw a body from rest in an unit of time.

Law of Force in a Circular Orbit.

153. The law of force may be expressed in terms of the distances SP, for SD, Sd being the greatest and least distances of the body from S, $SD . Sd = SP . SV$; see figure, page 176.

$$\therefore SP . PV = SP^2 \pm SD . Sd,$$

$+$ or $-$ according as S is within or without the circle;

$$\therefore F = \frac{2h^2 . AV^2 . SP}{(SP^2 \pm SD . Sd)^3}.$$

If S be on the circumference of the circle, $Sd = 0$,

$$\therefore F = \frac{2h^2 . AS^2}{SP^5}.$$

If S be exterior to the circle, $SD . Sd = SB^2$, and the lower sign is taken;

$$\therefore F = \frac{2h^2 AV^2 . SP}{(SP^2 - SB^2)^3}.$$

PROP. VII. PROBLEM II.

Periodic Time.

154. *To find the periodic time in a circular orbit described under the action of a force tending to a point in the circumference.*

Let P be the periodic time, R the radius of the circle, and let $\frac{\mu}{SP^5}$ be the measure of the accelerating effect of the force at P,

$$h \cdot P = \text{twice the area of the circle} = 2\pi R^2,$$

and $\mu = 2h^2 AS^2 = 8h^2 R^2$;

$$\therefore P = \frac{4\sqrt{2}\pi R^3}{\mu^{\frac{1}{2}}}.$$

155. *To compare the periodic times in the same circle when described under the action of a force tending to a point in the circumference, and a force tending to the center, of the same magnitude as the force at a distance equal to the radius of the circle.*

Let P' be the periodic time, and V the uniform velocity in the circle in the second case,

$$V^2 = \frac{\mu}{R^5} \cdot R; \therefore V = \frac{\mu^{\frac{1}{2}}}{R^2},$$

and $P' \cdot V = 2\pi R; \therefore P' = \frac{2\pi R^3}{\mu^{\frac{1}{2}}} = \frac{P}{2\sqrt{2}}.$

Illustrations.

1. *When the force in a circular orbit tends to a point within the circle, to find the point at which the true angular velocity is equal to the mean angular velocity.*

The true angular velocity is measured by $\frac{h}{SP^2}$, the mean angular velocity by $\frac{2\pi}{P}$, if P be the periodic time; but

$$h \cdot P = 2\pi R^2;$$

therefore at the required point, $\frac{h}{SP^2} = \frac{h}{R^2}$, and $SP = R$, or, the perpendicular from the required point upon the line joining S to O the center of the circle, bisects OS.

2. *If the measures of the accelerating effect of the force at the greatest and least distances* SD, Sd, *from the point to which the force tends, when a body describes a circular orbit, be the radius and twice the diameter respectively, the unit of time being a second, to find the number of seconds in passing from* D *to* d.

Since $\dfrac{8h^2R^2}{SD^2 \cdot Dd^3} = R$, and $\dfrac{8h^2R^2}{Sd^2 \cdot Dd^3} = 4R$;

$\therefore SD = 2Sd$, and $3Sd = Dd = 2R$,

and, if $T =$ the number of seconds from D to d,

$$h \cdot T = \pi R^2, \text{ and } \dfrac{h^2}{Sd^2} = 4R^2;$$

$$\therefore h = 2R \cdot Sd = \dfrac{4}{3}R^2; \quad \therefore T = \dfrac{3\pi}{4}.$$

XIV.

1. Compare the forces by which a body attracted separately to two centers of force may describe the same circle in different periodic times.

2. If SB (fig. page 176) be perpendicular to the diameter DSd, prove that the forces at D and d are as $dB^4 : DB^4$.

3. If μ be the absolute force in a circular orbit described under the action of a force tending to a point in the circumference, prove that the time in a quadrant commencing from the extremity of the diameter through the center of force is $(\pi + 2) R^3 \cdot \left(\dfrac{2}{\mu}\right)^{\frac{1}{2}}$.

In what unit of time is the result expressed?

4. Prove that $\dfrac{V^3}{F}$ is finite, however near the body approaches the tangent from S, if S be without the circular orbit.

5. Prove that, if the law of force tending to S, a point without a circle, be the law of force under which part of the circle can be described, the body will move near B as if acted on by a force tending to B and varying inversely as the cube of the distance from B.

Also give reasons for supposing that no force acts at the point B.

6. OE is a radius perpendicular to the diameter through S, in a circular orbit about a central force tending to a point S within the circle, SB an ordinate, perpendicular to OS, shew that, if the force at B be an arithmetic mean between the forces at the greatest and least distances, $OE^3 = SB \cdot SE^2$.

7. Prove that, if a circle be described about a force tending to a point in the circumference, and PQ be a chord parallel to the diameter through that point, the times of describing equal small arcs near P and Q differ by a quantity which varies as PQ.

8. A point describes a circle, with an acceleration tending to any point within the circle. Prove that, if three points be taken at which its velocities are in harmonical progression, the velocities at the other extremities of the diameters, passing through those points, will also be in harmonical progression.

9. Apply the proposition contained in Cor. 3, to prove that if in an elliptic orbit described under the action of a force tending to the center, the force varies as the distance from the center, then the force tending to the focus varies inversely as the square of the focal distances.

10. Deduce, by Cor. 3, the law of force, when a parabola is described under the action of a force tending to the focus, from the constant force parallel to the axis, under the action of which the same parabola may be described.

Prop. VIII. Problem III.

A body moves in a semicircle PQA *under the action of a force tending to a point* S *so distant that the lines* PS, QS *drawn from the body to that point may be considered parallel; to find the law of force.*

Let *CA* be a semidiameter of the semicircle drawn from the center perpendicular to the direction in which the force acts, cutting *PS, QS* in *M* and *N*, and join *CP*.

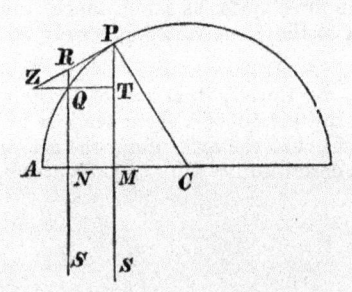

Let *PRZ* be the tangent at *P*, *ZQT* perpendicular to *PMS* meeting *PRZ* in *Z*, and let *SNQ* meet *PRZ* in *R*.

Then the force at $P \propto \dfrac{QR}{SP^2 \cdot QT^2}$ ultimately, if the arc *PQ* be indefinitely diminished, and *SP* may be considered constant; also by Euclid III. 36, $QR \cdot (RN + QN) = RP^2$, and, since *RQ* is parallel to *PT*, and the triangles *PZT*, *CPM* are similar, $RP : QT :: ZP : ZT :: CP : PM$;

$$\therefore \frac{QT^2}{QR} = \frac{QT^2}{RP^2} \cdot \frac{RP^2}{QR} = \frac{PM^2}{CP^2} \cdot (RN + QN)$$

$$= \frac{2PM^3}{CP^2}, \text{ ultimately;}$$

hence, force at *P*, which ultimately $\propto \dfrac{QR}{QT^2}, \propto \dfrac{1}{PM^3}$

Aliter.

In fig. page 176, draw OE a semidiameter perpendicular to SD, and let the distance SP cut the circle in V, and OE in M, then, by the preceding proposition,

$$F = \frac{8h^2R^2}{SP^2 \cdot PV^3},$$

and, if S be very distant, the ratio of $PM : SM$ or SO vanishes; therefore, $SP = SO$ ultimately, and PV is ultimately perpendicular to OE and equal to $2PM$;

$$\therefore F = \frac{h^2R^2}{SO^2 \cdot PM^3} \propto \frac{1}{PM^3}.$$

SCHOLIUM.

A body moves in an ellipse, hyperbola or parabola, under the action of a force tending to a point so situated and so distant that the lines drawn from the body to that point may be considered parallel, and perpendicular to the major axis of the ellipse, the axis of the parabola or the transverse axis of the hyperbola. To shew that the force varies inversely as the cube of the ordinates.

Let AMG be the axis to which the direction of the forces may be considered perpendicular, PM, PG the ordinate and normal, PO the diameter of curvature, PV the chord of curvature in direction PS.

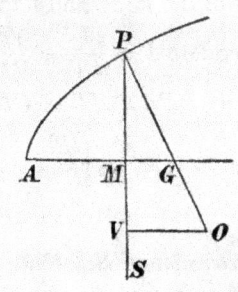

Then $F = \dfrac{2h^2}{SY^2 \cdot PV} = \dfrac{2h^2}{SP^2 \cdot PV} \cdot \dfrac{PG^2}{PM^2},$

since $SY : SP :: PM : PG$;

$$\therefore F \propto \frac{PG^2}{PM^2 \cdot PV} \propto \frac{PG^3}{PM^3 \cdot PO} \propto \frac{1}{PM^3},$$

since $PO \propto PG^3$, see Art. 86.

Observations on the Proposition.

156. It has been shewn in Art. 112, that the equable description of areas may, in the case of forces acting in parallel lines, be replaced by the uniformity of the resolved part of the velocity in the direction perpendicular to that of the forces. In the proof given in the text, when S is removed to an infinite distance h and SP are both infinite magnitudes, but the expression $\frac{h}{SP}$ is finite, for area SPQ described in the time T is ultimately equal to area SMN whose base is equal to uT, if u be the component of the velocity perpendicular to the direction of the forces, therefore $hT = uT \cdot SP$ ultimately, and $\frac{h^2}{SP^2} = u^2$, hence, the acceleration due to the force, when a body describes the semicircle, is $\frac{u^2 R^2}{PM^3}$.

157. The accelerating effect of the force, acting in parallel lines, may be obtained directly from the proposition of Art. 112, as follows.

Let u be the constant component of the velocity V, perpendicular to the direction of the force, and let F be the accelerating effect of the force, therefore $F = \frac{2V^2}{PV} = \frac{V^2}{PM}$,

also $V : u :: PZ : ZT :: CP : PM$;

$$\therefore F = \frac{u^2 \cdot CP^2}{PM^3}.$$

Extension of Scholium.

158. *When a body describes any curve under the action of a force tending to a point* S, *so distant that the lines drawn from* S

PROP. VIII. PROBLEM III. 187

to the body may be considered parallel, to find the law of force, and the velocity at any point.

Let AP be any curve, AMG the line to which the forces are perpendicular, PM, PG the ordinate and normal at the point P, PV the chord of curvature in the direction of the force, PO the diameter of curvature.

Let F be the accelerating effect of the force at P, u the component of the velocity V in the direction AMG;

$$\therefore V : u :: PG : PM,$$
also $PV : PO :: PM : PG$;

$$\therefore F = \frac{2V^2}{PV} = \frac{2u^2 . PG^2}{PM^2 . PO} \cdot \frac{PO}{PV} = \frac{2u^2 . PG^3}{PO . PM^3},$$

and the velocity $= u \cdot \dfrac{PG}{PM}$.

Illustrations.

1. *A cycloid is described by a particle, under the action of a force acting in a direction parallel to the axis; find the acceleration and the velocity at any point.*

In the cycloid $PO = 4PG$, and $PM . AB = PG^2$, AB being the length of the axis;

$$\therefore F = \frac{2u^2 . PG^2}{PM^3} \cdot \frac{PG}{PO} = \frac{u^2 . AB}{2PM^2} \propto \frac{1}{PO^4},$$

and the velocity at $P = u \cdot \dfrac{PG}{PM} = u \cdot \dfrac{AB}{PG} \propto \dfrac{1}{PO}$.

2. *A particle moves in a catenary under the action of forces acting in vertical lines; find the accelerating effect of the force, and the velocity at any point.*

Let AM be the directrix, AB the ordinate at the lowest point.

Then $PG : PM :: PM : AB$ and $PO = PG$;

$$\therefore F = \frac{2u^2 . PG^3}{PO . PM^3} = \frac{2u^2 . PM}{AB^2} \propto PM \propto PO^{\frac{1}{2}},$$

and the velocity at $P = u \cdot \dfrac{PG}{PM} = u \cdot \dfrac{PM}{AB} \propto PM$.

XV.

1. A body is moving in a semicircle under the action of a force tending to a point, so distant that the lines drawn from the body to that point may be considered parallel; if the center of force be transferred to the center of the circle, when the direction of the body's motion is perpendicular to that of the force, its magnitude at that point being unaltered, prove that the body will continue to move in the circle.

2. If a cycloid be described under the action of forces in the direction of the base, the force at any point varies inversely as $AM \cdot MQ$; AM, MQ being the abscissa and ordinate of the corresponding point of the generating circle.

3. A catenary is described under the action of a horizontal force, prove that the force varies as the distance from the directrix directly, and the cube of the arc from the lowest point inversely.

PROP. IX. PROBLEM IV.

If a body revolves in an equiangular spiral, required the law of centripetal force tending to the pole of the spiral.

Draw SY from S, the pole of the spiral, perpendicular to the tangent PY, and let PV be the chord of curvature at P, whose direction passes through S; then, since the angle SPY is constant, SY varies as SP, also PV varies as SP; therefore the centripetal force varies inversely as $SY^2 . PV$, and therefore inversely as SP^3.

Observations on the Proposition.

159. In the proof of the proposition, it is assumed that $PV \infty SP$; that this is the case may be shewn by the consideration that, if PQ, pq be any arcs of an equiangular spiral subtending equal angles at S, SPQ and Spq will be similar figures, and the subtenses QR, qr parallel to SP, Sp respectively, will be proportional to those radii, therefore $\dfrac{PQ^2}{QR} : \dfrac{pq^2}{qr} :: SP : Sp$.

160. *To find the measure of the accelerating effect of the force tending to the pole, under the action of which a body describes an equiangular spiral.*

Prove, first, as in Art. 90, that $PV = 2SP$, and then proceed as follows:

Let F be the measure of the accelerating effect of the force tending to the pole, α the angle of the spiral,

$$\text{then, } F = \frac{2h^2}{SY^2 . PV} = \frac{2h^2}{SP^2 \sin^2 \alpha . 2SP} = \frac{\mu}{SP^3},$$

where $\mu = h^2 \operatorname{cosec}^2 \alpha$.

161. *To find the velocity of a body describing an equiangular spiral under the action of a force tending to the pole.*

If $\dfrac{\mu}{SP^3}$ be the accelerating effect of the force tending to S;

the velocity at $P = \dfrac{h}{SY} = \dfrac{h}{SP.\sin\alpha} = \dfrac{\mu^{\frac{1}{2}}}{SP} \propto \dfrac{1}{SP}$.

162. *To find the time of describing any arc of the equiangular spiral.*

Let AL be any arc, SA, SL bounding radii, P the time of describing the arc. Then, as proved in page 31,

$$\text{area } SAL = \tfrac{1}{4}(SA^2 \sim SL^2)\tan\alpha = \tfrac{1}{2}h.P;$$

$$\therefore P = \dfrac{SA^2 \sim SL^2}{2h}\tan\alpha = \dfrac{SA^2 \sim SL^2}{2\mu^{\frac{1}{2}}\cos\alpha}.$$

Illustration.

In any orbit, described under the action of a force tending to any point S, *when the angle between the tangent* PY *and the radius* SP *is a maximum or minimum, the velocity is equal to the velocity in a circle at the same distance about the same force in the center.*

For, the curve, near this point, may be considered an equiangular spiral ultimately, since the angle is constant for a short time; therefore the chord of curvature is $= 2SP$, and $V^2 = F.SP$.

XVI.

1. In different equiangular spirals, described under the action of forces tending to the poles which are equal at equal distances, shew that the angular velocity varies at any point as the force and the perpendicular on the tangent conjointly.

2. The angular velocity of the perpendicular on the tangent is equal to that of radius.

3. The velocity of approach towards the focus, called the paracentric velocity, varies inversely as the distance.

4. A body is describing a circle, whose radius is a, with uniform velocity, under the action of a force, whose accelerating effect, at any distance r, is $\dfrac{\mu}{r^3}$. Prove that, if the direction of its motion be deflected inwards through any angle α, without altering the velocity, the body will arrive at the center of force after a time $\dfrac{a^2}{2\mu^{\frac{1}{2}}\sin\alpha}$.

5. Deduce from the time in an equiangular spiral, the time of passing from one point to another, when a body moves along a straight line with a velocity which varies inversely as the distance from a fixed point in that line.

PROP. X. PROBLEM V.

If a body is revolving in an ellipse, to find the law of centripetal force tending to the center of the ellipse.

Let CA, CB be the semiaxes of the ellipse, P the position of the body at any time, PCG, DCD' conjugate diameters, Q a point near P, QT, PF perpendiculars from Q and P on PG, DD'; draw QU an ordinate to PCG, QR a subtense parallel to CP.

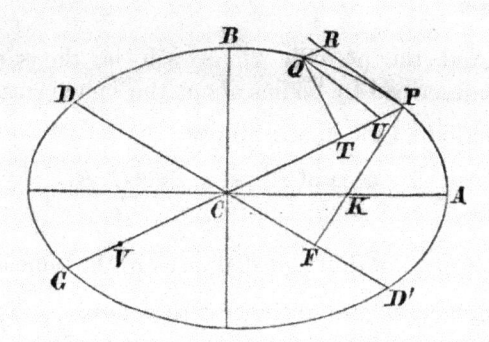

Then $F = \dfrac{2h^2}{CP^2} \cdot \dfrac{QR}{QT^2}$ ultimately.

But, by similar triangles QTU, PFC,

$$\frac{QT^2}{QU^2} = \frac{PF^2}{CP^2}, \text{ and } \frac{QU^2}{PU \cdot UG} = \frac{CD^2}{CP^2};$$

$$\therefore \frac{QT^2}{PU \cdot PU} = \frac{PF^2 \cdot CD^2}{CP^4} = \frac{AC^2 \cdot BC^2}{CP^4},$$

$UG = 2CP$ ultimately, and $PU = QR$;

$$\therefore \frac{QT^2}{2QR} = \frac{AC^2 \cdot BC^2}{CP^3} \text{ ultimately};$$

$$\therefore F = \text{limit of } \frac{2h^2 \cdot QR}{CP^2 \cdot QT^2} = \frac{h^2 \cdot CP}{AC^2 \cdot BC^2} \propto CP;$$

therefore the force is proportional to the distance from the center.

Aliter.

If CY be perpendicular on the tangent at P, and PV be the chord of curvature at P through the center $=\dfrac{2CD^2}{CP}$, Art. 81.

Then $F = \dfrac{2h^2}{CY^2 . PV} = \dfrac{h^2 . CP}{PF^2 . CD^2} = \dfrac{h^2}{AC^2 . BC^2} . CP.$

COR. 1. And conversely, if the force be as the distance, a body will revolve in an ellipse having its center in the center of force, or in a circle, which is a particular kind of ellipse.

COR. 2. And the periodic times will be the same in all ellipses described by bodies about the same center of force.

For the periodic time in any ellipse

$$= \frac{2 \times \text{area of ellipse}}{h} = \frac{2\pi AC . BC}{h},$$

and the forces, at different distances in the same or different ellipses, vary as the distance; therefore $\dfrac{h^2}{AC^2 . BC^2} = \mu$ is the same in different ellipses, therefore the periodic times in different ellipses is the same, and $= \dfrac{2\pi}{\sqrt{\mu}}.$

SCHOLIUM.

If the center of an ellipse be supposed at an infinite distance, the ellipse becomes a parabola, and the body will move in this parabola; and the force, now tending to a center at an infinite distance, will be constant and act in parallel lines. This theorem is due to Galileo. And, if the parabola be changed into a hyperbola, by the change of inclination of the plane cutting the cone, the body will move in this hyperbola under the action of a repulsive force tending from the center.

PROP. X. PROBLEM V. 193

Velocity in an Ellipse about the Center.

163. *To find the velocity in the elliptic orbit under the action of a force tending to the center, the measure of whose accelerating effect is $\mu \times$ distance.*

The velocity at $P = \dfrac{h}{CY} = \dfrac{h \cdot CD}{CY \cdot CD} = \dfrac{h \cdot CD}{AC \cdot BC}$,

and $\mu = \dfrac{h^2}{AC^2 \cdot BC^2}$;

therefore the velocity at $P = \sqrt{\mu} \cdot CD$.

Aliter.

(Vel.)^2 at $P = F \cdot \dfrac{PV}{2} = \mu \cdot CP \cdot \dfrac{CD^2}{CP}$;

$\therefore$ vel. at $P = \sqrt{\mu} \cdot CD$.

164. *To compare the velocity in an ellipse about the center with the velocity in a circle at the same distance.*

(Velocity)^2 in a circle, rad. $CP = \mu \cdot CP \cdot CP$;

$\therefore$ vel. at P : vel. in circle, rad. CP :: CD : CP.

165. *If a hyperbolic orbit be described under the action of a repulsive force tending from the center, the force varies as the distance, and the velocity at any point as the diameter of the conjugate hyperbola parallel to the tangent at the point.*

This may be proved exactly as in the case of the ellipse, employing the proper figure.

166. *To find the time in any arc of an elliptic orbit about a force tending to the center.*

Let P be any point of the orbit, Q the corresponding point in the auxiliary circle to the ellipse,

time from A to $P \propto$ area $ACP \propto$ area $ACQ \propto \angle ACQ$,

and periodic time $= \dfrac{2\pi}{\sqrt{\mu}}$;

$\therefore$ time in $AP : \dfrac{2\pi}{\sqrt{\mu}}$ :: $\angle ACQ$: four right angles;

$\therefore$ time in $AP =$ circular measure of $ACQ \div \sqrt{\mu}$.

Notes.

167. *If, at a given point, the velocity of a body be known, and the direction of its motion; to determine the curve which the body will describe under the action of a given centripetal force, which varies as the distance from the point to which it tends.*

Let Pt be the direction of motion at P, V the velocity at P, $\mu \cdot CP$ the measure of the accelerating effect of the force tending to C.

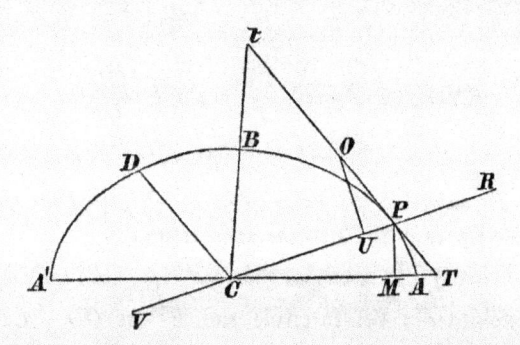

On PC produced, if necessary, take PV equal to four times the space through which a body must move from rest, under the action of the force at P continued constant, in order to acquire the given velocity V; so that $V^2 = 2\mu \, CP \cdot \frac{1}{4} PV$.

Draw CD parallel to Pt, a mean proportional to CP and $\frac{1}{2}PV$, and let an ellipse be constructed with CP, CD as semi-conjugate diameters, then PV is the chord of curvature at P through C.

In this ellipse let a body revolve under the action of a force tending to C, whose magnitude at P is that of the given force, see Arts. 121, 123, then, when it arrives at the point P, it will be moving in the direction Pt, also the square of the velocity at $P = \mu \cdot CD^2 = \mu \cdot CP \cdot \frac{1}{2}PV = V^2$, or the velocity at P, in the constructed ellipse, is V. Hence the body revolving in this ellipse is under the same circumstances as the proposed body, in all respects which can influence the motion of a body; therefore the proposed body will describe the ellipse constructed as above.

A direct solution of the problem, which is solved synthetically in the last Article, is given in pages 88 and 89.

168. *Geometrical construction for the position and magnitude of the axes of the elliptic orbit, described by a body about the center, when the velocity at a given point is known, and also the direction of motion.*

Produce CP to R, making PR a third proportional to CP and CD; bisect CR in U, and draw UO perpendicular to CR, meeting the tangent at P in O, and with center O describe a circle passing through C, R, and cutting the tangent in T and t;

$$\therefore PT \cdot Pt = CP \cdot PR = CD^2.$$

Let TC intersect the ellipse in A, A', and draw PM parallel to the diameter conjugate to ACA';

then $PT^2 : CD^2 :: TA \cdot TA' : CA^2$

$$:: CT^2 - CA^2 : CA^2,$$

$\therefore PT^2 : PT \cdot Pt :: CT^2 - CT \cdot CM : CT \cdot CM,$

$\therefore PT : Pt :: MT : CM;$

hence, Ct is parallel to PM, and CT, Ct are in the directions of conjugate diameters; but TCt is a right angle, therefore CT, Ct being in the direction of perpendicular conjugate diameters, are the directions of the axes of the ellipse, and if PM, Pm be perpendiculars from P upon these directions, the semiaxes are mean proportionals between CM, CT, and Cm, Ct.   Q.E.F.

169. *Equations for determining the position and dimensions of the orbit.*

Let $\mu \cdot R$ be the measure of the accelerating effect of the force at the distance $CP = R$, V the velocity, α the angle between CP and the direction of motion at the given point P. Let a, b be the semiaxes of the ellipse, ϖ the angle which the larger axis makes with the distance CP.

Then $V^2 = \mu \cdot CD^2$, and $CD^2 + CP^2 = a^2 + b^2$;

$$\therefore a^2 + b^2 = \frac{V^2}{\mu} + R^2. \qquad (1)$$

Also $V \cdot R \sin \alpha = h = \sqrt{\mu} \cdot ab$;

$$\therefore ab = \frac{V \cdot R \sin \alpha}{\sqrt{\mu}}, \qquad (2)$$

and, by the properties of the ellipse,

$$\frac{R^2}{a^2} \cos^2 \varpi + \frac{R^2}{b^2} \sin^2 \varpi = 1. \qquad (3)$$

The equations (1), (2) and (3) determine a, b and ϖ, whence the magnitude and position of the ellipse is determined.

We can obtain an equation for ϖ, immediately in terms of the data, as follows:

$$\left(\frac{R^2}{b^2} - 1\right) \sin^2 \varpi = \left(1 - \frac{R^2}{a^2}\right) \cos^2 \varpi, \text{ by (3)},$$

$$\frac{R^2}{a^2} + \frac{R^2}{b^2} = \operatorname{cosec}^2 \alpha \left(1 + \frac{\mu R^2}{V^2}\right), \text{ by (1) and (2)},$$

$$\frac{R^4}{a^2 b^2} = \operatorname{cosec}^2 \alpha \cdot \frac{\mu R^2}{V^2}, \text{ by (2)},$$

$$\therefore \left(\frac{R^2}{b^2} - 1\right)\left(1 - \frac{R^2}{a^2}\right) = \cot^2 \alpha;$$

$$\therefore \frac{\cos^2 \varpi}{\frac{R^2}{b^2} - 1} = \frac{\sin^2 \varpi}{1 - \frac{R^2}{a^2}} = \frac{\sin \varpi \cos \varpi}{\cot \alpha}$$

$$= \frac{\cos^2 \varpi - \sin^2 \varpi}{\operatorname{cosec}^2 \alpha \left(1 + \frac{\mu R^2}{V^2}\right) - 2};$$

$$\therefore \cot 2\varpi = \frac{1}{2} \tan \alpha \left(\cot^2 \alpha - 1 + \operatorname{cosec}^2 \alpha \cdot \frac{\mu R^2}{V^2}\right)$$

$$= \cot 2\alpha + \operatorname{cosec} 2\alpha \cdot \frac{\mu R^2}{V^2}; \qquad (4)$$

whence ϖ is known immediately from the initial circumstances of the motion.

170. If the force be repulsive, the equations for determining a, b, ϖ are

$$a^2 - b^2 = R^2 - \frac{V^2}{\mu}, \qquad (1)$$

PROP. X. PROBLEM V. 197

$$ab = \frac{VR \sin \alpha}{\sqrt{\mu}}, \quad (2)$$

and $\dfrac{R^2}{a^2} \cos^2 \varpi - \dfrac{R^2}{b^2} \sin^2 \varpi = 1.$ (3)

The direction and magnitude of the axes of the hyperbola may be determined geometrically, by observing that the asymptotes are the diagonals of the parallelograms of which the conjugate semi-diameters are sides, and that the axes bisect the angles between the asymptotes.

Resultant of any number of forces.

171. *When a particle is acted on by any number of forces, which tend to different centers, and vary as the distance from those centers, to find the resultant attraction.*

Let $\mu . R$, $\mu' . R$ be the magnitudes of two of the forces at the distance R; A, B the centers to which they tend, P the position of a particle acted on by the forces.

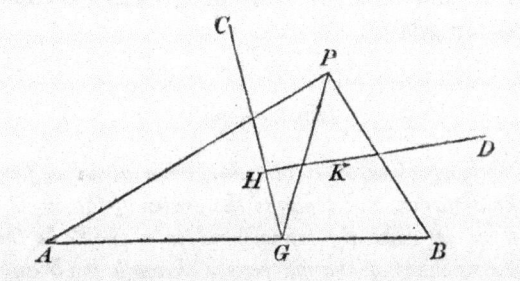

Let G be the center of gravity of two particles at A and B whose masses are in the ratio of μ to μ', join PA, PB, PG.

The components of the force $\mu . PA$, in the directions PG, GA, are $\mu . PG$ and $\mu . GA$, and those of the force $\mu' . PB$, in the directions PG, GB, are $\mu' . PG$ and $\mu' . GB$, but $\mu . GA = \mu' . GB$, therefore the resultant of the forces tending to A and B is $(\mu + \mu') PG$, which is a single force of magnitude $(\mu + \mu') R$, at the distance R, tending to the center of gravity of masses μ, μ' placed at A and B.

If $\mu''R$ be the magnitude of a force at the distance R, tending to C, the resultant attraction is that of a force tending to the center of gravity H of particles at C and G, whose masses are in the ratio $\mu'' : \mu + \mu'$, which varies as the distance from H, and whose magnitude at the distance R is $(\mu + \mu' + \mu'') R$.

And generally, the resultant of any number of forces is a single force, tending to the center of gravity of a system of particles whose masses are proportional to the magnitudes of the forces at the unit distance, and whose magnitude at any distance is the sum of those of the forces at the same distance.

172. COR. 1. If every particle of a solid of any form attract with a force which varies as the mass of the particle and the distance conjointly, the resultant attraction of the solid upon any body is the same as that of the whole mass of the solid collected into its center of gravity.

173. COR. 2. If any of the forces be repulsive, as that whose center is B, G will lie in AB or BA produced, according as μ' is greater or less than μ, and the resultant of the forces, tending to A and from B, will be $(\mu' - \mu) PG$ from G, or $(\mu - \mu') PG$ towards G.

Illustrations.

1. *A body revolves in a circular orbit about a force which varies as the distance, and tends to the center of the circle, and the center of force is suddenly transferred to a point in the radius which at the moment of change passes through the body; to find the subsequent motion of the body.*

(1) Since the force varies as the distance and is attractive, the orbit will be an ellipse.

(2) And, since the force is a finite force, the body will move in the same direction as before, at the moment of the change.

(3) Also, the velocity will, for the same reason, be unaltered, at that moment, since the force requires a finite time to produce an effect.

PROP. X. PROBLEM V. 199

Let CA be the radius passing through the body at the moment of change, CB perpendicular to CA, $\mu.CA$ the force at distance CA, V the velocity in the circle.

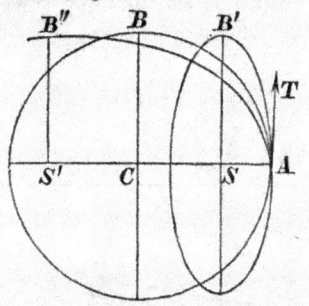

Then $V^2 = \mu.CA.CA = \mu.CA^2$; and if S, the new point to which the force tends, be in CA, let AB' be the ellipse described, by (1); SA is one of the semiaxes of the ellipse, since A is an apse, by (2), and, SB' being the other, if a body revolved in this ellipse round S, $\mu.SB'^2$ would be the square of the velocity at A, the same as in the circle, by (3); that is, $\mu.SB'^2 = \mu.CA^2$, and therefore $SB' = CA = CB$; hence the magnitude and position of the two semiaxes SA and SB' are known, and therefore the ellipse is completely determined.

The ellipse lies without the circle at A, because, the velocity being unaltered, the force has been diminished in the ratio of $SA : CA$, and therefore the curvature diminished in that ratio.

If S had been in AC produced, as at S', the force would have been increased, and the orbit AB'' would be within the circle near A.

The greatest distance from CA which the body reaches is in all cases the same for this law of force, because the component of the force perpendicular to CA is the same at the same distance from CA in whatever curve the body moves; therefore, in each orbit, the velocity being the same at A, the velocity perpendicular to AC is destroyed by the force at the same distance from AC.

2. *A body is describing a circle about a force which varies as the distance and tends to the center; if the center, to which the force tends, be suddenly transferred to a point in the circumference,*

at an angular distance of $60°$ from the position of the particle at any time, to determine the orbit described.

The orbit is an ellipse, since the force is attractive.

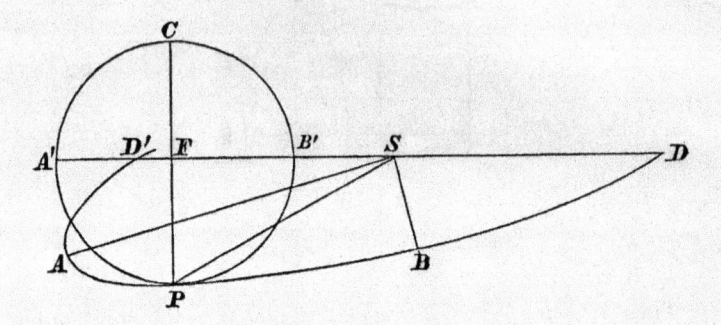

Let P be the position of the body at the instant the center of force is transferred from C, the center of the circle, to S, where SCP is an equilateral triangle.

The velocity at P is $\sqrt{\mu}.CP = \sqrt{\mu}.SP$; and, since it is unaltered by the change of the center of force, the semidiameter conjugate to SP is equal to SP.

Draw DSD' perpendicular to CP, meeting it in F, and take $SD = SD' = SP$. Construct an ellipse having SP, SD as equal conjugate semidiameters; SA, SB the semiaxes bisect the angles PSD, PSD'.

The ellipse so described is the orbit required.

Prove the following construction:

On CP as diameter describe a circle cutting SD' in B', A'; SA', SB' are the lengths of the semiaxes.

Explain why the orbit is exterior to the circle.

3. *Two bodies whose masses are* m, m' *revolve in an ellipse, under the action of a force tending to the center; shew that if they are at one time at the extremities of two conjugate diameters, they will always be so, and in this case find the locus of their center of gravity.*

Let P, D be their positions at any time, CP, CD being semi-conjugate diameters. Let the ordinates MPQ, NDR meet the auxiliary circle in Q and R.

PROP. X. PROBLEM V. 201

Since the angles ACQ, ACR are always proportional to the times; RCQ will always be a right angle; therefore the bodies will always be at the extremities of conjugate diameters.

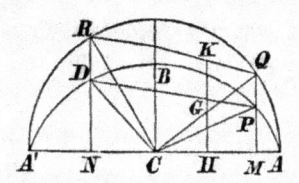

Let GH be the ordinate of their center of gravity.

Join RQ and produce HG to RQ in K;

$$\therefore KH : GH = QM : PM, \text{ a constant ratio,}$$
$$\text{also, } RK : KQ = DG : GP, \dots\dots\dots\dots\dots;$$

therefore CK is constant, or the locus of K is a circle,

hence, the locus of G is an ellipse, whose axes are proportional to those of APD.

Shew that the semi-major axis : $CA :: (m^2 + m'^2)^{\frac{1}{2}} : m + m'$.

4. *A body is composed of matter which attracts with a force varying as the distance; shew that, however a particle be projected, unless it strikes the body, it will describe its orbit in the same periodic time.*

This is obvious immediately from Art. 171, relating to the resultant of attracting forces.

5. *A body moves in an ellipse under the action of a force varying as the distance: if the velocity at any point be slightly increased by $\frac{1}{n}$ th of itself, find the consequent changes in the axes of the ellipse.*

If the body be at the end of one of the equal conjugate diameters, when the change takes place, shew that each axis is increased by $\frac{1}{2n}$ th of itself, and that the apse line regredes through a small angle, whose circular measure is $\frac{1}{n} \cdot \frac{ab}{a^2 - b^2}$.

When V is changed to $V\left(1+\dfrac{1}{n}\right)$, let the corresponding changes of a, b, and ϖ be $a\alpha$, $b\beta$, and γ: α, β, γ, and $\dfrac{1}{n}$ being so small that we may neglect their squares.

Then by the equations of Art. (169), and notes (1), (2), (3) in page 198,

$$a^2(1+\alpha)^2 + b^2(1+\beta)^2 = \frac{V^2}{\mu}\left(1+\frac{1}{n}\right)^2 + R^2,$$

and, $\quad a^2 + b^2 = \dfrac{V^2}{\mu} + R^2;$

$$\therefore a^2\alpha + b^2\beta = \frac{V^2}{\mu n}. \tag{1}$$

Again, $\quad a^2 b^2 (1+\alpha)^2 (1+\beta)^2 = \dfrac{V^2 R^2 \sin^2 \alpha}{\mu}\left(1+\dfrac{1}{n}\right)^2,$

and $\quad a^2 b^2 = \dfrac{V^2 R^2 \sin^2 \alpha}{\mu};$

$$\therefore \alpha + \beta = \frac{1}{n}, \tag{2}$$

whence it is easily shewn that

$$\frac{\alpha}{a^2 - R^2} = \frac{\beta}{R^2 - b^2} = \frac{1}{n(a^2 - b^2)}.$$

In the particular case proposed,

$$R^2 = \frac{a^2 + b^2}{2}, \quad \therefore \alpha = \frac{1}{2n} = \beta.$$

Also, $\quad \dfrac{R^2}{a^2}\cos^2(\varpi+\gamma) + \dfrac{R^2}{b^2}\sin^2(\varpi+\gamma) = 1 + \dfrac{1}{n},$

and $\quad \dfrac{R^2}{a^2}\cos^2\varpi + \dfrac{R^2}{b^2}\sin^2\varpi = 1;$

$$\therefore \left(\frac{R^2}{b^2} - \frac{R^2}{a^2}\right)\{\sin^2(\varpi+\gamma) - \sin^2\varpi\} = \frac{1}{n};$$

$$\therefore \left(\frac{R^2}{b^2} - \frac{R^2}{a^2}\right)\sin(2\varpi+\gamma)\sin\gamma = \frac{1}{n};$$

PROP. X. PROBLEM V.

and, since the axes bisect the angles between equal conjugate diameters,
$$ab = R^2 \sin 2\varpi,$$
therefore γ, being expressed in circular measure,
$$= \frac{ab}{n(a^2 - b^2)}.$$

6. *In any position of a particle describing an ellipse, under the action of a force tending to the center, the center of force is suddenly transferred to the focus, prove that the sum of the axes of the given ellipse is to the difference in the duplicate ratio of the sum to the difference of the axes of the new orbit. Find the eccentricity of the new orbit, and shew that its major axis bisects the angle between the focal distance and the major axis of the given ellipse.*

Employing the equations of Art. (169), if α, β be the semi-axes of the new orbit, P the position of particle when the center is transferred to S,

$$\alpha^2 + \beta^2 = CD^2 + SP^2 = SP \cdot HP + SP^2 = 2a \cdot SP$$

$$\alpha\beta = CD \cdot SY,$$

and $SY^2 : BC^2 :: SP : HP :: SP^2 : CD^2;$

$$\therefore 2\alpha\beta = 2b \cdot SP;$$

$$\therefore (\alpha + \beta)^2 : (\alpha - \beta)^2 :: a + b : a - b;$$

and, if e and ϵ be the eccentricities of the old and new orbits,

since $\dfrac{b}{a} = \dfrac{2\alpha\beta}{\alpha^2 + \beta^2},$

$$e^2 = 1 - \frac{b^2}{a^2} = \left(\frac{\alpha^2 - \beta^2}{\alpha^2 + \beta^2}\right)^2;$$

$$\therefore \epsilon^2 = \frac{\alpha^2 - \beta^2}{\alpha^2} = \frac{2e}{1 + e}.$$

Also, $\dfrac{SP^2}{\alpha^2} \cos^2 \varpi + \dfrac{SP^2}{\beta^2} \sin^2 \varpi = 1,$

$$(\alpha^2 - \beta^2)^2 = 4(a^2 - b^2) SP^2;$$

$$\therefore a^2 - \beta^2 = 2ae \cdot SP;$$
$$\therefore a^2 = a(1+e)SP,$$
$$\text{and} \quad \beta^2 = a(1-e)SP;$$
$$\therefore \frac{a(1-e^2)}{SP} = (1-e)\cos^2\varpi + (1+e)\sin^2\varpi$$
$$= 1 - e\cos 2\varpi;$$
$$\therefore 2\varpi = \angle PSA,$$

hence, the major axis of the new orbit bisects the angle between PS and the major axis of the original orbit.

Or, by the geometrical construction of Art. 168, since PR is a third proportional to SP and CD, and therefore is equal to HP, the circle, which determines T and t, passes through H, and the arcs HT, TR are equal, that is, ST bisects the angle PSA.

XVII.

1. Shew that the velocity in an ellipse about the center is the same as that in a circle at the same distance, at the points whose conjugate diameters are equal.

2. A body is revolving in a circle under the action of a force tending to the center, the law of force at different distances being that the force varies as the distance; find the orbits described when the circumstances are changed at any point as follows:

(1) If the force be increased in the ratio of $1 : n$.

(2) If the velocity be increased in the ratio $1 : n$.

(3) If the force become repulsive, remaining of the same magnitude.

(4) If the direction be changed by an impulse in the direction of the center, measured by the velocity which is equal to that in the circle.

3. If a body be projected from an apse, with a velocity double of that in a circle at the same distance, find the position and magnitude of the axes of its orbit.

4. A particle is revolving in a circle acted on by a force which varies as the distance; the center of force is suddenly transferred to the opposite extremity of the diameter through the particle, and becomes repulsive; shew that the eccentricity of the hyperbolic orbit $= \frac{1}{2}\sqrt{5}$.

5. An elastic ball, moving in an ellipse about the center, on arriving at the extremity of the minor axis strikes directly another ball at rest; find the orbits described by both bodies.

6. The particles of which a rectangular parallelopiped is composed attract with a force which varies as the distance, and a body is projected so as to describe a curve on one of the faces supposed smooth; find the periodic time.

7. A body is projected in a direction making an angle $\cos^{-1}\dfrac{1}{\sqrt{3}}$ with the distance from a point to which a force tends, varying as the distance from it, and the velocity $= \sqrt{\tfrac{3}{2}} \times$ velocity in the circle at the same distance; prove that one axis is double of the other and that the inclination of the major axis to the distance is $\tfrac{1}{2}\cos^{-1}\tfrac{1}{8}$.

8. CX, CY are straight lines inclined at any angle, and a force tends to C, and varies as the distance from C. If from various points in CY different particles are projected parallel to CX at the same moment, and with the same velocity, they will all arrive at CX at the same time and place; and they will also do so, if the force cease to act for any interval of time.

9. From points in a line CA between C and A particles are projected at right angles to CA, with velocities proportional to their distances from A, C being a center to which the force tends, and the force varying as the distance; find the ellipse of greatest area which is described.

10. A particle is projected from a point P, in a given ellipse, perpendicular to the major axis, and is acted on by a force which tends to the center C, and varies as the distance from it; and the velocity is that in a circle whose radius is CS; prove that the major axis of the orbit is equal to that of the given ellipse, and that $CP^2 =$ the sum of the squares of the semi-minor axes of the orbit and of the given ellipse; also that the tangents of the inclinations of CP to the major axes of the elliptic orbit and of the given ellipse are in the duplicate ratio of the minor axes.

11. A number of particles move in hyperbolas, under the action of the same repulsive force from their common center. Shew that, if the transverse axes coincide, and the particles start from the vertex at the same instant, they will always lie in a straight line perpendicular to the major axis. If the hyperbolas have all the same asymptotes, shew that the particles will at every instant be in a straight line passing through the center, if they be so at any given time.

12. Four equal bodies are placed in a smooth elliptic groove at the extremities of equal conjugate diameters, and are acted on by their mutual attraction, which varies as the distance. Shew that, if they be projected with the same velocity, equal to that with which they would revolve in a circle, passing through them all, they would

exert no pressure on the groove, and the sum of the squares of their velocities would never vary.

13. If a triangle ABC be inscribed in an elliptic orbit, described by a particle under the action of a force tending to the center, so that its center of gravity coincides with the center of the ellipse, prove that the velocities of the particle at A, B, C will be proportional to the opposite sides of the triangle, and also that the times from A to B, B to C and C to A will be equal to one another.

14. Two particles are projected in parallel directions from two points in a straight line passing through a center of force, the acceleration towards which varies as the distance, with velocities proportional to their distances from that center. Prove that all tangents to the path of the inner cut off, from that of the outer, arcs described in equal times.

15. A body is revolving in an ellipse under the action of a force tending to the center, and when it arrives at the extremity of the major axis, the force ceases to act until the body has moved through a distance equal to the semi-minor axis, it then acts for a quarter of the periodic time in the ellipse; prove that, if it again ceases to act for the same time as before, the body will have arrived at the other extremity of the major axis.

16. Two ellipses are described by two particles about a common center, the axes of the two are in the same directions, and the sum of the axes of one is equal to the difference of those of the other; prove that, if the particles be at corresponding extremities of the major axes at the same moment, and be moving in opposite directions, the line joining them will be of constant length during the motion, and will revolve with uniform angular velocity.

17. A small bead slides on a smooth wire in the form of an arc of a circle, under the action of a force, tending to a point in the circumference of the circle, and varying as the distance. If the bead be initially situated at the opposite extremity of the diameter passing through the center of force, and just displaced, prove that, whatever be the length of the arc, the sum of the squares on the axes of the elliptic orbit, which the bead will describe after leaving the wire, will be equal to the square on the diameter of the circle.

18. A point is moving in an equiangular spiral, its acceleration always tending to the pole S. When it arrives at a point P, the law of acceleration is changed to that of the direct distance, the actual acceleration being unaltered. Prove that the point will then move in an ellipse, whose axes make equal angles with SP and the tangent to spiral at P, and that the ratio of the axes is $\tan \dfrac{a}{2} : 1$, where a is the angle of the spiral.

SECTION III.

On the Motion of Bodies in Conic Sections, under the action of Forces tending to a Focus.

Prop. XI. Problem VI.

If a body is revolving in an ellipse, to find the law of force tending to a focus of the ellipse.

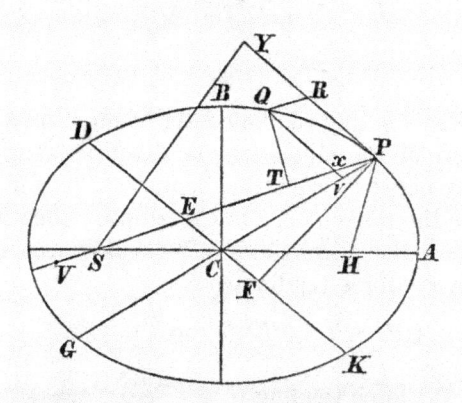

Let S be the focus to which the force tends, P the position of the body at any time, PCG, DCK conjugate diameters, Q a point near P, QT, PF perpendiculars on SP, DCK, from Q, P respectively, PR a tangent at P, QR parallel to SP, Qxv parallel to PR, meeting SP in x, and PC in v, and let SP, DCK intersect in E.

Then $F = \dfrac{2h^2}{SP^2} \cdot \dfrac{QR}{QT^2}$, ultimately, when QT is indefinitely diminished.

But, by similar triangles QTx, PFE,

$$\frac{QT^2}{Qx^2} = \frac{PF^2}{PE^2} = \frac{PF^2}{AC^2} = \frac{BC^2}{CD^2}.$$

Now, $\dfrac{Qv^2}{Pv \cdot vG} = \dfrac{CD^2}{CP^2}$, by the properties of the ellipse,

and $\dfrac{Pv}{QR} = \dfrac{Pv}{Px} = \dfrac{CP}{PE}$, by similar triangles;

$$\therefore \frac{Qv^2}{QR \cdot vG} = \frac{CD^2}{CP \cdot AC},$$

and $vG = 2CP$, $Qx = Qv$, ultimately;

$$\therefore \frac{QT^2}{QR} = \frac{2BC^2}{AC} = L, \text{ ultimately,}$$

if L be the latus rectum of the ellipse;

$$\therefore F = \frac{2h^2}{L} \cdot \frac{1}{SP^2} \propto \frac{1}{SP^2}.$$

Aliter.

Since the force tending to the center of an ellipse, under the action of which the ellipse can be described, varies directly as the distance CP from the center C; let CE be drawn parallel to the tangent PQ to the ellipse; then if S be any point within the ellipse, and SP, CE intersect in E, force tending to C : force tending to S

$$:: CP \cdot SP^2 : PE^3 \text{ (Prop. VII. Cor. 3);}$$

$\therefore$ force tending to $S \propto \dfrac{PE^3}{SP^2} \propto \dfrac{1}{SP^2}$,

since PE is constant.

Prop. XII. Problem VII.

If a body is revolving in a hyperbola, to find the law of force tending to a focus of the figure.

The investigation is exactly the same as in the last proposition, employing the subjoined figure.

Also, *repulsive* force from $C \varpropto CP$, and by Prop. VII. Cor. 3, force from C : force to S :: $CP.SP^2 : PE^3$, whence force to $S \varpropto \dfrac{1}{SP^2}$, since PE is constant.

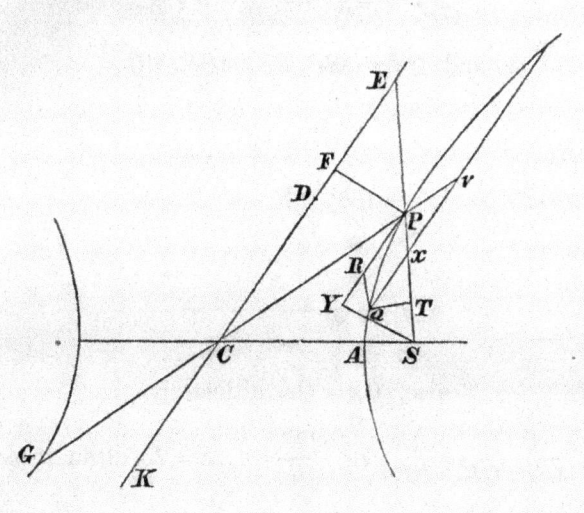

In the same manner as in these propositions, it can be shewn that the repulsive force tending from a focus, under the action of which the body describes the opposite branch of the hyperbola, varies inversely as the square of the distance.

Prop. XIII. Problem VIII.

If a body is moving in a parabola, to find the law of force tending to the focus.

Let S be the focus of the parabola, P the position of the body at any time, Q a point near P, PRY a tangent at P, QR parallel to SP, Qxv parallel to PR, meeting SP in x, and the diameter through P in v, QT, SY perpendicular to SP, PY respectively.

Then $F = \dfrac{2h^2}{SP^2} \cdot \dfrac{QR}{QT^2}$, ultimately, when QP is indefinitely diminished.

Since SP, Pv make equal angles with the tangent, Pxv is an isosceles triangle, therefore $Pv = Px = QR$, and by similar triangles

$$\frac{QT^2}{Qx^2} = \frac{SY^2}{SP^2} = \frac{AS \cdot SP}{SP^2} = \frac{AS}{SP},$$

and $Qv^2 = 4SP \cdot Pv = 4SP \cdot QR$;

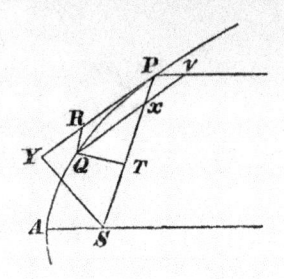

also, $Qx = Qv$, ultimately,

$$\therefore \frac{QT^2}{4SP \cdot QR} = \frac{AS}{SP}, \text{ or } \frac{QT^2}{QR} = 4AS = L, \text{ ultimately;}$$

$$\therefore F = \frac{2h^2}{L} \cdot \frac{1}{SP^2} \propto \frac{1}{SP^2}.$$

COR. 1. It follows from the last three propositions, that if any body move from the point P in any direction PR, with any velocity, and be at the same time acted on by a centripetal force, which is inversely proportional to the square of the distance, the body will move in some one of the conic sections, having a focus in the center of force, and conversely.

For when the focus, the point of contact, and the position of the tangent are given, a conic section can be described which will have a given curvature at that point. But when the force is given and the velocity of the body, the curvature is known; and two orbits touching one another cannot be described with the same centripetal force, and the same velocity at the point of contact.

COR. 2. If the velocity, with which a body leaves its position P, be such that the body would describe the small space PR in some very small time, and in the same time the centripetal force were able to move the same body through the space RQ, this body will move in some conic section whose latus rectum is the limit of $\dfrac{QT^2}{QR}$ when the lines PR, QR are indefinitely diminished.

In these corollaries the circle is included as a particular case of an ellipse; and the case is excepted in which the body moves in a straight line to the center of force.

Observations on the preceding Propositions.

174. If μ be the absolute force, in any conic section, whose latus rectum is L, described under the action of a force tending to the focus, $\mu = \dfrac{2h^2}{L}$, and μ is given, either when the force at any point is given, or when the velocity at any point in a given conic section is given, for, in the latter case, L and $V \cdot SY$ or h are given.

175. If we assume the chord of curvature through the focus for any point in an ellipse or hyperbola, we obtain the law of force from the expression $F = \dfrac{2h^2}{SY^2 \cdot PV}$.

For, $PV \cdot AC = 2CD^2 = 2SP \cdot HP$;

and $SY^2 : BC^2 :: SP : HP$;

$\therefore F = \dfrac{h^2 \cdot AC}{SY^2 \cdot HP \cdot SP} = \dfrac{h^2 \cdot AC}{BC^2 \cdot SP^2}$.

Similarly for the parabola,

since $PV = 4SP$, and $SY^2 = AS \cdot SP$,

$F = \dfrac{2h^2}{AS \cdot SP \cdot PV} = \dfrac{h^2}{2AS \cdot SP^2}$.

176. Cor. 1. It is assumed in this corollary that a conic section can be described under the action of a force tending to the focus: see Art. 121.

Prop. XIV. Theorem VI.

If any number of bodies revolve about a common center, and the centripetal force varies inversely as the square of the distance; the latera recta of the orbits described are in the duplicate ratio of the areas, which the bodies describe in the same time by radii drawn to the center of force.

For in each orbit the latus rectum is equal to the limit of $\frac{QT^2}{QR}$ (by Cor. 2, Prop. XIII.) when the arc PQ is made indefinitely small.

But QR in a given time is ultimately in the different orbits as the centripetal force, that is, reciprocally as the square of the distance SP.

Hence, ultimately, $\frac{QT^2}{QR} \propto QT^2 . SP^2$, or the latus rectum is in the duplicate ratio of $QT.SP$ or of twice the area PSQ described in the given small time, which, since the area in each orbit is proportional to the time, varies as the area described in any given time.

Cor. Hence the whole area of the ellipse, and the rectangle under the axes, which is proportional to it, varies in a ratio compounded of the subduplicate ratio of the latera recta and the ratio of the periodic time.

For the whole area is as $QT \times SP$ described in a given small time, multiplied by the periodic time.

Prop. XV. Theorem VII.

On the same supposition, the squares of the periodic times in ellipses are proportional to the cubes of the major axes.

For, by Prop. XIV. and the Corollary, since $QT.SP$, in each ellipse, described in a given small time varies as $\frac{BC}{AC^{\frac{1}{2}}}$, and the area $\propto AC.BC$, the periodic time, which varies as the area divided by $QT.SP$, $\propto AC^{\frac{3}{2}}$.

COR. Hence the periodic times in ellipses are the same as in circles whose diameters are equal to the major axes of the ellipses.

Observations on the preceding Propositions.

177. Prop. XIV. and its Corollary may be also proved as follows.

Let h, h' be the double areas described in the same time in any two of the orbits, L, L' the latera recta; then, since the absolute forces are the same in the different orbits,

$$\frac{2h^2}{L} = \frac{2h'^2}{L'};$$

$$\therefore L : L' :: h^2 : h'^2;$$

or the latera recta are in the duplicate ratio of the areas described in a given time.

COR. Let P, P' be the periodic times in any two of the orbits.

Then the areas are as $hP : h'P' :: L^{\frac{1}{2}}.P : L'^{\frac{1}{2}}.P$.

178. *To find the periodic time in an ellipse described under the action of a given force tending to the focus.*

Let P be the periodic time, μ the absolute force, then

$h.P =$ twice the area of the ellipse $= 2\pi AC.BC$;

$$\text{and } \mu = \frac{AC.h^2}{BC^2};$$

$$\therefore P = 2\pi AC.\frac{BC}{h} = 2\pi AC.\left(\frac{AC}{\mu}\right)^{\frac{1}{2}} = \frac{2\pi AC^{\frac{3}{2}}}{\mu^{\frac{1}{2}}}.$$

Therefore, in different ellipses described about the same center of force, the squares of the periodic time vary as the cubes of the major axes.

179. *To find the time from an apse to any point of an elliptic orbit described under the action of a force tending to the focus.*

Let ASa be the apsidal line, A being the further apse, AQa the circle on the major axis as diameter, P any point in the orbit, Q the corresponding point in the circle. Join SP, SQ, CQ.

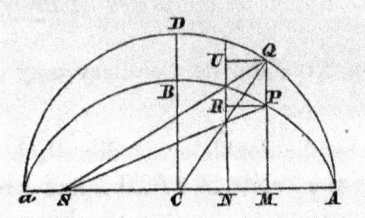

Time in AP : periodic time :: area ASP : $\pi AC.BC$
$$:: \text{area } ASQ : \pi AC^2,$$
and area ASQ = sector ACQ + triangle SCQ
$$= \frac{1}{2} AC.AQ + \frac{1}{2} SC.QM;$$

therefore, if u' be the circular measure of $\angle ACQ$, and e the eccentricity of the ellipse,
$$\text{area } ASQ = \frac{1}{2} AC^2 (u' + e \sin u')$$

and time in AP : $\dfrac{2\pi AC^{\frac{3}{2}}}{\mu^{\frac{1}{2}}}$ :: $u' + e \sin u'$: 2π,

i. e. the time from the further apse to P is $\dfrac{AC^{\frac{3}{2}}}{\mu^{\frac{1}{2}}} (u' + e \sin u')$.

Similarly, if u is the circular measure of aCQ, the time from the nearer apse is $\dfrac{AC^{\frac{3}{2}}}{\mu^{\frac{1}{2}}} (u - e \sin u)$.

180. DEF. $\angle aCQ$, from the nearer apse, is called the *eccentric anomaly*, $\angle aSP$ the *true anomaly*, and the *mean anomaly* is the angle which would be described in the same time as $\angle aSP$ by a body moving with uniform angular velocity equal to the mean angular velocity in the ellipse.

PROP. XV. THEOREM VII.

181. *To find the relations between the mean, the true, and the eccentric anomalies.*

Let m, v, and u be the three angles.

Since the mean angular velocity in the ellipse is 2π divided by the periodic time, or $\dfrac{\mu^{\frac{1}{2}}}{AC^{\frac{3}{2}}}$,

$$m = u - e \sin u, \text{ Art. 179,}$$

and if a, e be the semi major axis and eccentricity

$$SP \cos v = a \cos u - ae;$$

$$\therefore \cos u = \frac{(1-e^2) \cos v}{1 + e \cos v} + e = \frac{e + \cos v}{1 + e \cos v};$$

$$\therefore \frac{1 - \cos u}{1 + \cos u} = \frac{1-e}{1+e} \frac{1 - \cos v}{1 + \cos v};$$

$$\therefore \tan \frac{u}{2} = \sqrt{\frac{1-e}{1+e}} \tan \frac{v}{2}.$$

Also $SP = AC + e \cdot CM$

$$= a(1 - e \cos u).$$

182. *To find the time of describing any angle from the vertex, in a parabolic orbit.*

Let P be any point in a parabolic orbit whose axis is ASM, S being the center of force; draw PM an ordinate to ASM. Then $\sqrt{2\mu \cdot AS}$ is twice the area described in an unit of time.

Therefore time in $AP = \dfrac{2 \text{ area } ASP}{(2\mu \cdot AS)^{\frac{1}{2}}}$

$$\frac{1}{(2\mu \cdot AS)^{\frac{1}{2}}} \left(\frac{4}{3} AM \cdot MP - SM \cdot MP \right).$$

Let $\angle ASP = \theta$ and $AS = a$;

$$\therefore SP \cos^2 \frac{\theta}{2} = SY \cos \frac{\theta}{2} = AS;$$

$$\therefore AM = SP - AS = a \tan^2 \frac{\theta}{2},$$

$$PM = 2(a \cdot AM)^{\frac{1}{2}} = 2a \tan \frac{\theta}{2};$$

$$\therefore \text{ time in } AP = \frac{MP}{(2\mu a)^{\frac{1}{2}}} \left(\frac{4}{3} AM - AM + AS\right)$$

$$= \sqrt{\frac{2a^3}{\mu}} \left(\tan \frac{\theta}{2} + \frac{1}{3} \tan^3 \frac{\theta}{2}\right).$$

Kepler's Laws.

183. The three laws known by the name of Kepler's Laws are,

I. That planets move in ellipses having the Sun's center in one focus.

II. That the areas swept out by radii drawn from the planet to the Sun's center are, in the same orbit, proportional to the time of describing them.

III. That the squares of the periodic times are proportional to the cubes of the major axes.

These laws were discovered by Kepler from observations made on the planet Mars, and stated by analogy as general laws.

184. Kepler's laws, although not rigidly true, are sufficiently near to the truth to have led to the discovery of the law of attraction of the bodies of the solar system. The deviation from complete accuracy is due to the facts, that the planets are not of inappreciable mass, that, in consequence, they disturb each other's orbits about the Sun, and, by their action on the Sun itself, cause the periodic time of each to be shorter than if the Sun were a fixed body, in the subduplicate ratio of the mass of the Sun to the sum of the masses of the Sun and Planet; these errors are appreciable although very small, since the mass of the largest of the planets, Jupiter, is less than $\frac{1}{1000}$th of the Sun's mass.

Deductions from Kepler's Laws.

185. From the law of the equable description of areas, stated as the *second law*, it is deduced, by Prop. II., that the forces acting on the planets are centripetal forces tending to the Sun's center.

But this law gives no information regarding the nature or intensity of the forces.

186. From the elliptic motion of the planets, as asserted in the *first law*, it is deduced, by Prop. XI., that the force which acts upon each planet varies inversely as the square of the distance from the center of the Sun.

187. From the relation between the periodic times and lengths of the major axes, stated in the *third law*, it is inferred, by Prop. XV., that the planets are acted on by the same centripetal force; and that the attraction, being the same for all bodies, independently of their form and substance, is not of the nature of the elective action of chemical or magnetic forces.

188. The same laws hold for the motion of the satellites of Jupiter, Saturn, and Uranus, and the first two for our Moon, their respective primaries taking the place of the Sun in the statement of the laws.

Hence it is inferred that forces tend to the centers of the planets, varying according to the same law as the forces tending to the Sun.

189. By such deductions the law of gravitation is rendered probable, that *every particle attracts every other particle with a force which varies inversely as the square of the distance.*

The law thus suggested is assumed to be *universally* true, and calculations are made of the effects of the action of the bodies of the solar system upon one another in disturbing their elliptic motion; and also of the disturbances of the motion of the satellites due to the want of exact sphericity in the primaries; and these calculations have been found to agree with the results of most minute astronomical observations.

Predictions of the return of comets have been fulfilled, founded on the supposition of the truth of the law, and the existence and position of a planet have been recognized, before its discovery by actual observation, from its assumed action according to this law upon another planet.

Thus the law of gravitation has satisfied every test which could be applied to it, and it is therefore proved to be true as far as our system is concerned.

Prop. XVI. Theorem VIII.

On the same supposition, the velocities of the bodies are in the ratio compounded of the inverse ratio of the perpendiculars from the focus on the tangent and the subduplicate ratio of the latera recta.

For, in any two orbits,

$$V : V' :: \frac{h}{SY} : \frac{h'}{SY'}$$

$$:: \frac{L^{\frac{1}{2}}}{SY} : \frac{L'^{\frac{1}{2}}}{SY'}.$$

Cor. 1. The latera recta of the orbits are in the ratio compounded of the duplicate ratio of the perpendiculars and the duplicate ratio of the velocities.

For $L : L' :: h^2 : h'^2$
$$:: V^2 . SY^2 : V'^2 . SY'^2.$$

Cor. 2. The velocities of the bodies, at their greatest and least distances from their common focus, are in the ratio compounded of the ratio of the distances inversely, and the subduplicate ratio of the latera recta directly.

For the perpendiculars on the tangents are these very distances.

Cor. 3. And therefore the velocity in a conic section, at the greatest or least distance from the focus, is to the velocity in a circle at the same distance from the center in the subduplicate ratio of the latus rectum to twice that distance.

For the latus rectum of a circle is the diameter, therefore if SA be the greatest or least distance, velocity in the conic section : velocity in the circle

$$:: \frac{L^{\frac{1}{2}}}{SA} : \frac{(2SA)^{\frac{1}{2}}}{SA} :: L^{\frac{1}{2}} : (2SA)^{\frac{1}{2}}.$$

PROP. XVI. THEOREM VIII.

COR. 4. The velocities of bodies revolving in ellipses are, at their mean distances from the common focus, the same as the velocities of bodies revolving in circles at the same distances; that is, (by Cor. 6, Prop. IV.) in the inverse subduplicate ratio of the distances.

For the perpendiculars are now the semiaxes minor, that is $SY = BC$, and the distance $SB = AC$, therefore velocity in the ellipse at the mean distance : velocity in the circle at the same distance

$$:: \frac{L^{\frac{1}{2}}}{BC} : \frac{(2AC)^{\frac{1}{2}}}{AC} :: L^{\frac{1}{2}} : \left(\frac{2BC^2}{AC}\right)^{\frac{1}{2}},$$

therefore the velocities are equal.

COR. 5. In the same figure, or in different figures having their latera recta equal, the velocity varies inversely as the perpendicular from the focus on the tangent.

COR. 6. In the parabola, the velocity varies in the inverse subduplicate ratio of the distance of the body from the focus, in the ellipse it varies in a greater, and in the hyperbola in a less inverse ratio.

For the $(\text{velocity})^2 \propto \frac{1}{SY^2}$,

which in the parabola $\propto \frac{1}{SP}$,

in the ellipse $\propto \frac{HP}{SP} \propto \frac{2AC - SP}{SP}$,

in the hyperbola $\propto \frac{HP}{SP} \propto \frac{2AC + SP}{SP}$.

COR. 7. In the parabola, the velocity of the body at any distance from the focus is to the velocity of a body revolving in a circle at the same distance from the center, in the subduplicate ratio of 2 : 1; in the ellipse it is less, in the hyperbola greater than in this ratio.

For, velocity in the conic section : velocity in the circle at the same distance

$$:: \frac{L^{\frac{1}{2}}}{SY} : \frac{(2SP)^{\frac{1}{2}}}{SP} :: \left(\frac{L.SP}{2SY^2}\right)^{\frac{1}{2}} : 1$$

$$:: \sqrt{2} : 1 \text{ in the parabola,}$$

$$:: \left(\frac{BC^2.SP}{AC.SY^2}\right)^{\frac{1}{2}} : 1 :: \left(\frac{HP}{AC}\right)^{\frac{1}{2}} : 1 \text{ in the ellipse or hyperbola,}$$

and $HP < 2AC$ in the ellipse, and $> 2AC$ in the hyperbola.

Hence also, in the parabola, the velocity is everywhere equal to the velocity in a circle at half the distance, in the ellipse less, and in the hyperbola greater.

COR. 8. The velocity of a body revolving in any conic section, is to the velocity in a circle at the distance of half the latus rectum, as that distance is to the perpendicular from the focus on the tangent.

For, the velocity in the conic section : the velocity in the circle at distance $\frac{1}{2}L$ ::
$$\frac{L^{\frac{1}{2}}}{SY} : \frac{L^{\frac{1}{2}}}{\frac{1}{2}L} :: \frac{1}{2}L : SY.$$

COR. 9. Hence, since (Cor. 6, Prop. IV.) the velocity of a body revolving in a circle is to the velocity in any other circle in the inverse subduplicate ratio of the distances, the velocity of a body in a conic section will be to the velocity in a circle at the same distance as a mean proportional between that common distance and half the latus rectum to the perpendicular from the focus on the tangent.

For velocity in a circle at distance $\frac{1}{2}L$: velocity in a circle at distance SP :: $SP^{\frac{1}{2}} : (\frac{1}{2}L)^{\frac{1}{2}}$, therefore velocity in conic section : velocity in circle at distance SP

$$:: (\tfrac{1}{2}L.SP)^{\frac{1}{2}} : SY.$$

Notes.

190. *To find the velocity in a conic section described under the action of a force tending to the focus.*

In the central conic sections

$$V^2 = \frac{h^2}{SY^2} = \frac{\mu.BC^2}{AC.SY^2} = \frac{\mu.HP}{AC.SP};$$

or else, $V^2 = F.\tfrac{1}{2}PV = \dfrac{\mu}{SP^2}\cdot\dfrac{CD^2}{AC} = \dfrac{\mu.HP}{SP.AC};$

PROP. XVI. THEOREM VIII. 221

but, $HP = 2AC - SP$, in the ellipse,

and, $HP = SP - 2AC$, in the hyperbola, force repulsive,

$= SP + 2AC$, in the hyperbola, force attractive;

$$\therefore V^2 = \frac{\mu}{SP}\left(2 \mp \frac{SP}{AC}\right).$$

In the parabola,

$$V^2 = \frac{h^2}{SY^2} = \frac{\mu \cdot 2SA}{SA \cdot SP} = \frac{2\mu}{SP};$$

or else, $V^2 = F \cdot \frac{1}{2}PV = \frac{\mu}{SP^2} \cdot 2SP = \frac{2\mu}{SP}.$

191. The expression $\frac{\mu}{SP}\left(2 - \frac{SP}{AC}\right)$ for the square of the velocity in the ellipse, reduces itself to that for the hyperbola under an attractive force by changing the sign of CA, which corresponds to the opposite direction in which AC is measured in the hyperbola; it reduces to that for the hyperbola under a repulsive force by changing the sign of μ, which corresponds to changing the direction of the force; and to that for the parabola by making AC infinite.

192. *To compare the velocity in the ellipse or hyperbola with that in the circle at the same distance.*

Let U be the velocity in the circle,

$$U^2 = \frac{\mu}{SP^2} \cdot SP = \frac{\mu}{SP};$$

$$\therefore V^2 : U^2 :: 2 \mp \frac{SP}{AC} : 1,$$

$$V = U\sqrt{2 \mp \frac{SP}{AC}}.$$

The Hodograph.

193. DEF. If from any point lines be drawn representing in direction and magnitude the velocity of a particle describing

an orbit under the action of a force tending to a fixed center, the locus of the extremities of these lines is the *Hodograph*.

This name is given to the curve by Sir William Hamilton, in his work on Quaternions.

194. Since the velocity in a central orbit is $\dfrac{h}{SY}$, if SQ be taken in SY equal to $\dfrac{h}{SY}$, the locus of Q will be the polar reciprocal of the orbit with respect to a circle the square of whose radius is h; and if it be turned about S through a right angle will be the hodograph of the orbit.

195. PROP. *If a conic section be described under the action of a force tending to a focus, the Hodograph is a circle.*

For, in the case of the ellipse or hyperbola, the velocity varies inversely as SY, and therefore directly as HZ, to which its direction is perpendicular, and the locus of Z is a circle. And, in the case of a parabola, AY being the tangent at the vertex, AU perpendicular to SY,

$$SY : AS :: AS : SU,$$

therefore SU varies as the velocity, and the locus of U is a circle.

Illustrations.

1. *The hodograph for an ellipse, described under the action of a force tending to the center, is a similar ellipse.*

For CD is parallel to the direction of motion and proportional to the velocity.

2. *The hodograph for a hyperbola, described under the action of a force repelling from the center, is a hyperbola similar to the conjugate hyperbola.*

3. *The hodograph for a hyperbola, described under the action of a constant force parallel to the axis, is a straight line parallel to the axis.*

For the square of the velocity $\varpropto SP \varpropto SY^2$, and the locus of Y is a horizontal line, therefore, since SY is perpendicular to the direction of motion, and proportional to the velocity, turning the locus of Y through a right angle, the hodograph is a vertical line.

Prop. XVII. Problem IX.

Given that the centripetal force is inversely proportional to the square of the distance from the center, and that the absolute force of the center is known; it is required to find the curve which will be described by a body which is projected from a given point with a given velocity in a given direction.

Let V be the velocity, PY the direction of projection from P, S the point to which the force tends, and let PU be measured on PS, produced if necessary, equal to twice the space through which the body must be drawn from rest by the action of the force at P continued constant, in order that the velocity V may be generated; therefore since the absolute force is given, PU is given. Draw PG perpendicular to PY, and PH so that HP, or HP produced, and SP make equal angles with PG. Draw UG perpendicular to PG and join SG.

Here three distinct cases arise:

I. If PU is equal to $2SP$, S is the center of a circle described about PGU, and $\angle SGP = \angle SPG = \angle HPG$; therefore SG, produced either way, will not meet PH.

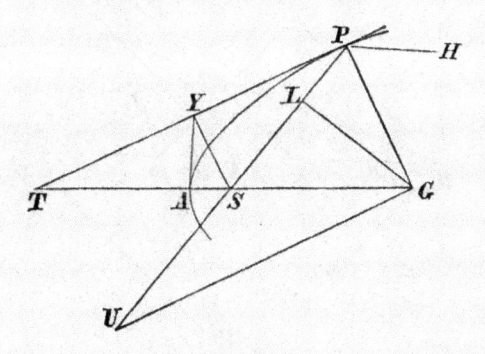

In this case, draw GL perpendicular to PS, and with S as focus, and $2PL$ as latus rectum describe a parabola, whose axis is in the direction SG.

224 NEWTON.

Then PU is half the chord of curvature at P through S.

II. If PU be less than $2SP$, $\angle SGP$ is greater than $\angle SPG$ or $\angle HPG$, therefore SG produced meets PH in H.

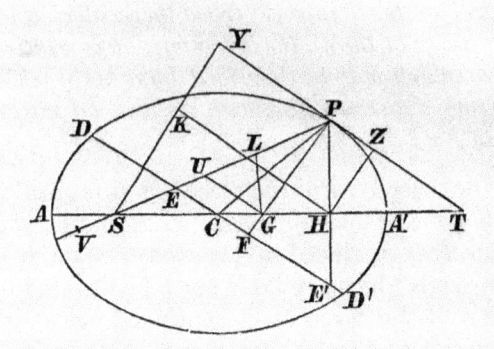

In this case, with S and H as foci, and $SP + PH$ as major axis, describe an ellipse, then PU is half the chord of curvature at P through S.

III. If PU be greater than $2SP$ $\angle SGP$ is less than $\angle SPG$, and angles SGP, HPG are together less than two right angles, therefore GS produced meets PH in H.

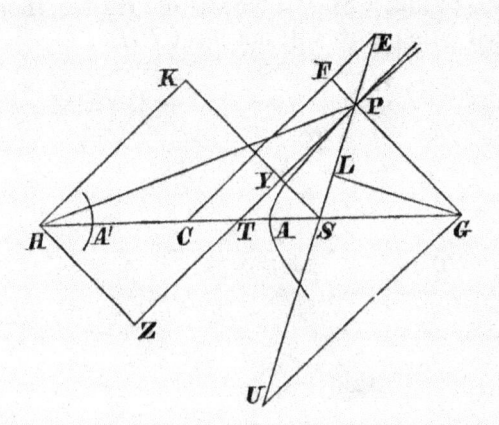

In this case, with S and H as foci, and $HP - SP$ as transverse axis, describe a hyperbola, then PU is half the chord of curvature at P through S.

PROP. XVII. PROBLEM IX. 225

In all these cases, a body may be supposed to revolve in the conic section described, under the action of the force tending to S, Art. 121, and the velocity at P is that due to falling through one-fourth of the chord of curvature through S, or half PU, under the action of the force at P supposed constant, and is therefore equal to V, the velocity of the projected body; also, since SP and HP, or HP produced, make equal angles with PG, PY is a tangent, therefore the direction of motion is that of the projected body.

Therefore, the circumstances of the two bodies are the same in all respects which can influence the motion at the point P, and they will therefore describe the same orbits; that is, the projected body will describe a conic section of that kind which corresponds to the velocity.

The orbit, therefore, will be an ellipse, parabola, or hyperbola, according as PU is less, equal to, or greater than $2SP$, that is, since $V^2 = F \cdot PU$, according as V^2 is less, equal to, or greater than $2F \cdot SP$ or twice the square of the velocity in a circle whose radius is SP.

Cor. 1. Hence if a body move in any conic section, and be disturbed from its orbit by any impulse, the orbit in which it will proceed to move may be discovered. For, by compounding the motion of the body with that motion which the impulse alone would generate, the motion and direction of motion will be found, with which the body will proceed from the point at which the disturbance took place.

Cor. 2. And if the body be disturbed by any continuous extraneous force, its course can be determined, approximately, by calculating the changes which the force produces at certain points, and estimating from analogy the changes which take place at the intermediate points.

SCHOLIUM.

If a body P move in the perimeter of any conic section, whose center is C, under the action of a centripetal force tending to any given point R, and the law of force be required,

NEWT. Q

draw CG parallel to RP and meeting in G the tangent PG to the conic section.

Then, by Prop. VII. Cor. 3, the force tending to R : the force tending to $C :: CG^3 : CP.RP^2$, but the force tending to C varies as CP, therefore the force tending to $R \propto \dfrac{CG^3}{RP^2}$.

Observations on the Proposition.

196. In the solution of Prob. IX. it is assumed that if, in any conic section, G be the intersection of the axis and normal at P, and GU, parallel to the tangent, meet SP in U, PU is half the chord of curvature at any point P of a conic section, drawn through the focus; this property may be proved as follows.

1. In the ellipse and hyperbola, let PG meet the conjugate diameter in F; then $CD.PF = AC.BC$, and $PG.PF = BC^2$;

$$\therefore \frac{PU}{PG} = \frac{PE}{PF} = \frac{CD}{BC};$$

$$\therefore \frac{PU}{CD} = \frac{PG}{BC} = \frac{BC}{PF} = \frac{CD}{AC};$$

$$\therefore PU = \frac{CD^2}{AC} = \text{half the chord of curvature at } P \text{ through } S.$$

Also, if GL be perpendicular to SP, PL is equal to the semi-latus rectum.

For, $\dfrac{PL}{PG} = \dfrac{PF}{PE}$; $\therefore PL = \dfrac{BC^2}{AC} =$ half the latus rectum.

2. In the parabola,

$$\frac{PU}{PG} = \frac{SP}{SY}, \text{ and } PG = 2SY;$$

$\therefore PU = 2SP = $ half the chord of curvature at P through S.

Also, $\dfrac{PL}{PG} = \dfrac{SY}{SP}$;

$$\therefore PL = \frac{2SY^2}{SP} = 2SA = \text{half the latus rectum.}$$

PROP. XVII. PROBLEM IX.

197. An elegant direct investigation of the path of a body projected at any inclination to the line drawn to a given center, to which a force tends which varies inversely as the square of the distance, is given in Goodwin's *Course of Mathematics*, being due to R. L. Ellis, Esq. of Trinity College; in that investigation the properties of the hodograph are introduced, and the path is shewn to be the locus of a point whose distance from a fixed straight line is in a constant ratio to its distance from the center of force.

For the outlines of the following demonstration, also depending on the properties of the hodograph, I am indebted to Professor Tait, of Edinburgh, to whom I proposed the problem to shew that the feet of the perpendiculars from the center of force on the direction of motion of the projected body always lie in a circle or straight line.

198. *General properties of the hodograph, connected with the motion of a body in a central orbit.*

Let ABC be a portion of a polygonal perimeter described under the action of impulses tending to S, as in Prop. I.

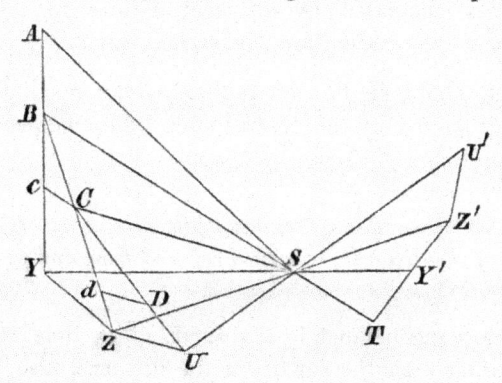

Draw SY, SZ, perpendicular to AB, BC; produce YS, ZS to Y', Z' making $YS \cdot SY' = ZS \cdot SZ'$.

Then SY', SZ' represent the velocities in AB, BC in magnitude, and are perpendicular to the directions of motion;

$$\therefore SY' : SZ' :: Bc : BC,$$
$$\text{and } \angle Y'SZ' = \angle YSZ = \angle YBZ;$$

therefore the triangles cBC, $Y'SZ'$ are similar, and $Y'Z'$ is perpendicular to BS produced.

Also, if $Y'Z'U'\ldots$ be the polygon corresponding to $ABCD\ldots$, making the same construction for each side successively,

$$Y'Z' : Cc :: Z'U' : Dd :: \ldots\ldots$$

therefore the perimeter $Y'Z'U'\ldots$ varies as the sum of the velocities generated by the impulses in the corresponding portion of the perimeter of the original polygon, and the line joining the extremities of the perimeter represents the resultant of those velocities in magnitude, and is perpendicular to its direction.

If we proceed to the limit, in which case $ABCD\ldots$ becomes the central orbit, and $Y''Z'U'\ldots$ the hodograph turned through a right angle, we obtain the following results:

1. If a body describe any curve under the action of a force tending to S, and YS, perpendicular to the tangent at any point P, be produced to Y', so that $SY'.SY$ is invariable, the tangent to the locus of Y' is perpendicular to PS.

2. Any finite arc of the locus of Y' varies as the sum of the velocities generated by the central force in the passage through the corresponding arc of the trajectory.

3. The chord of the arc represents the resultant of the velocities generated by the central force, and is perpendicular to its direction.

199. *To shew that if the central force vary inversely as the square of the distance, a body, projected from any point in any direction, will describe a conic section.*

The velocity generated in any small given time varies ultimately inversely as the square of the distance, also the angle described in the same time varies ultimately inversely as the square of the distance, therefore, the velocity generated varies as the angle described; hence, by Lemma IV., the velocity generated in a finite time varies as the whole angle described.

Now, by result (1) of the last proposition, the angle described is equal to the angle between the tangents at the extremities of the corresponding arc of the locus of Y', and, by (2), the velocity generated varies as the arc of that locus; therefore the locus is such that the angle between the tangents at the extremities of *any* arc varies as the arc, which is a property peculiar to the circle.

If the circular locus of Y' be constructed, and S be within or without the circle, let $Y'S$ meet the circle in y, then Sy varies inversely as SY' and therefore directly as SY, hence the locus of Y is similar to that of y, and therefore is a circle.

If S be upon the circle, let the extremity E' of the diameter through S correspond to E, so that $SE'.SE = SY'.SY$, therefore $SY : SE :: SE' : SY'$, hence $\angle SEY = \angle SY'E'$, therefore SY is perpendicular to SE, and the locus of Y is a straight line.

Hence, the feet of the perpendiculars from the center of force on a tangent to the body's path lie in a circle or straight line, which is a property of a conic section only, since straight lines drawn according to a fixed law can only have one envelope.

Therefore, the path will be an ellipse, parabola, or hyperbola, according as S lies within, upon, or without the perimeter of the locus of Y.

200. *Equations for determining the elements of the elliptic orbit, when* $V^2 < \dfrac{2\mu}{SP}$.

Let V be the velocity of projection, α the angle SPY between SP and PY, the direction of projection, fig. page 224, μ the absolute force, ψ the angle PTS between PY and the major axis, let a, b, e be the semiaxes and eccentricity of the orbit, L the latus rectum, and $SP = R$;

$$\therefore V^2 = \frac{\mu.HP}{SP.AC} = \frac{\mu}{R}\left(2 - \frac{R}{a}\right). \qquad (1)$$

Also, $\mu.\tfrac{1}{2}L = h^2 = V^2 R^2 \sin^2 \alpha$;

$$\therefore \frac{b^2}{a} = a(1-e^2) = \frac{V^2 R^2 \sin^2 \alpha}{\mu}. \qquad (2)$$

Draw SY, HZ perpendicular to the tangent, and HK to SY, then $SH \cos SHK = HK = YZ = (SP + PH) \cos SPY$;

$$\therefore 2ae \cos \psi = 2a \cos \alpha\,;$$
$$\therefore e \cos \psi = \cos \alpha. \qquad (3)$$

Also, $SH \sin SHK = SK = SY - HZ$;

$$\therefore 2ae \sin \psi = (SP - HP) \sin \alpha$$
$$= \{R - (2a - R)\} \sin \alpha;$$

$$\therefore e \sin \psi = \left(\frac{R}{a} - 1\right) \sin \alpha;$$

$$\therefore \tan \psi = \left(\frac{R}{a} - 1\right) \tan \alpha$$

$$= \left(1 - \frac{RV^2}{\mu}\right) \tan \alpha. \qquad (4)$$

The equations (1) and (2) determine a, b and e, and (4) determines ψ immediately from the given circumstances of projection, (3) is also a convenient equation for determining the position of the axes when e has been previously found.

Instead of (3) or (4) we might employ the equation

$$\frac{L}{2R} = 1 + e \cos ASP = \frac{V^2 R \sin^2 \alpha}{\mu}$$

to determine the angle ASP, which also gives the direction of the axes.

201. *Equations for determining the elements of the hyperbolic orbit, when* $V^2 > \dfrac{2\mu}{SP}$.

$$V^2 = \frac{\mu}{R}\left(2 + \frac{R}{a}\right), \qquad (1)$$

$$\mu \frac{b^2}{a} = \mu a (e^2 - 1) = V^2 R^2 \sin^2 \alpha, \qquad (2)$$

and $SH \cos SHK = HK = YZ = (HP - SP) \cos \alpha$; fig. p. 224,

$$\therefore e \cos \psi = \cos \alpha. \qquad (3)$$

Also, $SH \sin SHK = SK = SY + HZ$;

$$\therefore 2ae \sin \psi = \{R + (2a + R)\} \sin \alpha;$$

$$\therefore \tan \psi = \left(\frac{R}{a} + 1\right) \tan \alpha$$

$$= \left(\frac{RV^2}{\mu} - 1\right) \tan \alpha; \qquad (4)$$

PROP. XVII. PROBLEM IX. 231

or, as in the case of the ellipse,
$$\frac{L}{2R} = 1 + e \cos ASP = \frac{V^2 R \sin^2 \alpha}{\mu}.$$

202. *Equations for determining the elements of the parabolic orbit, when* $V^2 = \dfrac{2\mu}{SP}$.

$$SY^2 = AS \cdot SP, \text{ fig. page 223}; \quad \therefore AS = R \sin^2 \alpha, \qquad (1)$$
$$\text{and } PTS = \alpha, \qquad (2)$$

(1) and (2) are equations which completely determine the position and dimensions of the orbit.

203. *To find the elements of the orbit described under the action of a repulsive force varying inversely as the square of the distance from the point from which the force tends.*

Let H be the point from which the force tends, $HP = R$,
$$V^2 = \frac{\mu SP}{HP \cdot AC} = \frac{\mu}{HP} \frac{HP - 2AC}{AC} = \frac{\mu}{R}\left(\frac{R}{a} - 2\right). \qquad (1)$$

The other equations are similar to those in Art. 201.

Illustrations.

1. *A body is revolving in a circle under the action of a force which tends to the center and varies inversely as the square of the distance from it. When the body arrives at any point, if the force begin to tend to the point of bisection of the radius through the body, to determine the orbit described by the body.*

Let CA be the radius, S the new center of force. Then since the force is finite, the velocity at A is unaltered, and A is an apse of the new orbit.

Also (velocity)^2 in the circle $= \dfrac{\mu}{CA^2} \cdot CA = \dfrac{\mu}{CA} < \dfrac{2\mu}{SA}$; hence the body moves in an ellipse, and $\dfrac{\mu}{CA} = \dfrac{\mu}{SA}\left(2 - \dfrac{SA}{a}\right).$ (1)

$$\therefore a = \frac{2}{3} SA = \frac{1}{3} CA,$$
$$\text{and } \mu \frac{b^2}{a} = h^2 = \frac{\mu}{CA} \cdot SA^2; \qquad (2)$$

$$\therefore b^2 = \frac{1}{4} \cdot CA \cdot a = \frac{1}{12} CA^2.$$

Also $1 - \dfrac{b^2}{a^2} = 1 - \dfrac{3}{4} = \dfrac{1}{4}$; $\therefore e = \dfrac{1}{2}$.

Aliter.

Instead of equation (2) we might determine e from the consideration that A was one extremity of the major axis;

$$\therefore SA = a(1 \pm e);$$

$$\therefore 1 \pm e = \frac{3}{2}, \text{ and } e = \frac{1}{2},$$

since the upper sign must be taken, and therefore A is the greatest focal distance.

The orbit lies entirely within the circle, since the force at A is increased, and therefore the curvature is greater than that in the circle.

2. *If the new center of force be in the bisection of the radius which, if produced, passes through the body, to determine the orbit.*

The orbit must be elliptic, since $\dfrac{SA}{CA} = \dfrac{3}{2} < 2$;

hence $\dfrac{\mu}{CA} = \dfrac{\mu}{SA}\left(2 - \dfrac{SA}{a}\right)$,

$$\therefore \frac{SA}{a} = 2 - \frac{3}{2} = \frac{1}{2}; \therefore a = 3CA;$$

and $SA = a(1 \pm e)$; $\therefore e = \dfrac{1}{2}$,

and A, in the new orbit, is the nearest point to S.

In this case the force, and therefore the curvature, is diminished, which accounts for the orbit being exterior to the circle.

3. *A particle, acted on by a force which varies inversely as the square of the distance, is projected from a fixed point, with a velocity which is to the velocity in a circle at the same distance as $\sqrt{5} : 2$, making an angle whose sine is $\dfrac{2}{\sqrt{5}}$ with the line joining the point of projection to the fixed point; shew that the eccentricity*

PROP. XVII.   PROBLEM IX.   233

of the orbit is $\frac{1}{2}$, and that the major axis is perpendicular to the distance of projection.

$$V^2 = \frac{5}{4} \cdot \frac{\mu}{R} = \frac{\mu}{R}\left(2 - \frac{R}{a}\right), \qquad (1)$$

$$\mu a (1 - e^2) = V^2 \cdot R^2 \cdot \frac{4}{5} = \mu R; \qquad (2)$$

$\therefore a = \frac{4}{3} R$, and R is the semi-latus rectum, which proves the proposition.

Or, since
$$e \cos \psi = \cos \alpha; \qquad (3)$$

and by (1) and (2), $1 - e^2 = \frac{3}{4}$, and $e = \frac{1}{2}$;

$$\therefore \frac{1}{2} \cos \psi = \sqrt{1 - \frac{4}{5}} = \frac{1}{\sqrt{5}};$$

$$\therefore \cos \psi = \frac{2}{\sqrt{5}} = \sin \alpha;$$

hence, the angle between the direction of projection and major axis is $\frac{\pi}{2} - \alpha$, that is, the major axis is perpendicular to the distance of the point of projection.

4. *A body revolves in a circle under the action of a force tending to the center and varying inversely as the square of the distance. Find the orbit described, if the force suddenly tend to a point S in the circumference of the circle, at an angular distance* 60° *from the body.*

The square of the velocity at $A = \dfrac{\mu}{CA} = \dfrac{\mu}{SA}$, and, since the velocity is unaltered at A by the change,

$$\frac{\mu}{SA} = \frac{\mu}{SA}\left(2 - \frac{SA}{a}\right), \therefore a = SA,$$

that is, A is the extremity of the minor axis of the new orbit; hence, the major axis is parallel to the tangent at A, or perpendicular to CA, and the center is in the bisection of CA.

The curvature is less than that of the circle, because the normal force is diminished by the change.

5. *A body, revolving in an ellipse, under the action of a force tending to a focus S, has the direction of its motion altered at a given point of its path, the velocity remaining unaltered; to determine the corresponding change in the position of the major axis.*

Since the velocity, as well as the distance SP, in the new orbit is the same as in the old, the length of the major axis is the same; therefore PH is the same in the two orbits; that is, the other focus lies in a circle whose center is P, and SP, PH make equal angles with the new direction.

6. *To find at what point of an elliptic orbit a slight alteration may be made in the direction of motion, the velocity remaining unaltered, so that the direction of the major axis may be the same as before.*

The direction of the major axis being unaltered, SH must be a tangent to the locus of H, hence P must be at one of the extremities of that latus rectum which does not contain the center of force.

7. *Prove that if, when a body is at the extremity of the latus rectum which does not contain the center of force, the direction of motion is deflected through a small angle, without altering the velocity, the alteration of the eccentricity is to the circular measure of the angle of deflection as* $BC^2 : AC^2$.

For, let P be the position of the body, HH' the small arc of the circle described by H, which nearly coincides with the direction of the major axis, HPH' is double the angle of deflection, and $\dfrac{H'S}{2AC} - \dfrac{HS}{2AC}$, or $\dfrac{HH'}{2AC}$, is the change of eccentricity;

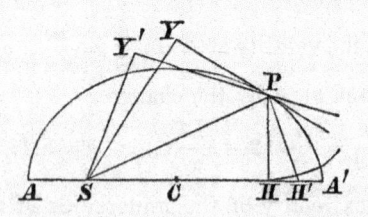

PROP. XVII. PROBLEM IX. 235

∴ change of eccentricity : deflection of direction

$$:: \frac{HH'}{2AC} : \frac{HH'}{2HP} :: HP : AC :: BC^2 : AC^2.$$

8. *If a body, moving in an ellipse about the focus, be acted on by an impulse towards the focus, when it arrives at the extremity of the latus rectum, the axis major will be unaltered in direction.*

For, the force being central, h is unaltered; therefore, if SL be the semi-latus rectum, $\mu \cdot SL$ is unaltered, or SL is the semi-latus rectum of the new orbit, and the axis major is perpendicular to SL.

9. *The velocity at any point of an ellipse about a force in the focus is compounded of two uniform velocities, $\frac{\mu}{h}$ perpendicular to the radius vector, and $\frac{\mu e}{h}$ perpendicular to the major axis.*

Let S be the center of force, HZ perpendicular on the tangent at P, join CZ. Then HZ, ZC parallel to PS, and CH are

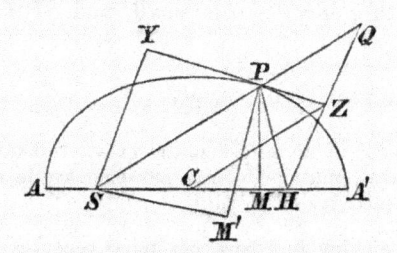

perpendicular to the three directions; therefore the velocity represented by HZ in magnitude is the resultant of the two represented by CZ and HC; but the velocity perpendicular to $HZ = \frac{h}{SY} = \frac{h}{b^2} \cdot HZ$; therefore the velocities, perpendicular to HC and CZ, are $\frac{h}{b^2} ae$, and $\frac{h}{b^2} a = \frac{\mu e}{h}$ and $\frac{\mu}{h}$, since $\mu \frac{b^2}{a} = h^2$.

10. *A particle moving in an ellipse under the action of a force tending to the focus has a very small velocity $\frac{n\mu}{h}$ impressed*

upon it in the direction of the focus; shew that the corresponding changes of the eccentricity and angular distance of the apse are given by the equations

$$e' - e = n \sin \theta,$$
$$e (\theta' - \theta) = n \cos \theta.$$

For, since the impressed velocity is towards S, $\frac{\mu}{h}$ in the new orbit is still the velocity perpendicular to the radius vector: and the velocity $\frac{e'\mu}{h}$, perpendicular to the new major axis, is compounded of the two velocities $\frac{e\mu}{h}$ in direction PM, and $\frac{n\mu}{h}$ in PS.

Let PM' be the perpendicular on the new major axis; then $\angle M'SM$ and $\angle M'PM$, being angles in the same arc of a circle about SPM, are equal, and the velocity in PM' and its components in PM and PS being as e', e and n,

$$e' \sin M'PM = n \sin SPM,$$
$$e' \cos M'PM = e + n \cos SPM;$$

therefore, since $M'PM = \theta' - \theta$ is small, and $SPM = 90° - \theta$, the proposition is proved.

XVIII.

1. The velocity in an ellipse at the greatest distance is half that with which a body would move in a parabola at the same distance; required the eccentricity of the ellipse.

2. A body, moving in a parabola about a center of force in the focus, meets at the vertex with an obstacle which diminishes the square of the velocity by one fourth, without altering the direction of the motion; shew that the body will afterwards move in an ellipse whose axis major is equal to the latus rectum of the parabola.

3. If, from each point of a hyperbola described under the action of a force in the farther focus, a particle moves from rest, under the action of the force at that point continued constant, until it acquires the velocity of the body moving in the hyperbola, and then stops; find the locus of the particles. If r, r' be the radii vectores for the hyperbola and locus, $2ar' = r^2$.

4. A body revolves in an ellipse about a center of force in the focus S. Shew that there is always some determinate point at

which the absolute force may be supposed to change suddenly from μ to $n\mu$, so that the subsequent path of the body may be a parabola about S in the focus, provided n is not situated beyond the limits $\frac{1}{2}(1+e)$ and $\frac{1}{2}(1-e)$. Prove also that the latus rectum of the ellipse : that of the parabola :: n : 1.

5. A particle, describing an ellipse about a force in the focus, comes to the point nearest to the center of force; find in what ratio the absolute force must then be diminished in order that the particle may proceed to describe a hyperbola, whose eccentricity is the reciprocal of that of the ellipse.

6. The ratio of the axes of the Earth's and Venus's orbits is 18 : 13; find the periodic time of Venus.

7. A body is projected, with a velocity of 100 feet per minute, from a point whose distance from a center of force, which varies inversely as the square of the distance, is 32 feet, the velocity in a circle at that distance being 80 feet per minute; find the periodic time.

8. If a body be projected with a given velocity about a center of force which varies inversely as the square of the distance, shew that the minor axis of the orbit described will vary as the perpendicular from the center of force upon the direction of projection; and determine the locus of the center of the orbit described.

9. The velocity in a parabola round the focus is suddenly diminished in the ratio of $\sqrt{2}$: 1; shew that the semi-major axis of the new orbit will be SP, and that the semi-minor axis will be a mean proportional between SP and AS.

10. A particle describes an ellipse under the action of a force tending to a focus; shew that the velocity at any point may be resolved into two velocities respectively perpendicular to the two focal distances, each of which varies as the distance from the focus to which the force is not tending.

11. A comet, moving in a parabola, is describing sectorial areas about the Sun at the same rate as a planet moving in a circle, of which the radius is half the latus rectum of the parabola; shew that the planet will move through about 76° 22' of longitude, while the comet passes from one extremity of the latus rectum to the other.

12. Two bodies describe the same ellipse, under the action of forces tending to the center and a focus respectively, the forces being such that, at the point where they are equal, the velocities of the bodies are also equal; shew that the periodic times of the two bodies are as $1 \pm e$: 1, e being the eccentricity of the ellipse.

13. Supposing the velocity of a body in a given elliptic orbit to be the same at a certain point, whether it describe the orbit in a time t about one focus, or in a time t' about the other, prove that,

$2a$ being the major axis, the focal distances of the point are equal to $\dfrac{2at'}{t+t'}$ and $\dfrac{2at}{t+t'}$.

14. The perihelion distance of a comet moving in a parabolic orbit is half the radius of the Earth's orbit, supposed circular. The planes of the orbits coinciding, find the time in days from perihelion to the point of intersection of the orbits.

15. Of all comets moving in the ecliptic in parabolic orbits, that which has the latus rectum of its orbit equal to the diameter of the Earth's orbit will remain within the latter for the longest period, the Earth's orbit being considered circular.

16. Two ellipses are described by two particles about the same center of force in the focus; the eccentricities are $\frac{1}{2}$ and $\frac{1}{2}\sqrt{3}$ respectively, and the major axes are coincident in direction and equal in length. Compare the times which each body spends within the orbit of the other.

17. A body is moving in a given parabola under the action of a force in the focus; and, when it comes to a distance from the focus equal to the latus rectum, the force suddenly becomes repulsive; determine the nature, position, and dimensions of the new orbit.

18. A particle is describing an ellipse under the action of a force tending to the focus; if, on arriving at the extremity of the minor axis, the force has its law changed, so that it varies as the distance, the magnitude at that point remaining unchanged, prove that the periodic time will be unaltered, and that the sum of the new axes will be to their difference as the sum of the old axes to the distance between the foci.

19. An ellipse and its auxiliary circle are described by two bodies in the same periodic time under the action of forces which vary inversely as the square of the distance. Prove that, if they are simultaneously at either extremity of the major axis, the difference of the times of arriving at equal distances from the minor axis varies as the distance of either from the major axis.

20. If the force, tending to the focus of an ellipse, become repulsive when a particle describing the ellipse is at an angular distance θ from the nearer apse, shew that the eccentricity of the hyperbola described after the change is $(e^2 + 4e \cos \theta + 4)^{\frac{1}{2}}$, e being the eccentricity of the ellipse.

21. A body revolves in a parabola under the action of a force tending to the focus, and when it arrives at a point whose distance from the axis is equal to the latus rectum, the force is suddenly transferred to the opposite extremity of the focal chord passing through the body. Shew that the new orbit will be a hyperbola

PROP. XVII. PROBLEM IX. 239

whose axes are as 2 : 1, and that the conjugate axis and the direction of motion at the point make equal angles with the focal chord.

22. A body moves in an ellipse about a focus, and is at the extremity of the minor axis when its velocity is doubled. Find the new orbit, and shew that the body will come to an apse after describing a right angle, if the ratio of the axes of the given ellipse be 2 : 1.

23. A body revolves in an ellipse about a center of force in its center. When the body comes to the extremity of the axis major, the law of the force is supposed to change suddenly to that of the inverse square of the distance, the magnitude at that point being unaltered; find the elements of the new orbit. Shew that the eccentricity of the new orbit is the square of that of the old.

24. If PO is perpendicular on the directrix from any point of an elliptic orbit described by a particle about the focus S, and when the particle is at P, the force suddenly tends to O instead of S, prove that the new orbit may be a parabola if $e > \frac{1}{3}$, and that, in this case, SP passes through the intersection of the two circles, one described on SH as diameter, and the other with center S and radius SA, the shortest focal distance.

25. A body, describing an ellipse about a center of force in S, has a velocity equal to its own communicated in the direction PH, which causes it to describe a circle; determine the eccentricity of the original orbit, and shew that the diameter of the circle is four times the latus rectum of the ellipse.

26. A body is revolving in an ellipse under the action of a force tending to the focus S, and, when it arrives at the point P, the center of force is suddenly transposed to the point S' in PS produced so that PS' is equal to the major axis of the ellipse, and the force becomes repulsive; shew that, if HP be produced to H', and $PH' = PH$, the length of the transverse axis of the hyperbola described is SP, and H' is the other focus.

27. Prove that the rate, at which areas are described about the center of a hyperbolic orbit described by a particle under the action of a force tending to a focus, will be inversely proportional to the distance of the particle from the center of force.

28. If the velocity of a particle at P, moving in an ellipse under the action of a force tending to the focus S, be slightly increased in the ratio $1 : 1 + n$, shew that the major axis will be increased slightly by $m \cdot HP$, where $m : 2n :: 2AC : SP$, and that it will revolve through a small angle whose circular measure is $m \cdot \dfrac{PM}{SH}$, PM being the ordinate at P.

29. A body revolves in an ellipse about the focus from nearer to farther apse, and the angle which its direction makes with the

focal distance is constantly being increased without altering the velocity; shew that the motion of the apse line will change from progression to regression, when the true anomaly of the instantaneous orbit is $\frac{\pi}{2} + 2\tan^{-1} e$, e being the eccentricity.

30. A particle is describing an ellipse about a center of force in the focus, and the absolute force is suddenly diminished one half; shew that the chance of the particle's new orbit being a hyperbola is $\pi - 2e : 2\pi$, all instants of time being supposed equally probable for the change.

31. Two particles are revolving in the same direction in an ellipse under the action of a force tending to the focus; prove that the direction of the motion of one as it appears to the other is parallel to the line bisecting the angle between their distances from the focus.

32. A force tends to the center of a given circle, and varies inversely as the square of the distance; prove that all elliptic orbits which can be inscribed in any triangle inscribed in the circle will be described by a particle, under the action of the force, in the same periodic time.

APPENDIX I.

SECTION VII.

ON RECTILINEAR MOTION.

PROP. XXXII. and PROP. XXXVI.

To find the time of motion and the velocity acquired, when a body falls through a given space from rest, under the action of a force which varies inversely as the square of the distance from a fixed point.

Let S be the center of force, A the point from which the body begins to fall.

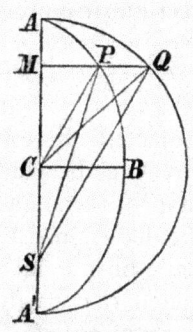

Let APA' be a semiellipse, whose focus is S, and axis major ASA', AQA' the circle upon AA' as diameter, MPQ a common ordinate; let C be the common center, and join CP, CQ, SP, SQ.

If a body revolve in the ellipse under the action of the force tending to S, the measure of whose accelerating effect at a distance SP is $\dfrac{\mu}{SP^2}$;

time in AP : time in APA' :: area ASQ : semicircle AQA'

:: sector $ACQ + \triangle SCQ$: semicircle AQA';

NEWT.   R

therefore, time in $AP = \dfrac{\pi AC^{\frac{3}{2}}}{\mu^{\frac{1}{2}}} \cdot \dfrac{AC \cdot \text{arc } AQ + SC \cdot QM}{\pi AC^2}$.

This is true, whatever be the magnitude of the minor axis BC, and therefore when it is indefinitely diminished, in which case the diameter of curvature at $A = \dfrac{2BC^2}{AC} = 0$, and therefore the body has no velocity at A; that is, the elliptic motion ultimately degenerates to a rectilinear motion in which the body starts from rest at A.

Also, since $AS \cdot SA' = BC^2$,

SA' ultimately $= 0$; $\therefore SC = AC = \tfrac{1}{2}SA$;

therefore, time in $AM = \left(\dfrac{SA}{2\mu}\right)^{\frac{1}{2}} \cdot (\text{arc } AQ + QM)$.

Again, the velocity in the ellipse at P is $\left\{\dfrac{\mu \cdot (2AC - SP)}{AC \cdot SP}\right\}^{\frac{1}{2}}$, and, when the minor axis is indefinitely diminished, the velocity at M, in the rectilinear motion of the body,

$$= \left\{\dfrac{2\mu (AS - SM)}{AS \cdot SM}\right\}^{\frac{1}{2}} = \left(\dfrac{2\mu \cdot AM}{AS \cdot SM}\right)^{\frac{1}{2}}.$$

COR. If a body be projected directly towards or from a center, to which a force tends which varies inversely as the square of the distance, the time and velocity acquired in a given space may be determined by means of an ellipse, parabola, or hyperbola, whose latus rectum is indefinitely diminished, so constructed that at the point of projection the velocity is properly represented.

Notes.

204. It must not be supposed that the motion will be represented throughout by the ultimate motion in an ellipse, whose axis minor is indefinitely diminished, in which case the body would return to A; for, since in this case the ellipse passes through S, we are precluded from applying the results of the second and third sections in determining the motion of the body after arriving at S; but we may correctly apply these results to determine the motion before arriving at S.

APPENDIX I. 243

In order to determine the motion after arriving at S, we must observe that at S the force is zero, since its direction is indeterminate, although, when the body is at any point very near to S, there will be a very great force tending towards S; on approaching S, therefore, the velocity will continually increase, and the body will pass through S with very great velocity; but the motion will be retarded, according to the same law, as rapidly as it was generated, and the body will proceed to a distance equal to SA on the opposite side of S.

Prop. XXXVIII.

To find the time of motion and the velocity acquired when a body falls through a given space from rest, under the action of a force which varies as the distance from a fixed point.

Let S be the center of force, A the place from which the body begins to move; make $SA' = SA$, and on ASA' as

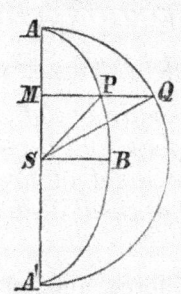

major axis describe a semiellipse APA', and a semicircle AQA', and let MPQ be a common ordinate.

Suppose a body to revolve in the ellipse, under the action of the force tending to S, the measure of whose accelerating effect at P is $\mu \cdot SP$, then, time in $AP \propto$ area ASP $\propto$ sector $ASQ \propto$ angle ASQ;

therefore time in AP : time in ABA' :: arc AQ : πAS,

and time in $AP = \dfrac{\pi}{\sqrt{\mu}} \cdot \dfrac{\text{arc } AQ}{\pi AS} = \dfrac{1}{\sqrt{\mu}} \times \dfrac{\text{arc } AQ}{AS}$;

and the same is true when the minor axis is indefinitely diminished, in which case the velocity at A vanishes, since the diameter of curvature vanishes.

R 2

Therefore the elliptic motion is reduced to the rectilinear motion of a body originally at rest at A, and the time in AM is thus shewn to be

$$\frac{1}{\sqrt{\mu}} \times \frac{\text{arc } AQ}{AS}.$$

Again, the velocity in the ellipse at P

$= \sqrt{\mu} \cdot SD$, where SD is conjugate to SP

$= \sqrt{\mu}(AS^2 + BS^2 - SP^2)^{\frac{1}{2}};$

therefore the velocity at M in the rectilinear motion

$$= \sqrt{\mu}(AS^2 - SM^2)^{\frac{1}{2}} = \sqrt{\mu} \cdot MQ.$$

Cor. Time from A to $S = \dfrac{\pi}{2\sqrt{\mu}}$,

or the time of reaching S is the same whatever be the initial distance.

SECTION VIII.

Prop. XL. Theorem XIII.

If the velocities of two bodies, one of which is falling directly towards a center of force and the other describing a curve about that center, be equal at any equal distances they will always be equal at equal distances, if the force depend only on the distance.

Let S be the center of force, and let one of the bodies be moving in the straight line APS, the other in the curve AQq. Suppose the velocities at P, Q to be equal, and

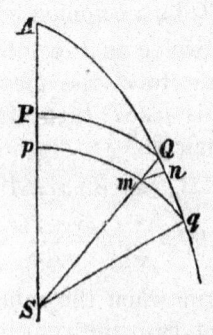

APPENDIX I. 245

let Qq be an arc of the curve described in a short time. With center S and radii SQ, Sq describe circular arcs QP, qP, let SQ meet pq in m, and draw mn perpendicular to Qq.

Since the centripetal forces at equal distances are equal, they will be so at P and Q, and Pp, Qm may represent them; Pp is wholly effective in accelerating P, Qn is the only effective part of Qm on Q, the component nm being employed in retaining the body in the curve.

Also since the velocities are equal at P and Q, the times of describing Pp, Qq are ultimately proportional to Pp, Qq, when the time is indefinitely diminished.

Hence, force at P in PS : force at Q in Qq :: Pp : Qn,

and time in Pp : time in Qq :: Pp : Qq,

$\therefore$ vel^y acquired at p : vel^y acquired at q :: Pp^2 : $Qn \cdot Qq$,

but $Qn \cdot Qq = Qm^2 = Pp^2$;

therefore the velocities added in Pp and Qq are equal, and the actual velocities at p and q are equal.

By proceeding in the same way through any number of small times, the proposition is proved.

XIX.

1. If a particle slide along a chord of a circle, under the action of a force tending to any fixed point, and varying as the distance, the time will be the same for all chords, provided they terminate at either extremity of the diameter which passes through the center of force.

2. If the velocity of the earth in its orbit were suddenly destroyed, find the time in which it would reach the sun.

3. A particle moves from any point in the directrix of a conic section, in a straight line towards a center of force, which varies inversely as the square of the distance, in the corresponding focus. Prove that when it arrives at the conic section, the velocity

$$= \left(\frac{4\mu}{L}\right)^{\frac{1}{2}},$$

L being the latus rectum.

4. A perfectly elastic ball falls from rest towards a center of force varying inversely as the square of the distance, and when it has

fallen half the distance it is reflected by a plane, so as to move in a direction making an angle a with its former direction; shew that the eccentricity of the ellipse subsequently described is $\cos a$.

5. A perfectly elastic ball falls from a distance a towards a center of force varying as the distance. When it has described a space $\frac{1}{2}a$ it impinges at an angle of $45°$ on a plane and is reflected. Shew that the semiaxes of the orbit subsequently described will be $a\cos 60°$ and $a\sin 60°$. Suppose that the ball again impinges on the opposite side of the same fixed reflecting plane, shew that it will be reflected to the center, and that the time of arriving at the center will be five times the time of falling directly to it.

6. Suppose e to be the elasticity of the ball in the last problem, prove that, if the angle of incidence $= \tan^{-1}\sqrt{e}$, the subsequent orbit will have its axis major or minor in the direction in which the ball was originally falling, according as the distance from the center C to the point of impact is greater or less than

$$a\sqrt{\frac{e}{1+e}}.$$

7. A particle of mass m is attached by an elastic string to the center of a repulsive force whose measure of acceleration is $\mu \times$ distance. If the natural length of the string be a, and the modulus of elasticity $\lambda \cdot ma$, shew that the greatest distance to which the particle will proceed, supposing it to start where the string is of its natural length, will be $\dfrac{\lambda+\mu}{\lambda-\mu}a$, and that the time of returning to its starting point will be $\dfrac{2\pi}{\sqrt{\lambda-\mu}}$.

APPENDIX II.

ON THE GEOMETRICAL PROPERTIES OF CERTAIN CURVES.

Cycloid.

205. DEF. If, in one plane, a circle be conceived to roll along a straight line, any point on its circumference will describe a curve called a Cycloid.

Let C, D be the points where the tracing point P meets the straight line, on which it rolls. A the point where it is furthest from CD, AB the corresponding diameter of the circle.

The revolving circle is called the *generating circle*, AB is called the *axis*, A the *vertex*, CD the *base*.

206. If RPS be the generating circle in any position, then, since the points of the base and circle come successively in contact, $CS = $ arc PS, CB and BD are each half of the circumference of the circle, and $BS = $ arc RP.

207. *To draw a tangent to a cycloid.*

Let the generating circle be in the position RPS, then considering a circle as the limit of a regular polygon of a large number of sides, it will roll by turning about the point of contact, which is at rest for an instant, being an angular point of the polygon; therefore P moves perpendicular to SP, for an instant, or in the direction PR of the supplemental chord, which is therefore the tangent at P.

If AQB be the circle on AB as diameter, PQM an ordinate perpendicular to AB the tangent at P is parallel to the chord QA.

208. *To find the length of the arc of a cycloid.*

Let RPS be the position of the generating circle corresponding to the point P in the cycloid, let P' be the position of P, when the circle has turned through a small angle POp, and therefore O moved through a space Pp, so that $P'p$ is parallel to the base, and equal to Pp; hence the triangle PpP' is

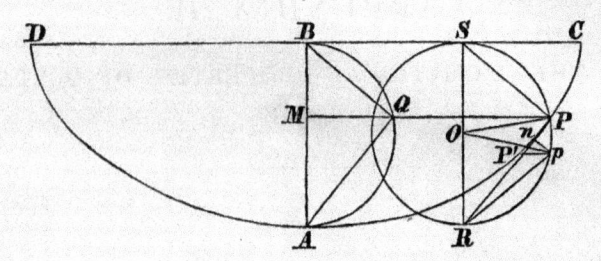

isosceles, and if pn be drawn perpendicular to RP, $PP' = 2Pn$ $= 2(RP - Rp)$ ultimately; therefore the cycloidal arc from the vertex decreases twice as fast as the supplemental chord, and they vanish together,

$$\therefore \text{ arc } AP = 2RP = 2AQ.$$

209. *To find the relation between the arc and abscissa.*

Let AM be the abscissa of the point P,
$$AM : AQ :: AQ : AB;$$
$$\therefore AP^2 = 4AQ^2 = 4AB \cdot AM.$$

210. *To find the area of the cycloid.*

Let P' be any point in the cycloid $CP'C'$ (see the figure in the next page), $P'S$ the chord of the generating circle which touches the cycloid, and let Q' be a point in the cycloid near P', then the arc $P'Q'$ ultimately coincides with $P'S$. Let $Q'N'$, $Q'N$ be the complements of the parallelogram whose diagonal is $P'S$, and sides parallel and perpendicular to the base, these are equal ultimately; therefore, by Lemma IV., the cycloidal area $CNP' = $ circular segment $SP'N'$.

211. COR. The exterior portion CBC' is equal to the area of the semicircle, and the whole parallelogram $BCB'C'$ is the rectangle under the diameter and semi-circumference of the generating circle, and is equal to four times the area of the semicircle; therefore the cycloidal area $CC'B'$ is three times the area of the semicircle.

APPENDIX II.

212. *To shew that the evolute of a given cycloid is an equal cycloid, and that the radius of curvature of a cycloid is twice the normal.*

Let APC be half the given cycloid, AB the axis, A the vertex, and BC the base. Produce AB to C', making BC' equal to AB, and complete the rectangle $BCB'C'$, and let the semicycloid $C'P'C$ be generated by a circle whose diameter is equal to that of the generating circle of the given cycloid, rolling on $C'B'$; C is the vertex, and CB' the axis of this cycloid.

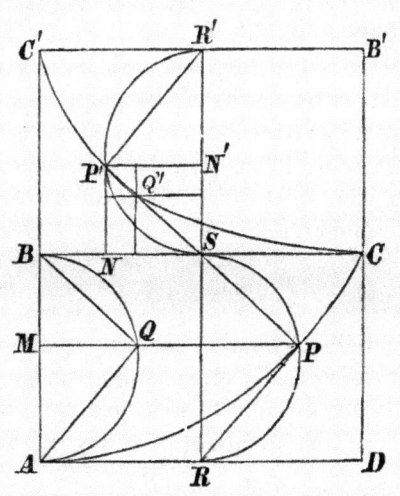

Let SPR, $SP'R'$ be two positions of the respective generating circles, having their diameters RS, SR' in the same straight line, P, P' the corresponding points of the cycloids.

Join SP, PR and SP', $P'R'$.

By the mode of generation, arc SP = SC, and arc SPR = BC;

$$\therefore \text{arc } PR = BS = C'R' = \text{arc } P'R';$$

$$\therefore \angle PSR = \angle P'SR'; \text{ and } PSP' \text{ is a straight line.}$$

Also, arc $P'S$ = arc PS; $\therefore$ chd. $P'S$ = chd. PS;

$$\therefore P'SP = 2P'S = P'C \text{ the cycloidal arc;}$$

also $P'SP$ touches the cycloid $C'P'C$ at P';

therefore, a string fixed to the cycloid at C', and wrapped over the arc of the semicycloid, will when unwrapped have its extremity in the arc of the given cycloid; hence, the evolute of a semicycloid is an equal semicycloid, and the radius of curvature at P is $2PS$ or twice the normal. If another equal semicycloid be described by the circle rolling on $B'C'$ produced, the extremity of the string wrapped on this curve will trace out the remainder of the given cycloid.

Thus a pendulum may be made to oscillate in a given cycloid.

213. *To find the time of oscillation of a heavy particle moving in a smooth cycloidal arc whose axis is vertical.*

A direct method of solving this problem is given in page 87, but it can be solved by means of the proposition given in Appendix I. Prop. XXXVIII.

The particle being in any position P is acted on by a force the measure of the accelerating effect of whose component in direction of the motion is

$$g \cdot \frac{RP}{RS} = \frac{g}{2RS} \cdot AP, \text{ and } \frac{g}{2RS}, \text{ or } \frac{g}{2AB} \text{ is constant.}$$

The tangential acceleration at every point is the same as if the particle moved in a straight line under the action of a force varying as the distance tending to a point in the line.

Therefore, the time of falling from any point to A is

$$\frac{\pi}{2}\sqrt{\frac{2AB}{g}},$$

and the time of an oscillation from rest to rest

$$= \pi\sqrt{\frac{2AB}{g}},$$

being the same for all arcs of vibration.

The length of the string which by the contrivance of the last article makes a particle oscillate in this cycloid is $2AB = l$ suppose; therefore the time of the oscillation of a pendulum of length $l = \pi\sqrt{\dfrac{l}{g}}$.

214. *To find the time of a very small oscillation of a simple pendulum suspended from a point.*

A simple pendulum is an imaginary pendulum consisting of a heavy particle called the *bob*, suspended from a point by means of a rod or string without weight.

In this case the pendulum describes the small arc of a circle which may be considered the same as a cycloidal arc the axis of which is half the distance of the bob from the point of suspension.

The time of oscillation from rest to rest is $\pi \sqrt{\dfrac{l}{g}}$.

215. *To count the number of oscillations made by a given pendulum in any long time.*

In consequence of the liability to error in counting a very great number of oscillations, since in the case of a seconds pendulum for each hour there would be 3600 oscillations, it becomes necessary to adopt some contrivance for diminishing the labour. For this purpose the pendulum is made to oscillate nearly in the same time as that of a clock; it is then placed in front of that of the clock, so that near the lowest positions the rod of the pendulum and a cross marked on the pendulum of the clock may be in the field of view of a fixed telescope.

Suppose that after n oscillations of the given pendulum they are again in coincidence close to the same position; if there be m such coincidences in the whole time of observation, the number of oscillations in that time is mn, and the only labour has been to count the n oscillations, and to estimate the number of the coincidences before the last one observed.

216. *To measure the accelerating effect of gravity by means of a pendulum.*

Let g be the measure of this effect or the velocity generated by the force of gravity in a second.

Let l be the length of a simple pendulum which makes n oscillations in m hours, then $\dfrac{3600m}{n}$ = number of seconds in one oscillation $= \pi \sqrt{\dfrac{l}{g}}$; $\therefore g = \dfrac{\pi^2 l n^2}{(3600)^2 m^2}$, in whatever unit of length l is estimated.

This would be a very exact method of determining g, if we could form a simple pendulum; but it is impossible to do this, and it is only by calculations of a nature too difficult to be explained here that it can be shewn how to deduce the length of the simple pendulum, which would oscillate in the same time as a pendulum of a more complicated structure.

217. The seconds pendulum at any place is the simple pendulum which at the mean level of the sea at that place would oscillate in one second.

If L be the length of the seconds pendulum, l the length of a pendulum making n oscillations in m hours;

$$\frac{3600m}{n} \cdot \pi \sqrt{\frac{L}{g}} = \pi \sqrt{\frac{l}{g}};$$

$$\therefore L = \frac{n^2 l}{(60)^4 m^2}.$$

218. *To determine the height of a mountain by means of a seconds pendulum.*

Let x be the height of the mountain above the mean level of the sea, L the length of the seconds pendulum for that place, a the Earth's radius, all expressed in feet; n the number of oscillations lost by the pendulum in 24 hours.

If g be the accelerating effect of gravity at the mean level of the sea, then $\frac{ga^2}{(a+x)^2}$ will be that at the top of the mountain, supposing the earth composed of spherical strata; therefore the time of oscillation at the top will be $\pi \sqrt{\frac{L}{g} \frac{(a+x)^2}{a^2}} = \frac{a+x}{a}$, in seconds, since $\pi \sqrt{\frac{L}{g}} = 1$;

$$\therefore (24 \times 60 \times 60 - n) \frac{a+x}{a} = 24 \times 60 \times 60,$$

hence $1 + \frac{x}{a} = \frac{24 \times 60 \times 60}{24 \times 60 \times 60 - n}$,

and $\frac{x}{a} = \frac{n}{24 \times 60 \times 60} + \frac{n^2}{(24 \times 60 \times 60)^2}$ nearly;

therefore, if $a = 4000 \times 1760 \times 3$,

$$x = \frac{4000 \times 1760 \times 3}{24 \times 60 \times 60} n + \ldots\ldots$$

$$= 245n + \frac{245 n^2}{24 \times 60 \times 60} \text{ nearly,}$$

and the height of the mountain will be $245n + \cdot 0027 \cdot n^2$.

If $n = 10$, the height $= 2450 \cdot 27$ feet.

APPENDIX II. 253

219. *To find the number of seconds lost in a day, in consequence of a slight error in the length of the seconds pendulum; and conversely.*

Let N be the number of seconds in a day, L the length of the seconds pendulum; $L+\lambda$ that of the incorrect pendulum; $N-n$ the number of oscillations in a day.

$$\therefore (N-n)\,\pi\sqrt{\frac{L+\lambda}{g}} = N\,.\,\pi\sqrt{\frac{L}{g}};$$

$$\therefore 1 + \frac{\lambda}{L} = \frac{N^2}{(N-n)^2};$$

$$\therefore \frac{\lambda}{L} = \frac{2nN - n^2}{(N-n)^2},$$

and $n = \dfrac{N\lambda}{2L}$ nearly;

whence n can be found from λ, or λ from n.

Epicycloid and Hypocycloid.

220. DEF. The curve traced out by a point on the circumference of a circle, which rolls upon that of a fixed circle, is called an *Epicycloid* if the rolling circle be on the exterior of the fixed circle, a *Hypocycloid*, if it be on the interior of the fixed circle.

221. *To find the radius of curvature of an epicycloid.*

Let AB, BC be consecutive sides of a regular polygon

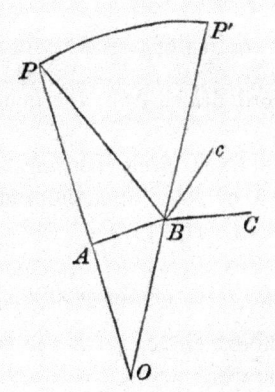

of m sides, AB, Bc of another regular polygon of n sides equal to those of the former, and which rolls on the outside of it, AB being the coincident sides in any position.

Let P be any angular point of the latter which generates a figure composed of a series of circular arcs such as PP', P' being the position of P when Bc, BC coincide.

Produce PA, $P'B$ to meet in O.

Then, $\angle APB = \dfrac{\pi}{n}$, and $\angle PBP' = \angle cBC = \dfrac{2\pi}{m} + \dfrac{2\pi}{n}$;

$$\therefore \angle POB = 2\pi \left(\frac{1}{m} + \frac{1}{n}\right) - \frac{\pi}{n};$$

$$\therefore \frac{PO}{PB} = \frac{\sin 2\pi \left(\dfrac{1}{m} + \dfrac{1}{n}\right)}{\sin \pi \left(\dfrac{2}{m} + \dfrac{1}{n}\right)}.$$

If we proceed to the limit, the polygons become circles, and the curve traced out by P is the epicycloid; and PO is ultimately the radius of curvature.

And if a, b be the radii of the fixed and rolling circles,

$$m : n :: a : b,$$

and ultimately $PO = PA \cdot \dfrac{2\pi \left(\dfrac{1}{m} + \dfrac{1}{n}\right)}{\pi \left(\dfrac{2}{m} + \dfrac{1}{n}\right)}$;

therefore the radius of curvature is $2PA \cdot \dfrac{a+b}{a+2b}$,

where PA is the chord drawn from the generating point to the point of contact.

If $a = \infty$, or the fixed circle becomes a straight line, the epicycloid becomes a cycloid, and the radius of curvature is twice the normal as in Art. 212.

222. *To find the form of the evolute of the epicycloid.*

Let FA be the fixed circle, APE the rolling circle in any position, P the generating point, CAE a line drawn from the center of the fixed circle, meeting the rolling circle in A, E. Produce PA to O, so that

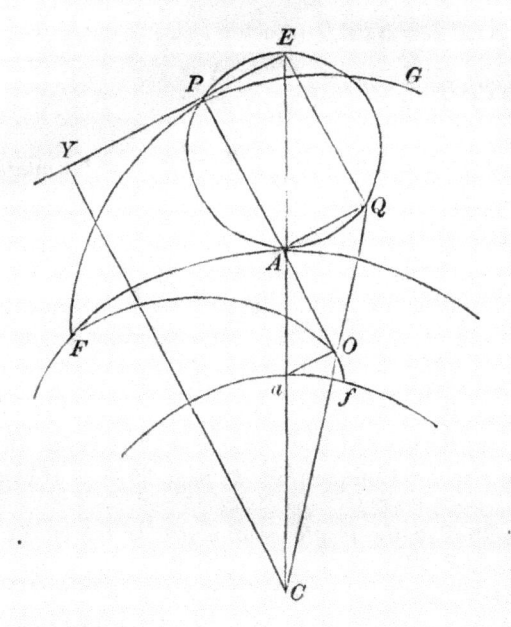

$$PAO : PA :: 2a+2b : a+2b,$$
$$\text{or } AO : PA :: a : a+2b.$$

Draw the chord EQ parallel to PA, and join CQ.

Then, since $AO : EQ :: AC : EC :: a : a+2b$, O, the center of curvature of the epicycloid FP at P, lies in CQ, and, since $CO : CQ :: CA : CE$, the curve traced out by O, is similar to that traced out by Q, and if a circle be drawn, whose radius $Ca : CA :: CA : CE$, the evolute is an epicycloid Ff, for which the fixed circle is af, and the diameter of the rolling circle is Aa; f being the centre of curvature corresponding to G, the position of P when furthest from C.

If $a = \infty$, FA and af become straight lines, and $Aa = AE$, whence the evolute of the cycloid is an equal cycloid; compare Art. 212.

223. *To find the area of the epicycloid.*

Recurring to figure, Art. 221,

Area $APP'B = \triangle PAB +$ sector PBP'

$$= \triangle PAB + \frac{1}{2} PB^2 . 2\pi \left(\frac{1}{m} + \frac{1}{n}\right)$$

$$= \triangle PAB + \frac{1}{2} PB . PA . \sin\frac{\pi}{n} . \frac{2(m+n)}{m}, \text{ ultimately,}$$

$$= \triangle PAB \left\{1 + \frac{2(a+b)}{a}\right\},$$

hence, by Lemma IV, Cor., the area of the segment AFP of the epicycloid is equal to the corresponding segment of the circle $\times \left(3 + \frac{2b}{a}\right)$.

If $a = \infty$, the area of the cycloid is three times that of the generating circle. Compare Ex. 5, page 39.

224. *To find the length of any arc of the epicycloid.*

By the properties of the evolute, see figure, Art. 222, the arc OF of the evolute $= OP = 2AP . \frac{a+b}{a+2b}$, and the arc of the epicycloid generated by Q from the highest point

$$= OF \frac{a+2b}{a} = 2AP . \frac{a+b}{a}.$$

Therefore, the arc GP from the highest point G of the epicycloid GPF

$$= 2EP . \frac{a+b}{a} = 2EP, \text{ when } a = \infty; \text{ compare Art. 208.}$$

225. The corresponding properties of the hypocycloid may be proved by adapting the investigations for the epicycloid to the case of the internal rolling; and the results will be obtained by writing $-b$ for b in the preceding results.

Thus, if the diameter of the fixed be double that of the rolling circle, the hypocycloid becomes a straight line, which coincides with the result of Art. 222, since $a + 2b = 0$, and therefore the radius of curvature at every point is infinite.

Equiangular Spiral.

226. DEF. 1. If a series of radii $SA, SB, SC, \ldots$ be drawn inclined at equal angles, and $AB, BC, CD, \ldots$ be drawn making equal angles $SAB, SBC, \ldots$ with these radii respectively, the curvilinear limit of the polygon $ABCD\ldots$, when the equal angles $ASB, BSC, \ldots$ are indefinitely diminished, is the *Equiangular Spiral*.

227. DEF. 2. If an indefinite line SP revolve uniformly about a fixed point S, while another point P advances or recedes on that line with a velocity which varies as the distance from S, it will trace out the *Equiangular* or *Logarithmic Spiral*.

The second definition follows immediately from the first, since, fig. page 31, $SA - SB : SB - SC :: SA : SB$, the triangles $SAB, SBC, \ldots$ being similar.

Since the limiting positions of the sides of the polygon are those of tangents to the curve, the inclination of the tangents to the radii at any point is a constant angle; whence the equiangular spiral is the spiral which cuts all the radii drawn from a fixed point at a constant angle.

228. *To find the length of an arc of an equiangular spiral contained between two radii.*

Let α be the angle SAB,

and let $SB : SA :: \lambda : 1$ a constant ratio, $\lambda < 1$;

$\therefore BC : AB :: CD : BC :: \ldots :: \lambda : 1$;

$\therefore AB + BC + \ldots : AB :: 1 + \lambda + \lambda^2 + \ldots : 1$,

$:: 1 - \lambda^n : 1 - \lambda$

$:: SA(1 - \lambda^n) : SA - SB$;

hence, proceeding to the limit, since $SL = \lambda^n . SA$,

arc $AL : SA - SL :: AB : SA - SB$ ultimately;

$\therefore$ arc $AL = (SA - SL) \sec \alpha$.

Catenary.

229. Def. The *Catenary* is the curve in which a uniform and perfectly flexible string, of which the extremities are suspended at two points, would hang under the action of gravity, supposed to be a constant force acting in parallel lines.

The *directrix* is a horizontal straight line whose depth below the lowest point is equal to the length of string whose weight is equal to the tension at the lowest point.

The *axis* is the vertical through the lowest point.

230. *The tension at any point of the catenary is equal to the weight of the string which if suspended from that point would extend to the directrix.*

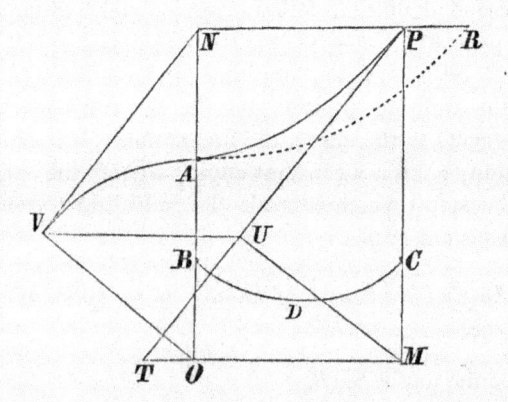

Let A be the lowest point of a uniform and perfectly flexible string hanging from two points under the action of gravity, P any other point, AO the length of string whose weight is equal to the tension of the string at A.

Take a point B in OA, or OA produced, and let OM, BC drawn horizontally meet a vertical PM in M and C.

If a string pass round pegs at $APCB$, it is evident that there will be a position of equilibrium whatever be the length of the string, or the position of BC, and for some length and some position of BC the tangent at A will be horizontal.

Also, since BDC will hang symmetrically, the tensions of the string on B and C will be equal, and BDC may be removed and replaced by equal lengths BO, CM of the string, without disturbing the equilibrium of AP, therefore the tension of the catenary at P is equal to the weight of a string of length PM.

231. The catenary may also be considered as the limit of the polygon formed by a series of equal rods of the same substances, jointed freely at the extremities and suspended from two fixed points, when the length of the rods is indefinitely diminished.

The proposition of the preceding article may then be proved as follows.

The equilibrium will be undisturbed if each rod be replaced by two weights at the extremities, each equal to half that of the rod, connected by a string without weight.

Let AB, BC, be two consecutive positions of the strings,

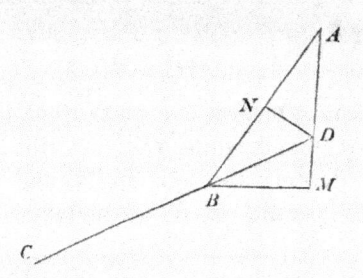

weights equal to those of the rods being placed at A, B, C; let AM be vertical and BM horizontal, and produce CB to meet AM in D, draw DN perpendicular to AB.

The forces which keep B in equilibrium act in the directions of the sides of the triangle ABD, and are proportional to them.

Therefore, ultimately, the difference of the tensions of AB and BC is to the weight of the rod AB as $AN : AD$, or as $AM : AB$; hence the difference of the tensions at A and B is the weight of a rod of length AM.

Therefore, proceeding to the limit, and summing by Lemma IV, the difference of tensions at any two points of the catenary is equal to the weight of string which is equal in length to the vertical depth of one point below the other, whence the truth of the proposition.

232. *If a circle be drawn on the ordinate perpendicular to the directrix as diameter, it will meet the tangent at a point whose distance from the point of contact is equal to the arc of the catenary.*

Let PT be the tangent at P, meeting the directrix MO in T, then, since the arc AP supposed to become rigid is kept at rest by the tensions at A and P, parallel to MT, TP and the weight parallel to PM, TPM is a triangle of forces;

$\therefore$ weight of AP : tension at P :: PM : PT;

$\therefore AP : PM :: PM : PT$;

and if MU be perpendicular to PT,

$PU : PM :: PM : PT$;

$\therefore PU = AP$.

Cor. Tension at A : weight of AP :: MT : PM;

$\therefore AO : PU :: MT : PM :: MU : PU$;

$\therefore AO = MU$.

233. *To draw a tangent to a catenary at any point.*

With center O, and radius OA, describe a circle AV, draw PN horizontal meeting the axis in N, and NV touching the circle in V, PT parallel to NV is a tangent to the catenary at P.

For, join OV, and draw MU perpendicular to PT, therefore OV is equal and parallel to MU;

$\therefore MU = OV = AO$; $\therefore PU$ is a tangent.

234. *If an equilateral hyperbola be described, having center O and AO the semi transverse axis, the ordinate of the hyperbola is equal to the arc of the catenary.*

For, let AR be the hyperbola,

then, $VN^2 = (NO + OA)\, AN = RN^2$;

$\therefore RN = VN = PU = AP$.

Lemniscate.

235. Def. The *Lemniscate* is the locus of the feet of the perpendiculars drawn from the center of a rectangular hyperbola upon the tangent.

APPENDIX II.

236. *To find the inclination of the radius from the center of the lemniscate to the tangent at any point.*

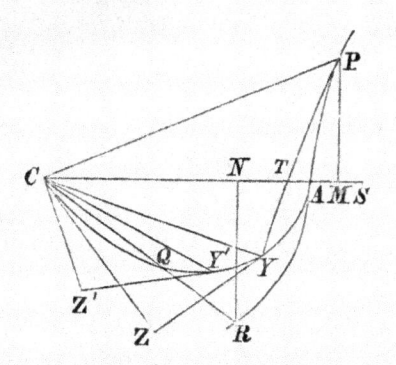

Let CY be perpendicular on PT the tangent at the point P in the hyperbola. $CY = PF$;

$$\therefore CY.CP = PF.CD = AC^2,$$

since $CP = CD$ in the rectangular hyperbola,

Draw the ordinate PM, then $CT.CM = AC^2 = CY.CP$;

$$\therefore CY : CT :: CM : CP;$$

and CMP, CYP are right angles; $\therefore \angle PCM = \angle ACY$.

Draw CZ perpendicular on the tangent at Y to the lemniscate.

Therefore ZCY and YCP are similar triangles, see page 61, 6;

$$\therefore \angle ZYC = \angle CPY = \text{complement of twice } \angle YCA.$$

237. *To find the perpendicular on the tangent at any point of the lemniscate.*

$$CZ.CP = CY^2, \text{ and } CY.CP = AC^2;$$
$$\therefore CZ : CY :: CY^2 : AC^2;$$
$$\therefore CZ.AC^2 = CY^3.$$

238. *To find the chord of curvature through the center.*

Let YV be the chord of curvature;

$$\therefore YV : 2CZ :: CY - CY' : CZ - CZ', \text{ ultimately, (Art. 88),}$$
$$\text{and } (CZ - CZ')AC^2 = CY^3 - CY'^3;$$

$$\therefore CY - CY' : CZ - CZ' :: AC^2 : 3CY^2;$$
$$\therefore YV : 2CZ :: CY : 3CZ;$$
$$\therefore YV = \tfrac{2}{3}CY.$$

239. *To find the radius of curvature.*

The radius of curvature

$$= \tfrac{1}{2}YV \cdot \frac{CY}{CZ} = \frac{CY^2}{3CZ} = \frac{AC^2}{3CY} = \tfrac{1}{3}CP$$

$= \tfrac{1}{3}$ of the radius of curvature at the corresponding point of the hyperbola.

240. *To find the area of the lemniscate.*

The sectorial area ACQ may be shewn by Lemma IV. to be equal to the triangle CRN where CQ meets the auxiliary circle in R, and RN is perpendicular to CA.

241. *To find the law of force tending to the center, under the action of which the lemniscate may be described.*

$$F = \frac{2h^2}{CZ^2 \cdot YV} = \frac{3h^2}{CZ^2 \cdot CY} = \frac{3h^2 AC^4}{CY^7} \propto \frac{1}{CY^7}.$$

242. *The velocity varies inversely as the cube of the distance.*

243. *To find the time in any arc of the lemniscate.*

$$\text{Time in } AQ = \frac{CN \cdot NR}{h} = \sqrt{3} \cdot \frac{AC^2 \cdot CN \cdot NR}{\mu^{\frac{1}{2}}}.$$

244. *To find the poles of the lemniscate.*

Let S, H be the foci of the hyperbola, s, h the middle points of CS and CH.

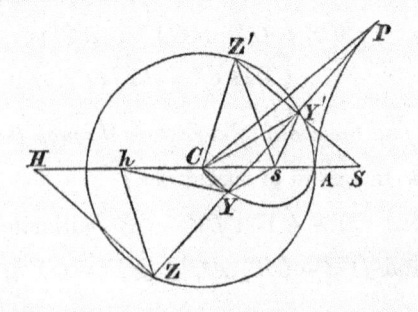

Draw $SY'Z'$ perpendicular to the tangent to the hyperbola, meeting the auxiliary circle in Y', Z', and join sY', sZ', sY, hY.

Since $Cs = sS$, the perpendicular from s on YY' bisects it; therefore $sY' = sY$, and similarly $hY = hZ = sZ'$.

The altitude of the triangle $Y'CZ'$ is double that of $Y'sZ'$, upon the same base;

$$\therefore \triangle Y'CZ' = 2.\triangle Y'sZ',$$

and $CS.Ss = \tfrac{1}{2}CS^2 = AC^2 = SY'.SZ'$;

therefore a circle may be drawn circumscribing $CsY'Z'$;

$$\therefore \angle Y'CZ' = \angle Y'sZ';$$
$$\therefore sY'.sZ' = \tfrac{1}{2}CY'.CZ' = \tfrac{1}{2}CA^2;$$
$$\therefore sY.hY = \tfrac{1}{2}CA^2,$$

which is the property of the poles of the lemniscate.

For this proof I am obliged to Professor Tait.

XX.

1. If the base of a smooth cycloidal arc be horizontal, and its plane inclined at an angle of 30° to the horizon, and a smooth heavy particle make a complete oscillation in n seconds, find the radius of the generating circle.

2. A particle describes a cycloid with uniform velocity; prove that, if, through any point, straight lines are drawn parallel in direction, and proportional in magnitude, to the acceleration at each point of the cycloid, the locus of their extremities is a straight line parallel to the base of the cycloid.

3. A particle describes a cycloid under the action of a constant force, which tends from the center of the generating circle; supposing the particle to be projected along the curve with such a velocity that it comes to rest at the vertex, find the velocity and pressure on the curve at any point.

4. A cycloidal arc is placed with its axis vertical, and vertex upwards, and a particle is projected from the cusp up the curve with a velocity due to a height h, shew that, if a be the length of the axis, the length of the latus rectum of the parabola described after leaving the curve will be $\dfrac{h^2}{a}$, h being less than $2a$.

5. If, along the several normals to an epicycloid, a system of particles move from the curve under the action of a force, tending to the center of the fixed circle, and varying as the distance, prove that they will all arrive at the fixed circle at the same instant.

6. Two equal circles roll on the circumference of a third fixed equal circle, the centers of the three being always in the same straight line; prove that the straight line joining the two points of the rolling circles, one of which was initially in contact with the fixed circle, and the other at the opposite extremity of the diameter passing through its point of contact, always passes through a fixed point.

7. Prove that the diameter through the point of a rolling circle which generates an epicycloid, always touches another epicycloid generated by a circle of half the dimensions.

8. Prove that the locus of the middle point of the tangent to an epicycloid having three cusps at any point, limited by the points in which it again meets the epicycloid, will be a circle.

9. A hypocycloid of n cusps has at any point a tangent drawn, prove that the length of the tangent, intercepted between the generating circle and the point of contact, is to the arc measured from the point to the vertex of the branch in which the point is taken, as $n : 2(n-1)$.

10. A bead slides on a hypocycloid being acted on by a force which varies as the distance from the center of the hypocycloid and tending to it; prove that the time of oscillation will be independent of the arc of oscillation.

11. A plane curve rolls along a straight line, shew that the radius of curvature of the path of any point, fixed with respect to the curve, is $\dfrac{r^2}{r - \rho \sin \phi}$, r being the distance of the fixed point from the point of contact, ϕ the angle between this line and the fixed line, and ρ the radius of curvature of the curve at the point of contact.

12. An equiangular spiral rolls along a straight line, shew that its pole describes a straight line.

13. A particle describes an equiangular spiral with uniform velocity, prove that its acceleration at any point is inversely proportional to the distance of that point from the pole.

14. If a perfectly elastic particle, describing an equiangular spiral under the action of a force tending to the pole, impinge on a smooth plane, it will describe after impact another equiangular spiral.

15. If the velocities of two particles describing different equiangular spirals, under the action of forces tending to the poles, be the same at a given time, and the ratio of the absolute forces be that

of the squares of the cosines of the angles of the spirals, prove that the velocities will be always equal at the same time.

16. A particle moves in an equiangular spiral about a force in the pole, shew that the hodograph is a similar spiral; and if it be traced by a point, shew that the velocity of the point varies as the cube of that of the particle.

Shew also that the hodograph might be described freely in the same manner under the action of a force varying as the fifth power of the distance from the pole, and inclined at a constant angle to the radius vector.

17. Prove that, if a catenary roll on a fixed straight line, its directrix will always pass through a fixed point.

18. Prove that the portion of the tangent to that involute of a catenary which passes through the lowest point of the catenary, intercepted between the directrix and the point of contact, is of constant length.

19. A particle slides down a tube in the form of a catenary, whose plane is vertical, and vertex upwards, the velocity at the vertex being that due to falling from the directrix; prove that the pressure at any point varies inversely as the distance from the directrix.

20. If a parabola be described touching the asymptotes of a rectangular hyperbola, and having its focus in the corresponding lemniscate, its chord of contact will touch the hyperbola.

GENERAL PROBLEMS.

XXI.

1. Find the limit of $\dfrac{1.2 + 2.3 + \ldots + n(n+1)}{n^3}$, when n is indefinitely increased.

2. Prove, without finding the actual values, that the chords of curvature through the focus and center, and the diameter of curvature at any point of an ellipse, are as $\dfrac{1}{AC} : \dfrac{1}{CP} : \dfrac{1}{PF}$.

How does it appear that the chords of curvature through the two foci are equal?

3. A body describes an ellipse about one focus; prove that it always moves as fast *towards* one focus as *from* the other.

4. A particle describes a parabola round a force in the focus. A is the vertex, L the extremity of the latus rectum, P a point whose distance from the axis is the length of the latus rectum. Prove that the time in AL : time in LP :: 2 : 5.

5. A body perfectly elastic, revolving in an ellipse about the focus, strikes a hard plane; if ϕ, θ be the angles which the direction of its motion makes respectively with the focal distance and the plane, shew that the periodic time will be unaffected, and that the new minor axis will equal the former minor axis
$$\times \dfrac{\sin(\phi + 2\theta)}{\sin \phi}.$$

6. In question 5, find what would be the eccentricity of the new orbit if the old orbit were a circle. And if the old orbit were a parabola, find what would be the inclination of the axis of the new orbit to the axis of the old one.

7. A balloon was found to be sailing steadily before the wind at an invariable elevation above the earth. A seconds

pendulum suspended in the car was observed in 50 minutes to make 2997 oscillations; at what height was the balloon, supposing the radius of the earth to be 4000 miles, nearly?

8. Shew how to find the weights of equal bodies on planets which have secondaries.

XXII.

1. If the sides of a right-angled triangle vary, while its area remains constant, determine the ultimate ratio of the changes in the sides adjacent to the right angle.

2. The curvatures at the extremities of the major and minor axes of an ellipse are as 8 to 1; find the eccentricity.

3. If a particle describe an ellipse under the action of a force tending to the focus, and v, v' be the velocities at two points equally distant from the axis on the same side, V the velocity at the extremity of the minor axis; prove that $vv' = V^2$.

4. Shew that, an ellipse being described under the action of a force tending in a direction perpendicular to the major axis, the velocity varies as the secant of the angle which the direction of motion makes with the major axis.

5. A hyperbola and its conjugate are described by particles round a force in the center. They are at an apse at the same instant; shew that they will always be at the extremities of conjugate diameters. Also if v, v' be their velocities,

$$v^2 - v'^2 = \mu (a^2 - b^2).$$

6. A body is projected with a velocity equal to that in a circle at the same distance at an angle of 30°, and acted on by a central force varying as the distance; determine the position, form, and magnitude of the orbit.

7. When force $\propto$ (dist.)$^{-2}$, shew that however the absolute force be altered so that similar ellipses are described, the proportionate alterations of the absolute force and mean distance are the same.

8. Find the time of oscillation in a cycloid; and the height of a mountain to the top of which if a seconds pendulum

be carried, 43 oscillations are lost in a day; prove that it is about two miles high.

9. Shew that in the elliptic orbit described under the action of a force tending to a focus, the angular velocity round the other focus varies inversely as the square of the diameter parallel to the direction of motion.

XXIII.

1. AB is an arc of finite curvature in any curve; the tangents at A and B intersect each other in T; and around the triangle ABT a circle is described; when B moves up to A, this circle ultimately bisects the diameter of curvature and all the chords of curvature.

2. Deduce the expression for the diameter of curvature at any point of a plane curve from the definition, that the circle of curvature is the limiting position of the circle passing through three consecutive points of a curve.

3. If the eccentricity of an ellipse be $\frac{1}{2}$, the time of moving under the action of a force tending to the center from one extremity of the latus rectum to the other is $\dfrac{\pi}{3\sqrt{\mu}}(3 \pm 1)$.

4. Given the velocity and direction at two points of a central orbit, find the locus of the center of force.

5. If at any point of an ellipse, described under the action of a force tending to the focus, the velocity be increased in the ratio $n : 1$, prove that the latus rectum will be increased in the ratio $n^2 : 1$.

6. If a closed string, lying on a smooth horizontal plane, pass loosely round three vertical pegs in the angles of an equilateral triangle, and if a bead be projected along the string so as to keep it stretched tightly, shew that the tension of the string will have two minimum values, and that they will be inversely proportional to the free lengths of the string in the two cases.

7. If the earth's orbit be taken an exact circle, and a comet be supposed to describe round the sun a parabolic orbit in the plane of the ecliptic; shew that this comet cannot

possibly continue within the earth's orbit longer than the $\left(\dfrac{3\pi}{2}\right)^{\text{th}}$ part of a year.

8. A body describes a hyperbola, under a repulsive force tending from the farther focus, and when the body arrives at the vertex, the force suddenly becomes attractive; shew that, if the new orbit be a parabola, e' the eccentricity of the hyperbola $= 3$; if the new orbit be an ellipse of eccentricity e, $e' \pm e = 2$.

9. A particle slides down the arc of a vertical circle, starting from rest at a given point; find the point where it will leave the curve.

XXIV.

1. Find the ultimate ratio of the area of a segment of a circle to the area of a triangle on the same base, and whose vertex divides the arc in a given ratio when the arc is diminished without limit.

2. From a point in the circumference of a vertical circle a chord and tangent are drawn, the one terminating at the lowest point and the other in the vertical diameter produced; compare the velocities acquired by a heavy body in falling down the chord and tangent when they are indefinitely diminished.

3. A flat ring is revolving about its center with a given angular velocity; find the law of force under the action of which it would continue to revolve exactly as before if cohesion among the particles of which it is composed were destroyed.

4. A hollow cylinder consists of particles attracting with force varying as the distance; shew that, if a particle be projected along the interior with any velocity, in a plane perpendicular to the axis, it will continue to make isochronous oscillations between points at equal distances above and below the middle section.

5. If a body be projected with a velocity $= \sqrt{2} \times$ velocity in a circle at the same distance at an angle of $45°$, determine the orbit completely. Force $\propto (\text{dist.})^{-2}$.

6. Supposing the major axis of an ellipse $= 200$ feet, the

eccentricity $=\frac{1}{10}$, and the periodic time 10 days; find the number of square inches in the area swept out by the radius vector in 1".

7. A particle describes an ellipse, the center of force being situated at any point within the figure. Shew that at the point where the *true* angular velocity is equal to the *mean* angular velocity, the radius vector is a mean proportional between the semiaxes.

8. A body describes an ellipse about a center of force in the center; prove that if r, r' be two radii vectores and α the angle between them, the time of describing the intercepted arc

$$= \frac{1}{\sqrt{\mu}} \sin^{-1}\left(\frac{rr' \sin \alpha}{ab}\right).$$

What is this time when $rr' \sin \alpha = \frac{1}{2} ab$, and the periodic time in the ellipse $= 12$ days?

9. A body describes a circle to the center of which it is connected by a string; it is attracted to a point in the circumference by a force varying as the distance; shew that if the string be always kept stretched, the greatest and least velocities are in a ratio less than $\sqrt{3}$: 1.

10. A particle moves from any point in the directrix of a conic section, in a straight line towards a center of force, which $\propto \frac{1}{(\text{dist.})^2}$, in the nearer focus. Prove that, when it arrives at the conic section, its velocity $= \left(\frac{4\mu}{\text{latus rectum}}\right)^{\frac{1}{4}}$.

XXV.

1. ACB is an arc of a curve of continued curvature; find the ultimate ratio of the area of the triangle, formed by joining the points A, B, C, to that of the triangle included between the tangents at those points.

2. Apply Lemma IV. to prove that the area included between a hyperbola and the tangents at the vertices of the conjugate hyperbola is equal to the area included between the conjugate hyperbola and the tangents at the vertices of the hyperbola.

GENERAL PROBLEMS. 271

3. The circle of curvature at any point of an ellipse cannot pass through the center unless the eccentricity be greater than $\dfrac{1}{\sqrt{2}}$.

4. Having given rad. of earth = 4000 miles nearly, shew that gravity in latitude $\lambda = G\left(1 - \dfrac{\cos^2 \lambda}{289}\right)$, the earth being considered spherical, and G gravity at the pole.

5. The sides a, b, c of a triangle are composed of matter attracting directly as the distance, with an intensity which would equal μx at the distance x, if the whole matter were collected at a point; from D, E, F, the middle points of the sides, three particles are projected in the directions DE, EF, FD, with velocities whose squares are μc, μa, μb. If S be the sum of the areas of the three orbits, and A be the area of the triangle, shew that $S = \pi A$.

6. A particle is attached by an elastic string to a center of attractive force of constant intensity, and of such magnitude that it would exactly double the length of the elastic string. The string is now stretched and the particle projected at right angles to it. Shew that the particle will begin to move in an ellipse; but if the velocity of projection be less than the velocity in a circle at the same distance, the ellipse will be deserted after a certain interval of time.

In the latter case find the velocity and direction of motion at the moment of leaving the ellipse.

7. The latus rectum of a comet's parabolic orbit is equal to the diameter of the earth's orbit supposed circular; if the earth describe an arc of its orbit equal to the radius in $58\frac{1}{2}$ days, find how long the comet takes to move from one extremity of the latus rectum to the other.

8. Shew that if a body describe an ellipse of very small eccentricity under the action of a force tending to a focus, the angular velocity about the other focus will be very nearly uniform.

9. Shew that the intersection of the string of a cycloidal pendulum, which makes complete oscillations with the base of the cycloid, moves uniformly along the latter.

10. If two points describe the same ellipse in opposite directions with accelerations tending to the center, prove that the chord joining them will move parallel to itself, with a velocity proportional to its length.

11. A particle, describing an ellipse about the focus, impinges upon a plane placed at the extremity of the latus rectum through the center of force perpendicular to the major axis. If the coefficient of elasticity be equal to the eccentricity of the ellipse, prove that the major axis of the new orbit is half that of the old.

12. A body is describing an ellipse about the focus S, and, when it arrives at the mean distance, the force is doubled, shew that the new line of apses passes through the foot of the perpendicular from the other focus upon the tangent.

XXVI.

1. If AB, $A'B'$, two chords of a curve of equal length, cut each other in T, shew that if $A'B'$ approach to and coincide with AB, then $AT : BT = \tan \alpha : \tan \beta$, ultimately, where α, β, are the angles that AB makes with the tangents at A and B.

2. PQR is an equilateral triangle, in which P, Q are points on a parabola, of which the focus lies on PQ, and PR is parallel to the axis; shew that the circle described about PQR is the circle of curvature to the parabola at P.

3. The angular velocities of a body moving in an ellipse about a force in the center are $4°$ and $9°$ per hour at the extremities of the major and minor axes respectively; find the periodic time.

4. A particle is to be projected from a given point, and in a given direction, and to be acted upon by a central force varying as the distance; the eccentricity of the orbit described will be least if the velocity of projection be such that the line joining the point of projection with the center of force is one of the equi-conjugate semi-diameters.

5. When a body describes a parabola about the focus, the intersection of its direction with the axis of the parabola moves

most rapidly when the body is at the extremity of the latus rectum.

6. Sir John Herschel states that the great comet of 1843 passed within a distance equal to ¼th of the sun's radius from the sun's surface. Taking the sun's diameter as 882,000 miles, and the earth's distance from the sun as 95,000,000 miles, find the velocity of the comet at perihelion.

7. AB is the vertical axis of a cycloid, A the highest point, AM, AN are the abscissæ of points at which a body begins to slide down the arc of the cycloid, and at which it leaves the curve; prove that N is the middle point of MB.

8. A particle moves in a smooth elliptic tube, at the foci of which are situated two centers of force of unequal intensity, the one attracting and the other repelling, according to the law of the inverse square; find the pressure. Shew that there exists a certain circle, such that a particle placed anywhere on its circumference, and abandoned to the free action of the forces, will describe an ellipse having those centers of force for the foci.

9. A body, acted on by a central force which varies inversely as the square of the distance, is constrained to move in a circle whose radius is a, and center is at distance b from the center of force; it is projected with velocity V from the nearer extremity of the diameter which passes through the center of force; shew that, in order that it may complete the circuit, V^2 must at least $= \dfrac{2\mu}{a-b} - \dfrac{2\mu}{a+b}$.

10. In an elliptic orbit about the focus, when a particle is at a distance r from the focus, the direction of motion is turned through a small angle, shew that the corresponding change in the apsidal line is $\dfrac{\delta\alpha}{ae^2}\left(1+e^2-\dfrac{r}{a}\right)$, $2a$ being the major axis, and e the eccentricity.

11. Find the locus of a point, in order that the resultant attraction of a uniform rod upon it may pass through a given point, equidistant from the extremities of the rod; the law of attraction being that of the inverse square.

NEWT.   T

12. A body moves in elliptic arcs about a center of force varying as $\frac{1}{(\text{dist.})^2}$ situated in a perfectly elastic plane perpendicular to the plane of the orbits; shew that those arcs are portions of similar ellipses whose major axes are equally inclined to the elastic plane, and that the time between the first and third impact is equal to that between the second and fourth.

XXVII.

1. ABC is an isosceles triangle, base BC; P, Q are points on CA, CB such that $AP = 2BQ$; find O, the point of ultimate intersection of PQ, AB as P and Q move up respectively to A and B. Prove that $OB : AB :: AB : 2BC - AB$.

2. If a line move parallel to the base of a cycloid, find the limiting ratio of the segment of the cycloid to the corresponding segment of the generating circle, as the line becomes infinitely near to the vertex.

3. A body revolves in an ellipse under the action of a force tending to the focus; if α, β be the angular velocities at the extremities of any chord parallel to the major axis, the periodic time will be $\frac{\pi b}{2a}\left(\frac{1}{\sqrt{\alpha}} + \frac{1}{\sqrt{\beta}}\right)^2$.

4. A heavy particle is projected horizontally from any point in the interior of a surface of revolution, whose axis is vertical; the velocity being that due to the height above a given horizontal plane of the point of projection, find the form of the surface so that the particle may always remain in the horizontal plane of projection.

5. Shew that from the moon's periodic time of 27 days we may deduce that gravity is the force which keeps her in her orbit; her distance from the earth's center being 60 times the earth's radius.

6. Two straight lines AB and BC are united at B, and AB revolves about A, BC about B with the same uniform angular velocity, shew that the acceleration on C tends to A and varies as CA.

GENERAL PROBLEMS. 275

7. An elastic string just fits a fixed straight tube when it is of its natural length; it is fixed at one end, and pulled out at the other, so as to double its length; a particle, fixed at the free end, is then projected at right angles to the string along a smooth horizontal plane with the velocity which it would acquire in falling freely, under the action of gravity, through a space equal to the length of the tube; prove that the weight of the particle must be $\frac{3}{8}$ of that which would double the length of the string, in order that it may describe an ellipse whose eccentricity is $\frac{1}{2}$.

8. A particle is describing a parabola under the action of gravity; when it is at one extremity of the latus rectum, gravity is replaced by a force tending to the other extremity of the latus rectum and varying as the distance, such that the accelerating effort in that position is equal to that of gravity. Shew that the ratios of the axes of the ellipse described to the latus rectum of the parabola are $2\sqrt{2}\cos\frac{\pi}{8}$ and $2\sqrt{2}\sin\frac{\pi}{8}$.

9. A body is revolving in an ellipse about the center of force tending to a focus, and, when it arrives at the farther apse, another body is projected with the velocity which the first body had at the extremity of the minor axis. Shew that the eccentricities of the two orbits will be equal, and that the bodies will meet at the same point, after m revolutions of one, and n of the other, if the eccentricity is $\dfrac{m^{\frac{2}{3}} - n^{\frac{2}{3}}}{m^{\frac{2}{3}} + n^{\frac{2}{3}}}$.

10. A particle describes an ellipse round a force in one focus; at what point of the orbit may a given *finite* change be made in the *direction* of the motion without changing the position of the apse line?

11. If P be a point in a cycloid and O the corresponding position of the center of the generating circle, shew that PO touches another cycloid of half the dimensions.

12. Prove that it is possible that an equiangular spiral may be described by the action of a constant force, acting at a constant angle β to the radius vector, if $\cos\alpha\cos\beta = 1 - \frac{1}{3}\cosec^2\alpha$, α being the spiral angle.

XXVIII.

1. Prove that, in an ellipse, the sum of the chord of curvature at any point through the focus, and the focal chord parallel to the diameter through the point, is constant.

2. A given curve is freely described with an acceleration, tending to a given point S, and equal at any point P to $\phi(SP)$. Prove that, if SY be drawn perpendicular to the tangent at P, and on SY, produced if necessary, a point Q be taken, such that $SQ \cdot SY = $ a constant, then the locus of Q may be freely described by a point of which the acceleration tends to S, the normal component of which acceleration is proportional to $\dfrac{1}{\phi(SP)}$.

3. The number of oscillations lost by a second's pendulum at the top of a mountain is found to be 10 in 24 hours, shew that the height of the mountain is about 2444 feet.

4. An ellipse and a hyperbola have the same center and foci. They are described by particles, under the action of forces in the center of equal intensity. If a, a' be their semi-transverse axes, the square of the velocity of each body at a point where the curves cut $= \mu(a^2 - a'^2)$.

5. A particle describes an ellipse about a center of force in the focus, and another particle describes the circle upon the major axis about another force in the same point in the same periodic time. If the particles start simultaneously from the vertex, prove that the line joining them is always perpendicular to the axis.

Also shew that the velocity at any point in the circle is inversely proportional to the corresponding focal distance in the ellipse.

6. Bodies describing ellipses about a given center of force which $\infty \, (\text{dist.})^{-2}$ pass through a given point with the velocity in a circle at that distance; the locus of the vertices of the ellipses is a cardioid, the center of force being the pole.

7. Two particles move in different planes about a center which attracts with a force varying inversely as the square of

the distance, the one in a circle, the other in an ellipse; the orbits have two points in common, and at either of these points the velocity of one particle is to that of the other as n to 1. Determine the eccentricity of the ellipse.

8. If an imperfectly elastic particle fall from an infinite distance, under the action of a central force varying inversely as the square of the distance, and impinge, before arriving at the center of force, on a small plane area inclined to the direction of its motion, shew that, if the orbit after the first impact be a circle, the elasticity is $\frac{1}{2}$; and shew that after an infinite number of impacts, twice the major axis of the final orbit is three times the distance of the area from the center of force.

9. An ellipse is described about a center of force in the focus. A parabola is described with its axis coincident in direction with the minor axis, so as to pass through the points X, X', where the axis-major produced meets the directrices, the latus rectum being $2ae^{-2}$. If we draw any line parallel to the axis-minor cutting the ellipse in P, the parabola in Q, and the axis-major in N, then will QN be the space due to the velocity at the point P.

10. The envelope of a series of circles, whose centers are on the circumference of a given ellipse, and which all pass through a focus, is a circle whose center is the other focus.

11. A body is attached to the end of a string, which just winds round the circumference of a circle, in whose center there is a repulsive force $= \mu$ (dist.). Prove that the time of unwinding $= \dfrac{2\pi}{\sqrt{\mu}}$. Also, find the tension of the string at any time.

12. A particle is projected from a given point P, with a given velocity V, and is acted on by a force which varies inversely as the square of the distance, and tends to a point S; prove that there are two directions of projection for which the direction of the major axis will be the same; if α be the angle between these directions and e, e' the eccentricities, then $\mu(e'-e) = V^2 . SP \sin \alpha$.

XXIX.

1. Shew that the limit of the whole length of the hypocycloid or epicycloid corresponding to a complete revolution of the generating circle is eight times the radius of the fundamental circle, when that of the generating circle is indefinitely diminished.

2. A particle describes with uniform velocity an equiangular spiral whose constant angle is $45°$; shew that its motion may result from the attraction of a center of force varying as $\frac{1}{\text{dist.}}$, which itself moves with the same uniform velocity in a certain other similar and equal spiral.

3. The circle of curvature at the point P of a parabola cuts the curve in Q, PM is an ordinate at P; prove that the area PAQ is sixteen times that of PAM.

4. The velocity of a body describing a hyperbola by the action of a repulsive force in the center is at any point the same as if it had been repelled to that point in a straight line from rest when at a distance from the center $= \sqrt{a^2 - b^2}$.

5. Two bodies describing the same ellipse about the same center of force in the focus start together from the two extremities of the major axis. The angles which they have described will have the greatest difference, when the area included between their distances from the focus is half the area of the ellipse.

6. One body is describing a parabola about the focus, and another a circle whose center is in the focus, and $4n$ times the radius of the circle is equal to the latus rectum of the parabola.

Prove that, if the bodies are simultaneously at both points of intersection,

$$\sqrt{2}\,(2n+1)\sqrt{1-n} = 6\sin^{-1}\sqrt{n}, \text{ or } 6\cos^{-1}\sqrt{n}.$$

7. A given quantity of matter, consisting of particles which attract with forces varying as the distance, is formed into a thin hemispherical shell. Shew that, whatever be the size of the hemisphere, a particle placed at a given angular

distance from the vertex will always reach that point in the same time.

8. A particle moves in an elliptic tube under the attraction of a material line joining the foci, each element of which attracts with a force varying inversely as the square of the distance. Shew that the velocity is constant; and find the pressure on the tube when the particle is at the extremity of the minor axis.

9. From a given point S, within a given closed curve, perpendiculars are let fall on the several tangents to the curve, let the locus be the curve Y. The given closed curve then rolls on a given straight line, so that S traces out a curve X.

Prove that the lengths of X and Y are equal, and that the area included between X, the given straight line, and two ordinates, is double of the sectorial area of the corresponding portion of Y.

10. If a particle move in such a manner that its acceleration is constant in direction, shew that the hodograph is a straight line parallel to the direction of the acceleration.

XXX.

1. If any number of particles be moving in an ellipse about a force in the center, and the force suddenly cease to act, shew that, after the lapse of $\frac{1}{2\pi}$ of the period of a complete revolution, all the particles will be in a similar, concentric, and similarly situated ellipse.

2. If a particle in a smooth elliptic groove, under the action of two centers of force in the foci, each varying inversely as the square of the distance, the absolute forces being the same, be placed at the extremity of the axis-minor, prove that the equilibrium will be unstable; but if at the extremity of the axis-major it will be stable, and in this latter case shew that the time of a small oscillation is $\pi \left(\dfrac{b^2}{a}\right)^{\frac{3}{2}} \div 2e\mu^{\frac{1}{2}}$.

3. Two bodies of equal mass and whose coefficient of elasticity is $\frac{1}{2}$, are revolving in the same ellipse (eccentricity $= \frac{3}{5}$)

but in opposite directions round a center of force in the focus: they impinge upon one another at the nearest apse: determine the distances at which they will afterwards impinge on each other: and shew that the whole time from the first impact to their falling into the center of force is $\frac{\pi}{14} \cdot \sqrt{\frac{(5p)^3}{2\mu}}$, where p is the least distance at first, and μ the absolute force.

4. A body is projected about a center of force $\propto (\text{dist.})^{-2}$ perpendicular to the distance: shew that as the velocity of projection is increased the center of the curve moves through the center of force to infinity, it then suddenly starts back to the other side of the point of projection and goes off to infinity in that direction. But when the force $\propto$ dist. the nearer focus moves to a given point and then suddenly starts at right angles to its previous direction.

5. Two perfectly elastic balls are moving in concentric circular tubes in opposite directions and with velocities proportional to the radii: at an instant when they are in the same diameter and on opposite sides of the center the tubes are removed and the balls move in ellipses under the action of a force of attraction in the common center of the circles varying inversely as the square of the distance. After one has performed in its orbit a complete revolution and the other a revolution and a half, a direct collision takes place between the balls and they interchange orbits: find the relation between the radii of the circles and between the masses of the balls.

6. A body describes an ellipse in a free medium under the attraction of two equal forces, one in each focus, varying at any point as $\frac{1}{c^3}$, c being the semiconjugate diameter at that point: if the medium were to resist with a force varying as any function of the velocity, the body might be made to describe the same ellipse in the same manner by increasing the force in one focus and diminishing that in the other by a quantity which varies as $\frac{c}{\sqrt{c^2 - b^2}}$, b being the semiaxis-minor.

GENERAL PROBLEMS.

7. An attractive force equal to $\dfrac{\mu}{(\text{dist.})^2}$ resides in each focus of a smooth elliptic groove; if a particle start from the end of the major axis with a velocity $\dfrac{2\sqrt{\mu a}}{b}$, it will reach the end of the minor axis in a time $\dfrac{\pi a^{\frac{3}{2}}}{4\sqrt{\mu}}\left(1-\dfrac{e^2}{2}\right)$,

a, b, e being the semi-axes and eccentricity.

8. A curve is traced out by a point P in a straight line of given length, which moves with its extremities in the arc of an ellipse; shew that the area included between the ellipse and the locus of P is $\pi cc'$, c and c' being the distances of P from the extremities of the line.

SOLUTIONS OF PROBLEMS.

I.

1. The limits are zero in (1), ∞ in (2), and a in (3).
2. The limit is 3 for case (1), and $\frac{1}{8}$ for case (2).
3. $a : b$.
8. The chord of intersection ultimately makes the same angle with one of the fixed sides, which the straight line joining the middle point of the moving side with the opposite angle makes with the other.
11. The circles, which have their centers between the vertex and focus, do not intersect.

II.

6. The distance from the base is one-fourth of the height.
8. The mass is half that of a uniform rod whose density is equal to the greatest density of the given rod.
9. The mass is to that of a homogeneous circle, whose density is that of the given circle at the circumference, as $2 : m + 2$.
10. The volume generated by the closed portion of the curve is $\dfrac{\pi b^4}{4a}$.

III.

1. Shew that the volumes generated by the quadrant and the portion of the square exterior to it are as $2 : 1$, by inscribing in them rectangles whose finite sides are respectively perpendicular and parallel to the axis about which the figure revolves.
4. Prove that the two centers of gravity coincide.
5. The mass is one-third of that of a uniform rod of density equal to the greatest density of the given rod.
6. The volume is a quarter of that of a cylinder on the same base and of equal height.

IV.

10. The constant angle between the radius and tangent must be the same in both.

VI.

1. Only if the curves have the same curvature at P.
4. The velocities are as $1 : \sqrt{2}$.

VII.

7. The curve will be a parabola passing through A, whose center is at a distance a below AK, and whose axis meets KA produced at an unit of distance from A, the latus rectum is $\frac{1}{a}$, and the space described in time $t = \frac{1}{3} a \left(3t^2 + t^3\right)$.

10. If μSM be the accelerating effect at M, the square of the velocity at $M = \mu \left(SM^2 - SA^2\right)$, A being the starting point.

11. If μD, $\mu' D$ be the accelerations at a distance D, the time is $\dfrac{\pi}{\sqrt{\mu + \mu'}}$.

IX.

1. The fixed point is in UA produced, (fig. page 117), at a distance from $A = UA$.
2. The focus of the parabola is in the chord perpendicular to the subtenses, at a distance from the point of contact equal to a quarter of the chord, and the directrix is parallel to the chord, meeting the common normal at a distance from the point of contact equal to half the radius.
3. The focus is in the base of the cycloid, and the locus required is the circle on the axis as diameter.
4. $1 : 2$.

X.

2. The direction will not be changed, but the curvature will be changed in the ratio of the new force to the old.

9. $4\pi - 3\sqrt{3} : 8\pi + 3\sqrt{3}$.

12. The eccentricity $= \dfrac{1-m}{1+m} \cdot \dfrac{\pi}{2}$.

XI.

2. $\left(\dfrac{ga^2 P^2}{4\pi^2}\right)^{\frac{1}{3}}$, P being the periodic time, a the Earth's radius, and g the accelerating effect of gravity.

3. The areas vary in the subduplicate ratios of the radii.

6. The days would be shortened nearly in the ratio 17 : 1.

7. $54\pi^2 : 161$.

8. The square of the velocity is $3FR$.

11. The velocity $= (\mu g l)^{\frac{1}{2}}$.

XII.

3. The circle touches the two tangents at the points where they are intersected by the third.

XIII.

2. $\cos^{-1}\left(\dfrac{3W' - W}{2W'}\right)$.

3. If α be the inclinations of the moving portions of the string to the horizontal line, the tension required is to the weight of the ring as $2 - \cos 2\alpha : 2 \sin \alpha$.

4. If horizontal lines through the positions of the body at starting and at any given time meet the axis AB in N and M, the pressure at that time is to the weight of the body as $MN + BN$ is to the normal.

10. The eccentricity is ·01686.

13. The pressure at P is to the pressure if the particle were at rest at B, as the curvature at P is to that at B.

14. Let $CS = c$, and a be the length of the string, and let A, B be the points nearest to and farthest from S in the circle described.

If S be within the circle, the minimum tension being at A, the least velocity, at A, is $\dfrac{(\mu a)^{\frac{1}{2}}}{a - c}$, and the greatest tension, at D, is

$$\frac{\mu}{a}\left\{\frac{1}{\sqrt{a^2 - c^2}} - \frac{a - 2c}{(a - c)^2}\right\}.$$

If S be without the circle, the minimum tension is at B, and the least velocity of projection from A is $\dfrac{\mu a (3a + 5c)}{(c + a)^2 (c - a)}$, the greatest tension at A is $\dfrac{2\mu (3c^2 - a^2)}{(c^2 - a^2)^2}$, which becomes $6g$ if S is at an infinite distance, remaining finite in magnitude, so that

SOLUTIONS OF PROBLEMS.

$\frac{\mu}{c^2} = g$, in which case the force acts in parallel lines; compare page 170, Cor. 1.

XIV.

1. If P, P' be the periodic times about two centers of force S and S', PSV being drawn as in page 175, the forces will be in the ratio $P'^2 . SP'^2 . P'V'^3 : P^2 . SP^2 . PV^3$.

3. The unit of time is the same which is employed in fixing the measure of the accelerating force.

XVII.

2. If the change take place at A, C being the center;

(1) The semi-axes are CA and $\frac{1}{\sqrt{n}} . CA$.

(2) The semi-axes are CA and $n . CA$.

(3) The orbit is a rectangular hyperbola, whose vertex is at A.

(4) The axes are $(\sqrt{5} \pm 1) CA$, and the inclination of the major axis to CA is $\frac{1}{2} \tan^{-1} 2$.

3. The axes are $2CA$ and $4CA$.

5. The minor axis of the ellipse is one of the axes of each orbit, and the other axes are respectively $\frac{m - em'}{m + m'}$ and $\frac{m(1 + e)}{m + m'}$ times the major axis of the original ellipse.

6. If μD be the measure of the accelerating effect of an unit of mass at a distance D, and m be the number of units of mass in the parallelopiped, the periodic time will be $\frac{2\pi}{\sqrt{m\mu}}$.

9. The point of projection corresponding to the greatest ellipse is the point of bisection of CA.

XVIII.

1. $\frac{1}{2}$.

5. It must be diminished in the ratio $1 : e$.

6. Nearly 225 days.

7. About $8'\ 40''$.

8. The locus of the center is a circle.

14. Nearly 39 days.

16. The angles of the circle on the major axes as diameter corresponding to the points of intersection of the orbit are $30°$ and $60°$, and the ratio is $\sqrt{3}\,(2\pi+3) : 8\pi-9$.

17. The transverse axis is equal to the semi-latus rectum, and is perpendicular to the axis of the parabola, the eccentricity is $\sqrt{3}$.

25. The eccentricity $= \dfrac{\sqrt{21}}{6}$.

XIX.

2. The time to the sun is 64 days and a half.

XX.

1. The radius is $\dfrac{4n^2}{\pi^2}$.

3. If f be the constant acceleration from the center, the square of the velocity is $AB.AM$, and the pressure $= \dfrac{AB}{PG}\cdot f$.

XXI.

1. The limit is $\tfrac{1}{3}$.

6. The eccentricity would be sin 2θ; the inclination $=4\theta$.

7. The height was 4 miles 7 yards.

XXII.

1. The required ratio will be that of the sides.

2. The eccentricity $= \tfrac{1}{2}\sqrt{3}$.

6. The axes are $\sqrt{3}\pm 1$ times the distance of the point of projection, and are inclined to it at $15°$ and $75°$.

XXIII.

4. A straight line passing through the intersection of the tangents, and making with them angles whose sines are inversely proportional to the velocities.

9. The particle starting from a given distance from the horizontal diameter leaves the curve at two-thirds of that distance.

XXIV.

1. If $m : n$ be the given ratio, the required ratio will be $(m+n)^2 : 3mn$.

2. One is double of the other.

3. The force tends to the center, and varies as the distance.

6. The number required is $4\pi\sqrt{11}$.

8. One day.

XXV.

1. The former is double of the latter.

6. If c be the initial, a the natural length, f the constant acceleration, u the velocity of projection in the latter case, v, α the required velocity and angle,

$$v^2 = \frac{f}{a}(c^2 - a^2) + u^2, \text{ and } \sin\alpha = \frac{cu}{av}.$$

7. 78 days.

XXVI.

3. Two days and a half.

6. 366 miles per second.

11. The locus is a circle passing through the extremities of the rod and the given point.

XXVII.

2. The ratio is $2 : 1$.

4. A paraboloid of revolution.

10. If β be the finite change, PM perpendicular to the axis, and $\angle HPM = \beta$, $HP = \dfrac{a(1-e^2)}{1 - e\sin\beta}$.

XXVIII.

7. The eccentricity is $\sqrt{n^2 - 1}$.

11. The tension : weight of the body :: $2a\mu^{\frac{3}{2}}t : g$ at the time t.

XXIX.

2. The path of the center of force is the evolute of the given spiral.

8. If $\dfrac{\mu}{D^2}$ be the accelerating effect of the attraction of an unit of mass collected in a point upon a body at a distance D,

n the number of units of mass in the material line, W the weight of the body, v its velocity, the pressure on the tube

$$= W \times \left(\frac{v^2 b}{a^2 g} - \frac{\mu n}{abg}\right).$$

XXX.

1. The ellipse is the locus of the angular points of the circumscribing parallelogram whose sides are parallel to conjugate diameters: the semi-axes are $a\sqrt{2}$, $b\sqrt{2}$.

2. If ϕ be the inclination of the normal at a point P near A, shew that the force in the tangent has an accelerating effect $\frac{4\mu e a^2}{b^4} \cdot \sin\phi$, and $\phi = \frac{a \cdot AP}{b^2}$.

3. Shew that at every impact the major axis is diminished to $\frac{1}{4}$th, that the eccentricity is unaltered, and that the greatest distance in each orbit is the least in the preceding. The distances at which they impinge are p, $\frac{1}{4}p$, $\frac{1}{16}p$, $\frac{1}{64}p$, &c.

5. The masses are equal, and if r, s be the radii of the circles $\frac{r^3}{s^3} - \frac{s}{r} = 1 - \left(\frac{2}{3}\right)^{\frac{2}{3}}$.

6. The motion being the same in both cases, the velocity in the resisting medium is constant, and therefore the resistance constant also. Hence, shew that $\frac{\mu}{c^2} \pm f$ being the two new focal forces, $f \cos\alpha$ is constant, and thence deduce the result.

7. If PP' be an arc described in a small time, PMQ, $Q'P'M'$ common ordinates for the ellipse and auxiliary circle, DN that of the extremity of the conjugate diameter to CP; shew that velocity at $P = \frac{2\sqrt{\mu a}}{CD}$, or $\frac{2\sqrt{\mu a}}{CD} \cdot \frac{CN}{CD} = \frac{2\sqrt{\mu a}\, QM}{CD^2}$ parallel to AC;

$\therefore$ time in $PP' = \frac{MM'}{2\sqrt{\mu a}} \cdot \frac{CD^2}{QM} = \frac{MM'}{2\sqrt{\mu a}} \cdot \frac{e^2 QM^2 + b^2}{QM}$,

and making the summation from A to B,

$\Sigma (MM' \cdot QM) = \frac{\pi a^2}{4}$, and $\Sigma \left(\frac{MM'}{QM}\right) = \Sigma \frac{QQ'}{a} = \frac{\pi}{2}$, ultimately;

$\therefore$ time from A to $B = \frac{1}{2\sqrt{\mu a}} \left(\frac{\pi a^2 e^2}{4} + b^2 \cdot \frac{\pi}{2}\right) = \frac{\pi a^{\frac{3}{2}}}{4\sqrt{\mu}} \left(1 - \frac{e^2}{2}\right).$

CAMBRIDGE: PRINTED AT THE UNIVERSITY PRESS.

CATALOGUE OF BOOKS

PUBLISHED BY

MACMILLAN AND CO.

ACROSS THE CARPATHIANS. In 1858—60.
With a Map. Crown 8vo. cloth, 7s. 6d.

ÆSCHYLI Eumenides.
The Greek Text with English Notes, and an Introduction, containing an Analysis of Müller's Dissertations. By BERNARD DRAKE, M.A. late Fellow of King's College, Cambridge. 8vo. cloth, 7s. 6d.

AIRY.—Treatise on the Algebraical and Numerical Theory of
Errors of Observations, and the Combination of Observations. By G. B. AIRY, M.A. Crown 8vo. cloth, 6s. 6d.

ANSTED.—The Great Stone Book of Nature.
By DAVID THOMAS ANSTED, M.A. F.R.S. F.G.S. &c. Late Fellow of Jesus College, Cambridge; Honorary Fellow of King's College, London. Fcap. 8vo. cloth, 5s.

ARISTOTLE on the Vital Principle.
Translated, with Notes. By CHARLES COLLIER, M.D. F.R.S. Fellow of the Royal College of Physicians. Crown 8vo. cloth, 8s. 6d.

ARTIST AND CRAFTSMAN; A Novel.
Crown 8vo. cloth, 6s.

BACON'S ESSAYS AND COLOURS OF GOOD AND EVIL.
With Notes and Glossarial Index by W. ALDIS WRIGHT, M.A. Trinity College, Cambridge. With Vignette of WOOLNER's Statue of LORD BACON. 4s. 6d.; morocco, 7s. 6d.; extra, 10s. 6d. Large paper copies, cloth, 7s. 6d.; half morocco, 10s. 6d.

BEASLEY.—An Elementary Treatise on Plane Trigonometry:
with a numerous Collection of Examples. By R. D. BEASLEY, M.A. Fellow of St. John's College, Cambridge, Head-Master of Grantham Grammar School. Crown 8vo. cloth, 3s. 6d.

BIRKS.—The Difficulties of Belief in connexion with the
Creation and the Fall. By THOMAS RAWSON BIRKS, M.A. Rector of Kelshall, and Author of "The Life of the Rev. E. Bickersteth." Crown 8vo. cloth, 4s. 6d.

BIRKS.—On Matter and Ether; or the Secret Laws of Physi-
cal Change. By THOMAS RAWSON BIRKS, M.A. Crown 8vo. cloth, 5s. 6d.

BLAKE.—The Life of William Blake, the Artist.
By ALEXANDER GILCHRIST, Author of "The Life of William Etty." Medium 8vo. with numerous Illustrations from Blake's Designs and Fac-similes of his Studies of the "Book of Job." 2 vols. 32s.

BLANCHE LISLE, and Other Poems.
Fcap. 8vo. cloth, 4s. 6d.

BOOLE.—A Treatise on Differential Equations.
By GEORGE BOOLE, D.C.L. Crown 8vo. cloth, 14s.

BOOLE.—A Treatise on the Calculus of Finite Differences.
By GEORGE BOOLE, D.C.L. Crown 8vo. cloth, 10s. 6d.

BRIMLEY.—Essays, by the late GEORGE BRIMLEY, M.A.
Edited by W. G. CLARK, M.A., Tutor of Trinity College, and Public Orator in the University of Cambridge. With Portrait. **Second Edition.** Fcap. 8vo. cloth, 5s.

BROCK.—Daily Readings on the Passion of Our Lord.
By Mrs. H. F. BROCK. Fcap. 8vo. cloth, red leaves, 4s.

BROKEN TROTH, The.—A Tale of Tuscan Life. From the
Italian. By Philip Ireton. 2 vols. Fcap. 8vo. cloth, 12s.

BROOK SMITH.—Arithmetic in Theory and Practice.
For Advanced Pupils. Part First. By J. BROOK SMITH, M.A. of St. John's College, Cambridge. Crown 8vo. cloth, 3s. 6d.

BUTLER (Archer).—WORKS by the Rev. WILLIAM
ARCHER BUTLER, M.A. late Professor of Moral Philosophy in the University of Dublin:—

1. Sermons, Doctrinal and Practical.
Edited, with a Memoir of the Author's Life, by the Very Rev. THOMAS WOODWARD, M.A. Dean of Down. With Portrait. **Fifth Edition.** 8vo. cloth, 12s.

2. A Second Series of Sermons.
Edited by J. A. JEREMIE, D.D. Regius Professor of Divinity in the University of Cambridge. **Third Edition.** 8vo. cloth, 10s. 6d.

3. History of Ancient Philosophy.
A Series of Lectures. Edited by WILLIAM HEPWORTH THOMPSON, M.A. Regius Professor of Greek in the University of Cambridge. 2 vols. 8vo. cloth, 1l. 5s.

4. Letters on Romanism, in Reply to Mr. Newman's Essay
on Development. Edited by the Very Rev. T. WOODWARD, Dean of Down. **Second Edition,** revised by the Ven. Archdeacon HARDWICK. 8vo. cloth, 10s. 6d.

BUNYAN.—The Pilgrim's Progress from this World to that
which is to Come. By JOHN BUNYAN. With Vignette, by W. HOLMAN HUNT. 18mo. cloth, 4s. 6d.; morocco plain, 7s. 6d.; extra, 10s. 6d. The same on large paper, crown 8vo. cloth, 7s. 6d.; half-morocco, 10s. 6d.

BUTLER (Montagu).—Sermons Preached in the Chapel of
Harrow School. By the Rev. H. MONTAGU BUTLER, Head Master of Harrow School, and late Fellow of Trinity College, Cambridge. Crown 8vo. cloth, 7s. 6d.

BUTLER.—Family Prayers.
By the Rev. GEORGE BUTLER, M.A. Vice-Principal of Cheltenham College; late Fellow of Exeter College, Oxford. Crown 8vo. cloth, red edges, 5s.

BUTLER.—Sermons Preached in Cheltenham College Chapel.
By the Rev. GEORGE BUTLER, M.A. Crown 8vo. cloth, red edges, 7s. 6d.

CAIRNES.—The Slave Power; its Character, Career, and
Probable Designs. Being an Attempt to Explain the Real Issues Involved in the American Contest. By J. E. CAIRNES, M.A. Professor of Jurisprudence and Political Economy in Queen's College, Galway. **Second Edition.** 8vo. cloth, 10s. 6d.

CALDERWOOD.—Philosophy of the Infinite. A Treatise on
Man's Knowledge of the Infinite Being, in answer to Sir W. Hamilton and Dr. Mansel. By the Rev. HENRY CALDERWOOD, M.A. **Second Edition.** 8vo. cloth, 14s.

CAMBRIDGE SCHOOL CLASS BOOKS.
Uniformly printed and bound in 18mo.

I.—**An Elementary Latin Grammar.** By H. J. ROBY, M.A. Under Master of Dulwich College Upper School; late Fellow and Classical Lecturer of St. John's College, Cambridge. 18mo. bound in cloth, 2s. 6d.

II.—**Euclid for Colleges and Schools.**
By I. TODHUNTER, M.A. F.R.S. Fellow and Principal Mathematical Lecturer of St. John's College, Cambridge. 18mo. bound in cloth, 3s. 6d.

III.—**An Elementary History of the Book of Common**
Prayer. By FRANCIS PROCTER, M.A. Vicar of Witton, Norfolk; late Fellow of St. Catharine's College, Cambridge. 18mo. bound in cloth, 2s. 6d.

IV.—**Algebra for Beginners.**
By I. TODHUNTER, M.A. F.R.S. 18mo. bound in cloth, 2s. 6d.

V.—**Mythology for Latin Versification: a brief Sketch**
of the Fables of the Ancients, prepared to be rendered into Latin Verse for Schools. By F. C. HODGSON, B.D. late Provost of Eton College. 18mo. bound in cloth, 3s.

CAMBRIDGE SENATE-HOUSE PROBLEMS and RIDERS, with SOLUTIONS:—

1848—1851.—Problems.	By N. M. FERRERS, M.A. and J. S. JACKSON, M.A. of Caius College. 15s. 6d.
1848—1851.—Riders.	By F. J. JAMESON, M.A. of Caius College. 7s. 6d.
1854—Problems and Riders.	By W. WALTON, M.A. of Trinity College, and C. F. MACKENZIE, M.A. of Caius College. 10s. 6d.
1857—Problems and Riders.	By W. M. CAMPION, M.A. of Queen's College, and W. WALTON, M.A. of Trinity College. 8s. 6d.
1860—Problems and Riders.	By H. W. WATSON, M.A. Trinity College, and E. J. ROUTH, M.A. St. Peter's College. 7s. 6d.

MACMILLAN & CO.'S PUBLICATIONS.

CAMBRIDGE. — Cambridge Scrap Book: containing in a Pictorial Form a Report on the Manners, Customs, Humours, and Pastimes of the University of Cambridge. With nearly 300 Illustrations. Second Edition. Crown 4to. half-bound, 7s. 6d.

CAMBRIDGE.—Cambridge and Dublin Mathematical Journal. The Complete Work, in Nine Vols. 8vo. cloth, 7l. 4s.
ONLY A FEW COPIES OF THE COMPLETE WORK REMAIN ON HAND.

CAMBRIDGE SENATE-HOUSE EXAMINATION PAPERS, 1860-61. Being a Collection of all the Papers set at the Examination for the Degrees, the various Triposes and the Theological Examination. Crown 8vo. limp cloth, 2s. 6d.

CAMBRIDGE YEAR-BOOK and UNIVERSITY ALMANACK, FOR 1863. Containing an account of all Scholarships, Exhibitions, and Examinations in the University. Crown 8vo. limp cloth, 2s. 6d.

CAMPBELL.—Thoughts on Revelation, with special reference to the Present Time. By JOHN M'LEOD CAMPBELL, Author of "The Nature of the Atonement and its Relation to the Remission of Sins and Eternal Life." Crown 8vo. cloth, 5s.

CAMPBELL.—The Nature of the Atonement and its Relation to Remission of Sins and Eternal Life. By JOHN M'LEOD CAMPBELL, formerly Minister of Row. 8vo. cloth, 10s. 6d.

CATHERINES, The Two; or, Which is the Heroine? A Novel. 2 vols. crown 8vo. cloth, 21s.

CHALLIS.—Creation in Plan and in Progress: Being an Essay on the First Chapter of Genesis. By the Rev. JAMES CHALLIS, M.A. F.R.S. F.R.A.S. Crown 8vo. cloth, 3s. 6d.

CHEYNE.—An Elementary Treatise on the Planetary Theory. With a Collection of Problems. By C. H. H. CHEYNE, B.A. Scholar of St. John's College, Cambridge. Crown 8vo. cloth, 6s. 6d.

CHILDE.—The Singular Properties of the Ellipsoid and Associated Surfaces of the Nth Degree. By the Rev. G. F. CHILDE, M.A. Author of "Ray Surfaces," "Related Caustics." 8vo. half-bound, 10s. 6d.

CHILDREN'S GARLAND. From the Best Poets. Selected and Arranged by COVENTRY PATMORE. With a vignette by T. WOOLNER. 18mo. cloth, 4s. 6d.; morocco plain, 7s. 6d.; extra, 10s. 6d.

CHRETIEN.—The Letter and the Spirit. Six Sermons on the Inspiration of Holy Scripture, Preached before the University of Oxford. By the Rev. CHARLES P. CHRETIEN, Rector of Cholderton, Fellow and late Tutor of Oriel College. Crown 8vo. cloth, 5s.

CICERO.—THE SECOND PHILIPPIC ORATION. With an Introduction and Notes, translated from Karl Halm. Edited with corrections and additions. By JOHN E. B. MAYOR, M.A. Fellow and Classical Lecturer of St. John's College, Cambridge. Fcap. 8vo. cloth, 5s.

CLARK.—Four Sermons Preached in the Chapel of Trinity College, Cambridge. By W. G. CLARK, M.A. Fellow and Tutor of Trinity College, and Public Orator in the University of Cambridge. Fcap. 8vo. limp cloth, red leaves, 2s. 6d.

MACMILLAN & CO.'S PUBLICATIONS.

CLAY.—**The Prison Chaplain. A Memoir of the Rev. John** CLAY, B.D. late Chaplain of the Preston Gaol. With Selections from his Reports and Correspondence, and a Sketch of Prison-Discipline in England. By his Son, the Rev. W. L. CLAY, M.A. 8vo. cloth, 15s.

CLOUGH.—**The Poems of Arthur Hugh Clough, sometime** Fellow of Oriel College, Oxford. Reprinted and Selected from his unpublished Manuscripts. With a Memoir by F. T. PALGRAVE. **Second Edition.** Fcap. 8vo. cloth, 6s.

CLOUGH.—**The Bothie of Toper-Na-Fuosich. A long** Vacation Pastoral. By ARTHUR HUGH CLOUGH. Royal 8vo. cloth limp, 3s.

COLENSO.—**WORKS by the Right Rev. J. W. COLENSO,** D.D. Bishop of Natal:—

1. **The Colony of Natal.** A Journal of Ten Weeks' Tour of Visitation among the Colonists and Zulu Kafirs of Natal. With a Map and Illustrations. Fcap. 8vo. cloth, 5s.

2. **Village Sermons.** **Second Edition.** Fcap. 8vo. cloth, 2s. 6d.

3. **Four Sermons on Ordination, and on Missions.** 18mo. sewed, 1s.

4. **Companion to the Holy Communion,** containing the Service, and Select Readings from the writings of Mr. MAURICE. *Fine Edition,* rubricated and bound in morocco, antique style, 6s.; or in cloth, 2s. 6d. *Common Paper,* limp cloth, 1s.

5. **St. Paul's Epistle to the Romans.** Newly Translated and Explained, from a Missionary point of View. Crown 8vo. cloth, 7s. 6d.

6. **Letter to His Grace the Archbishop of Canterbury,** upon the Question of the Proper Treatment of Cases of Polygamy, as found already existing in Converts from Heathenism. Second Edition. Crown 8vo. sewed, 1s. 6d.

COTTON.—**Sermons and Addresses delivered in Marlborough** College during Six Years by GEORGE EDWARD LYNCH COTTON, D.D. Lord Bishop of Calcutta, and Metropolitan of India. Crown 8vo. cloth, 10s. 6d.

COTTON.—**Sermons: chiefly connected with Public Events** of 1854. Fcap. 8vo. cloth, 3s.

CROSSE.—**An Analysis of Paley's Evidences.** By C. H. CROSSE, M.A. of Caius College, Cambridge. 24mo. boards, 2s. 6d.

DAVIES.—**St. Paul and Modern Thought:** Remarks on some of the Views advanced in Professor Jowett's Commentary on St. Paul. By Rev. J. LL. DAVIES, M.A. Rector of Christ Church, Marylebone. 8vo. sewed, 2s. 6d.

DAVIES.—**The Work of Christ; or the World Reconciled to** God. Sermons Preached in Christ Church, St. Marylebone. With a Preface on the Atonement Controversy. By the Rev. J. LL. DAVIES, M.A. Fcap. 8vo. cloth, 6s.

MACMILLAN & CO.'S PUBLICATIONS.

DAYS OF OLD: Stories from Old English History of the
Druids, the Anglo-Saxons, and the Crusades. By the Author of "Ruth and her Friends." Royal 16mo. cloth, gilt leaves, 3s. 6d.

DEMOSTHENES DE CORONA.
The Greek Text with English Notes. By B. DRAKE, M.A. late Fellow of King's College, Cambridge. **Second Edition**, to which is prefixed AESCHINES AGAINST CTESIPHON, with English Notes. Fcap. 8vo. cloth, 5s.

DE TEISSIER.—Village Sermons, by G. F. De Teissier, B.D.
Rector of Brampton, near Northampton; late Fellow and Tutor of Corpus Christi College, Cambridge. Crown 8vo. cloth, 9s.

DICEY.—Six Months in the Federal States.
By EDWARD DICEY, Author of "Cavour, a Memoir;" "Rome in 1860," &c. &c. 2 Vols. crown 8vo. cloth, 12s.

DICEY.—Rome in 1860.
By EDWARD DICEY. Crown 8vo. cloth, 6s. 6d.

DREW.—A Geometrical Treatise on Conic Sections, with
Copious Examples from the Cambridge Senate House Papers. By W. H. DREW, M.A. of St. John's College, Cambridge, Second Master of Blackheath Proprietary School. **Second Edition.** Crown 8vo. cloth, 4s. 6d.

DREW.—Solutions to Problems contained in Mr. Drew's
Treatise on Conic Sections. Crown 8vo. cloth, 4s. 6d.

EARLY EGYPTIAN HISTORY FOR THE YOUNG. With
Descriptions of the Tombs and Monuments. By the Author of "Sidney Grey," etc. **New Edition,** with Frontispiece. Fcap. 8vo. cloth, 5s.

FAIRY BOOK, THE—The Best Popular Fairy Stories Selected
and Rendered Anew. By the Author of "John Halifax, Gentleman." Fcap. 8vo. cloth, 4s. 6d.
*** This forms one of the Golden Treasury Series.

FAWCETT.—Manual of Political Economy.
By HENRY FAWCETT, M.A. Fellow of Trinity Hall, Cambridge. Crown 8vo. cloth, 12s.

FERRERS.—A Treatise on Trilinear Co-ordinates, the
Method of Reciprocal Polars, and the Theory of Projections. By the Rev. N. M. FERRERS, M.A. Fellow of Gonville and Caius College. Crown 8vo. cloth, 6s. 6d.

FORBES.—Life of Edward Forbes, F.R.S.
Late Regius Professor of Natural History in the University of Edinburgh. By GEORGE WILSON, M.D. F.R.S.E. and ARCHIBALD GEIKIE, F.G.S. of the Geological Survey of Great Britain. 8vo. cloth, with Portrait, 14s.

FREEMAN. — History of Federal Government, from the
Foundation of the Achaian League to the Disruption of the United States. By EDWARD A. FREEMAN, M.A. late Fellow of Trinity College, Oxford. Vol. I. General Introduction.—History of the Greek Federations. 8vo. cloth, 21s.

FROST.—The First Three Sections of Newton's Principia.
With Notes and Problems in illustration of the subject. By PERCIVAL FROST, M.A. late Fellow of St. John's College, Cambridge, and Mathematical Lecturer of Jesus College. **Second Edition.**

FROST & WOLSTENHOLME.—Plane Co-ordinate Geometry.
By the Rev. PERCIVAL FROST, M.A. of St. John's College, and the Rev. J. WOLSTENHOLME, M.A. of Christ's College, Cambridge.

GALTON.—Meteorographica, or Methods of Mapping the Weather. Illustrated by upwards of 600 Printed Lithographed Diagrams. By FRANCIS GALTON, F.R.S. 4to. 9s.

GARIBALDI AT CAPRERA. By COLONEL VECCHJ.
With Preface by Mrs. GASKELL, and a View of Caprera. Fcap. 8vo. 3s. 6d.

GOLDEN TREASURY SERIES.
Uniformly printed in 18mo. with Vignette Titles by T. WOOLNER, W. HOLMAN HUNT, J. E. MILLAIS, &c. Bound in extra cloth, 4s. 6d.; morocco plain, 7s. 6d.; morocco extra, 10s. 6d. each Volume.

1. **The Golden Treasury of the best Songs and Lyrical** Poems in the English Language. Selected and arranged, with Notes, by FRANCIS TURNER PALGRAVE.

2. **The Fairy Book: the Best Popular Fairy Stories.** Selected and Rendered Anew by the Author of "John Halifax."

3. **The Children's Garland from the Best Poets.** Selected and arranged by COVENTRY PATMORE.

4. **The Pilgrim's Progress from this World to that which** is to Come. By JOHN BUNYAN.
    ** Large paper Copies, crown 8vo. cloth, 7s. 6d.; or bound in half morocco, 10s. 6d.

5. **The Book of Praise. From the best English Hymn** Writers. Selected and arranged by ROUNDELL PALMER.

6. **Bacon's Essays and Colours of Good and Evil.** With Notes and Glossarial Index by W. ALDIS WRIGHT, M.A., Trinity College, Cambridge. Large paper Copies, crown 8vo. 7s. 6d.; or bound in half morocco, 10s. 6d.

GEIKIE.—Story of a Boulder; or, Gleanings by a Field Geologist. By ARCHIBALD GEIKIE. Illustrated with Woodcuts. Crown 8vo. cloth, 5s.

GROVES.—A Commentary on the Book of Genesis.
For the Use of Students and Readers of the English Version of the Bible. By the Rev. H. C. GROVES, M.A. Perpetual Curate of Mullavilly, Armagh. Crown 8vo. cloth, 9s.

HAMERTON.—A Painter's Camp in the Highlands; and Thoughts about Art. By P. G. HAMERTON. 2 vols. crown 8vo. cloth, 21s.

HAMILTON.—The Resources of a Nation. A Series of Essays. By ROWLAND HAMILTON. 8vo. cloth, 10s. 6d.

HAMILTON.—On Truth and Error: Thoughts, in Prose and Verse, on the Principles of Truth, and the Causes and Effects of Error. By JOHN HAMILTON, Esq. (of St. Ernan's), M.A. St. John's College, Cambridge. Crown 8vo. cloth, 5s.

MACMILLAN & CO.'S PUBLICATIONS.

HARDWICK.—Christ and other Masters.
A Historical Inquiry into some of the chief Parallelisms and Contrasts between Christianity and the Religious Systems of the Ancient World. With special reference to prevailing Difficulties and Objections. By the Ven. ARCHDEACON HARDWICK. **New Edition,** revised with the Author's latest Corrections and a Prefatory Memoir by Rev. FRANCIS PROCTER. Two vols. crown 8vo. cloth, 15s.

HARDWICK.—A History of the Christian Church, during the Middle Ages and the Reformation. (A.D. 590–1600.)
By ARCHDEACON HARDWICK. Two vols. crown 8vo. cloth, 21s.

Vol. I. **Second Edition.** Edited by FRANCIS PROCTER, M.A. Vicar of Witton, Norfolk. History from Gregory the Great to the Excommunication of Luther. With Maps.

Vol. II. History of the Reformation of the Church.
Each volume may be had separately. Price 10s. 6d.
*** These Volumes form part of the Series of Theological Manuals.

HARDWICK.—Twenty Sermons for Town Congregations.
Crown 8vo. cloth, 6s. 6d.

HARE.—WORKS by JULIUS CHARLES HARE, M.A. Sometime Archdeacon of Lewes, and Chaplain in Ordinary to the Queen.

1. **Charges delivered during the Years 1840 to 1854.** With Notes on the Principal Events affecting the Church during that period. With an Introduction, explanatory of his position in the Church with reference to the parties which divide it. 3 vols. 8vo. cloth, 1l. 11s. 6d.

2. **Miscellaneous Pamphlets on some of the Leading Questions** agitated in the Church during the Years 1845–51. 8vo. cloth, 12s.

3. **The Victory of Faith.**
Second Edition. 8vo. cloth, 5s.

4. **The Mission of the Comforter.**
Second Edition. With Notes. 8vo. cloth, 12s.

5. **Vindication of Luther from his English Assailants.**
Second Edition. 8vo. cloth, 7s.

6. **Parish Sermons.**
Second Series. 8vo. cloth, 12s.

7. **Sermons Preached on Particular Occasions.**
8vo. cloth, 12s.

8. **Portions of the Psalms in English Verse.**
Selected for Public Worship. 18mo. cloth, 2s. 6d.

*** The two following Books are included in the Three Volumes of Charges, and may still be had separately.

The Contest with Rome.
With Notes, especially in answer to Dr. Newman's Lectures on Present Position of Catholics. **Second Edition.** 8vo. cloth, 10s. 6d.

Charges delivered in the Years 1843, 1845, 1846.
Never before published. With an Introduction, explanatory of his position in the Church with reference to the parties which divide it. 6s. 6d.

HAYNES.—Outlines of Equity. By FREEMAN OLIVER HAYNES, Barrister-at-Law, late Fellow of Caius College, Cambridge. Crown 8vo. cloth, 10s.

HEBERT.—Clerical Subscription, an Inquiry into the Real Position of the Church and the Clergy in reference to—I. The Articles; II. The Liturgy; III. The Canons and Statutes. By the Rev. CHARLES HEBERT, M.A. F.R.S.L. Vicar of Lowestoft. Crown 8vo. cloth, 7s. 6d.

HEMMING.—An Elementary Treatise on the Differential and Integral Calculus. By G. W. HEMMING, M.A. Fellow of St. John's College, Cambridge. **Second Edition.** 8vo. cloth, 9s.

HERVEY.—The Genealogies of our Lord and Saviour Jesus Christ, as contained in the Gospels of St. Matthew and St. Luke, reconciled with each other and with the Genealogy of the House of David, from Adam to the close of the Canon of the Old Testament, and shown to be in harmony with the true Chronology of the Times. By Lord ARTHUR HERVEY, M.A. Archdeacon of Sudbury, and Rector of Ickworth. 8vo. cloth, 10s. 6d.

HISTORICUS.—Letters on some Questions of International Law. Reprinted from the *Times*, with Considerable Additions. 8vo. cloth, 7s. 6d. Also, ADDITIONAL LETTERS, 8vo. 1s.

HODGSON.—Mythology for Latin Versification: a Brief Sketch of the Fables of the Ancients, prepared to be rendered into Latin Verse for Schools. By F. HODGSON, B.D. late Provost of Eton. New Edition. revised by F. C. HODGSON, M.A. Fellow of King's College, Cambridge. 18mo. bound in cloth, 3s.

HOMER.—The Iliad of Homer Translated into English Verse. By I. C. WRIGHT, M.A. Translator of "Dante." Vol. I. containing Books I.—XII. Crown 8vo. cloth, 10s. 6d., also sold separately, Books I.—VI. in Printed Cover, price 5s. also, Books VII.—XII. price 5s.

HOWARD.—The Pentateuch; or, the Five Books of Moses. Translated into English from the Version of the LXX. With Notes on its Omissions and Insertions, and also on the Passages in which it differs from the Authorised Version. By the Hon. HENRY HOWARD, D.D. Dean of Lichfield. Crown 8vo. cloth. GENESIS, 1 vol. 8s. 6d.; EXODUS AND LEVITICUS, 1 vol. 10s. 6d.; NUMBERS AND DEUTERONOMY, 1 vol. 10s. 6d.

HUMPHRY.—The Human Skeleton (including the Joints). By GEORGE MURRAY HUMPHRY, M.D. F.R.S. Surgeon to Addenbrooke's Hospital, Lecturer on Surgery and Anatomy in the Cambridge University Medical School. With Two Hundred and Sixty Illustrations drawn from Nature. Medium 8vo. cloth, 1l. 8s.

HUMPHRY.—The Human Hand and the Human Foot. With Numerous Illustrations. Fcap. 8vo. cloth. 4s. 6d.

HYDE.—How to Win our Workers. An Account of the Leeds Sewing School. By Mrs. HYDE. Dedicated by permission to the Earl of Carlisle. Fcap. 8vo. cloth, 1s. 6d.

JAMESON.—Life's Work, in Preparation and in Retrospect. Two Sermons preached before the University of Cambridge. By the Rev. F. J. JAMESON, M.A. Rector of Coton, Late Fellow and Tutor of St. Catharine's College, Cambridge. Fcap. 8vo. limp cloth, 1s. 6d.

JAMESON.—Brotherly Counsels to Students. Four Sermons
preached in the Chapel of St. Catharine's College, Cambridge. By F. J. JAMESON, M.A. Fcap. 8vo. limp cloth, red edges, 1s. 6d.

JANET'S HOME.
A Novel. 2 Vols. crown 8vo. cloth, 21s.

JUVENAL.—Juvenal, for Schools.
With English Notes. By J. E. B. MAYOR, M.A. Fellow and Classical Lecturer of St. John's College, Cambridge. Crown 8vo. cloth, 10s. 6d.

KINGSLEY.—WORKS by the Rev. CHARLES KINGSLEY,
M.A. Rector of Eversley, Chaplain in Ordinary to the Queen and the Prince of Wales, and Professor of Modern History in the University of Cambridge:—

1. Two Years Ago.
   Third Edition. Crown 8vo. cloth, 6s.

2. "Westward Ho!"
   Fourth Edition. Crown 8vo. cloth, 6s.

3. Alton Locke, Tailor and Poet. New Edition, with a New Preface. Crown 8vo. cloth, 4s. 6d.

4. Hypatia; or, New Foes with an Old Face.
   Fourth Edition. Crown 8vo. cloth, 6s.

5. The Water Babies, a Fairy Tale for a Land Baby.
   With Two Illustrations by J. NOEL PATON, R.S.A. square 8vo. cloth, 7s. 6d.

6. Glaucus; or, the Wonders of the Shore.
   New and Illustrated Edition, containing beautifully Coloured Illustrations of the Objects mentioned in the Work. Elegantly bound in cloth, with gilt leaves, 5s.

7. The Heroes; or, Greek Fairy Tales for my Children.
   With Eight Illustrations, Engraved by WHYMPER. **New Edition**, printed on toned paper, and elegantly bound in cloth, with gilt leaves, Imp. 16mo. 3s. 6d.

8. Alexandria and Her Schools: being Four Lectures delivered at the Philosophical Institution, Edinburgh. With a Preface. Crown 8vo. cloth, 5s.

9. The Limits of Exact Science as Applied to History.
   An Inaugural Lecture delivered before the University of Cambridge. Crown 8vo. boards, 2s.

10. Phaethon; or Loose Thoughts for Loose Thinkers.
    Third Edition. Crown 8vo. boards, 2s.

KINGSLEY.—Austin Elliot.
By HENRY KINGSLEY, Author of "Ravenshoe," &c. **Third Edition.** 2 vols. crown 8vo. cloth, 21s.

KINGSLEY.—The Recollections of Geoffry Hamlyn.
By HENRY KINGSLEY. **Second Edition.** Crown 8vo. cloth, 6s.

KINGSLEY.—Ravenshoe.
By HENRY KINGSLEY, Author of "Geoffry Hamlyn." **Second Edition.** 3 vols. 31s. 6d.

KINGTON.—History of Frederick the Second, Emperor of
the Romans. By T. L. KINGTON, M.A. of Balliol College, Oxford, and the Inner Temple. 2 vols. demy 8vo. cloth, 32s.

KIRCHHOFF.—Researches on the Solar Spectrum and the
Spectra of the Chemical Elements. By G. KIRCHHOFF, Professor of Physics in the University of Heidelberg. Translated by HENRY E. ROSCOE, B.A. Professor of Chemistry in Owen's College, Manchester. 4to. boards, 5s.

LANCASTER.—Præterita: Poems.
By WILLIAM LANCASTER. Royal fcap. 8vo. 4s. 6d.

LATHAM.—The Construction of Wrought-Iron Bridges,
embracing the Practical Application of the Principles of Mechanics to Wrought-Iron Girder Work. By J. H. LATHAM. Esq. Civil Engineer. 8vo. cloth. With numerous detail Plates. **Second Edition.**

LEAVES FROM OUR CYPRESS AND OUR OAK.
Square 8vo. cloth, 7s. 6d.

LECTURES TO LADIES ON PRACTICAL SUBJECTS.
Third Edition, revised. Crown 8vo. cloth, 7s. 6d. By Reverends F. D. MAURICE, PROFESSOR KINGSLEY, J. Ll. DAVIES, ARCHDEACON ALLEN, DEAN TRENCH, PROFESSOR BREWER, DR. GEORGE JOHNSON, DR. SIEVEKING, DR. CHAMBERS, F. J. STEPHEN, Esq., and TOM TAYLOR, Esq.

LUDLOW and HUGHES.—A Sketch of the History of the
United States from Independence to Secession. By J. M. LUDLOW, Author of "British India, its Races and its History," "The Policy of the Crown towards India," &c.
To which is added, **The Struggle for Kansas.** By THOMAS HUGHES, Author of "Tom Brown's School Days," "Tom Brown at Oxford," &c. Crown 8vo. cloth, 8s. 6d.

LUDLOW.—British India; its Races, and its History,
down to 1857. By JOHN MALCOLM LUDLOW, Barrister-at-Law. 2 vols. fcap. 8vo. cloth, 9s.

LUSHINGTON.—The Italian War 1848-9, and the Last
Italian Poet. By the late HENRY LUSHINGTON. With a Biographical Preface by G. S. VENABLES. Crown 8vo. cloth, 6s. 6d.

LYTTELTON.—The Comus of Milton rendered into Greek
Verse. By LORD LYTTELTON. Royal fcap. 8vo. 5s.

MACKENZIE.—The Christian Clergy of the first Ten Centuries, and their Influence on European Civilization. By HENRY MACKENZIE, B.A. Scholar of Trinity College, Cambridge. Crown 8vo. cloth, 6s. 6d.

MACLEAR.—A History of Christian Missions during the
Middle Ages. By G. F. MACLEAR, M.A. Formerly Scholar of Trinity College, and Classical Master at King's College School, London. Crown 8vo. cloth, 10s. 6d.

MACMILLAN.—Footnotes from the Page of Nature. A
Popular Work on Algæ, Fungi, Mosses, and Lichens. By the Rev. HUGH MACMILLAN, F.R.S.E. With numerous Illustrations, and a Coloured Frontispiece. Fcap. 8vo. cloth, 5s.

MACMILLAN'S MAGAZINE. Published Monthly, Price
One Shilling. Volume I. to VIII. are now ready, handsomely bound in cloth, 7s. 6d. each.

MACMILLAN & CO.'S PUBLICATIONS.

MACMILLAN'S SERIES OF BOOKS FOR THE YOUNG.
Handsomely bound in cloth. Three Shillings and Sixpence each.

1. **Our Year.** By the Author of "John Halifax." With Numerous Illustrations. Gilt leaves.
2. **Professor Kingsley's Heroes; or Greek Fairy Tales.** With Eight Illustrations. Gilt leaves.
3. **Ruth and Her Friends.** A Story for Girls. Gilt leaves.
4. **Days of Old. Stories from Old English History.** By the Author of "Ruth and Her Friends." Gilt leaves.
5. **Agnes Hopetoun's Schools and Holidays.** By the Author of "Margaret Maitland." Gilt leaves.
6. **Little Estella, and other Fairy Tales.** Gilt leaves.
7. **David, King of Israel. A History for the Young.** By J. WRIGHT, M.A. Gilt leaves.
8. **My First Journal.** By G. M. Craik. Gilt leaves.

McCOSH.—**The Method of the Divine Government, Physical and Moral.** By JAMES McCOSH, LL.D. Professor of Logic and Metaphysics in the Queen's University for Ireland. **Eighth Edition.** 8vo. cloth, 10s. 6d.

McCOSH.—**The Supernatural in Relation to the Natural.** By the Rev. JAMES McCOSH, LL.D. Crown 8vo. cloth, 7s. 6d.

M'COY.—**Contributions to British Palæontology; or, First Descriptions** of several hundred Fossil Radiata, Articulata, Mollusca, and Pisces, from the Tertiary, Cretaceous, Oolitic, and Palæozoic Strata of Great Britain. With numerous Woodcuts. By FREDERICK M'COY, F.G.S. Professor of Natural History in the University of Melbourne. 8vo. cloth, 9s.

MANSFIELD.—**Paraguay, Brazil, and the Plate.** With a Map, and numerous Woodcuts. By CHARLES MANSFIELD, M.A. of Clare College, Cambridge. With a Sketch of his Life. By the Rev. CHARLES KINGSLEY. Crown 8vo. cloth, 12s. 6d.

MARRINER.—**Sermons Preached at Lyme Regis.** By E. T. MARRINER, Curate. Fcap. 8vo. cloth, 4s. 6d.

MARSTON.—**A Lady in Her Own Right.** By WESTLAND MARSTON. Crown 8vo. cloth, 6s.

MASSON.—**Essays, Biographical and Critical; chiefly on the English Poets.** By DAVID MASSON, M.A. Professor of English Literature in University College, London. 8vo. cloth, 12s. 6d.

MASSON.—**British Novelists and their Styles;** being a Critical Sketch of the History of British Prose Fiction. By DAVID MASSON, M.A. Crown 8vo. cloth, 7s. 6d.

MASSON.—**Life of John Milton, narrated in Connexion** with the Political, Ecclesiastical, and Literary History of his Time. Vol. I. with Portraits. 18s.

MAURICE.—WORKS by the Rev. FREDERICK DENISON MAURICE, M.A. Incumbent of St. Peter's, St. Marylebone:—

1. **The Claims of the Bible and of Science;** a Correspondence between a LAYMAN and the Rev. F. D. MAURICE, on some questions arising out of the Controversy respecting the Pentateuch. Crown 8vo. cloth, 4s. 6d.

2. **Dialogues between a Clergyman and Layman** on Family Worship. Crown 8vo. cloth, 6s.

3. **Expository Discourses on the Holy Scriptures:**
   I.—**The Patriarchs and Lawgivers of the Old Testament.** Second Edition. Crown 8vo. cloth, 6s.
   This volume contains Discourses on the Pentateuch, Joshua, Judges, and the beginning of the First Book of Samuel.

   II.—**The Prophets and Kings of the Old Testament.** Second Edition. Crown 8vo. cloth, 10s. 6d.
   This volume contains Discourses on Samuel I. and II., Kings I. and II., Amos, Joel, Hosea, Isaiah, Micah, Nahum, Habakkuk, Jeremiah, and Ezekiel.

   III.—**The Gospel of St. John; a Series of Discourses.** Second Edition. Crown 8vo. cloth, 10s. 6d.

   IV.—**The Epistles of St. John; a Series of Lectures** on Christian Ethics. Crown 8vo. cloth, 7s. 6d.

4. **Expository Sermons on the Prayer-Book:**
   I.—**The Ordinary Services.**
   Second Edition. Fcap. 8vo. cloth, 5s. 6d.

   II.—**The Church a Family. Twelve Sermons on the** Occasional Services. Fcap. 8vo. cloth, 4s. 6d.

5. **Lectures on the Apocalypse, or, Book of the Revelation** of St. John the Divine. Crown 8vo. cloth, 10s. 6d.

6. **What is Revelation? A Series of Sermons on the Epiphany;** to which are added Letters to a Theological Student on the Bampton Lectures of Mr. MANSEL. Crown 8vo. cloth, 10s. 6d.

7. **Sequel to the Inquiry, "What is Revelation?"** Letters in Reply to Mr. Mansel's Examination of "Strictures on the Bampton Lectures." Crown 8vo. cloth, 6s.

8. **Lectures on Ecclesiastical History.**
   8vo. cloth, 10s. 6d.

9. **Theological Essays.**
   Second Edition, with a new Preface and other additions. Crown 8vo. cloth, 10s. 6d.

10. **The Doctrine of Sacrifice deduced from the Scriptures.** With a Dedicatory Letter to the Young Men's Christian Association. Crown 8vo. cloth, 7s. 6d.

11. **The Religions of the World, and their Relations to** Christianity. Fourth Edition. Fcap. 8vo. cloth, 5s.

14   MACMILLAN & CO.'S PUBLICATIONS.

WORKS by the Rev. F. D. MAURICE—continued.

12. **On the Lord's Prayer.**
Fourth Edition. Fcap. 8vo. cloth, 2s. 6d.

13. **On the Sabbath Day: the Character of the Warrior:**
and on the Interpretation of History. Fcap. 8vo. cloth, 2s. 6d.

14. **Learning and Working.**—Six Lectures on the Foundation of Colleges for Working Men, delivered in Willis's Rooms, London, in June and July, 1854. Crown 8vo. cloth, 5s.

15. **The Indian Crisis. Five Sermons.**
Crown 8vo. cloth, 2s. 6d.

16. **Law's Remarks on the Fable of the Bees.**
Edited, with an Introduction of Eighty Pages, by FREDERICK DENISON MAURICE, M.A. Fcp. 8vo. cloth, 4s. 6d.

MAYOR.—Cambridge in the Seventeenth Century: Auto-
biography of Matthew Robinson. By JOHN E. B. MAYOR, M.A. Fellow and Classical Lecturer of St. John's College, Cambridge.

₊ The Autobiography of Matthew Robinson may be had separately, price 5s. 6d.

MAYOR.—Early Statutes of St. John's College, Cambridge.
Now first edited with Notes. Royal 8vo. 18s.

₊ The First Part is now ready for delivery.

MELIBŒUS IN LONDON.
By JAMES PAYN, M.A. Trinity College, Cambridge. Fcap. 8vo. cloth, 5s.

MERIVALE.—Sallust for Schools.
By C. MERIVALE, B.D. Author of "History of Rome." Second Edition. Fcap. 8vo. cloth, 4s. 6d.

₊ The Jugurtha and the Catilina may be had separately, price 2s. 6d. each, bound in cloth.

MERIVALE.—Keats' Hyperion rendered into Latin Verse.
By C. MERIVALE, B.D. **Second Edition.** Royal fcap. 8vo. 3s. 6d.

MOOR COTTAGE.—A Tale of Home Life.
By the Author of "Little Estella." Crown 8vo. cloth, 6s.

MOORHOUSE. — Some Modern Difficulties respecting the Facts of Nature and Revelation. Considered in Four Sermons preached before the University of Cambridge, in Lent, 1861. By JAMES MOORHOUSE, M.A. of St. John's College, Cambridge, Curate of Hornsey. Fcap. 8vo. cloth, 2s. 6d.

MORGAN.—A Collection of Mathematical Problems and
Examples. Arranged in the Different Subjects progressively, with Answers to all the Questions. By H. A. MORGAN, M.A. Fellow of Jesus College. Crown 8vo. cloth, 6s. 6d.

MORSE.—Working for God, and other Practical Sermons.
By FRANCIS MORSE, M.A. Incumbent of St. John's, Ladywood, Birmingham. **Second Edition.** Fcap. 8vo. cloth, 5s.

MORTLOCK.—Christianity agreeable to Reason. To which
is added Baptism from the Bible. By the Rev. EDMUND MORTLOCK, B.D. Rector of Moulton, Newmarket. **Second Edition.** Fcap. 8vo. cloth, 3s. 6d.

MACMILLAN & CO.'S PUBLICATIONS. 15

NOEL.—Behind the Veil, and Other Poems. By the Hon.
RODEN NOEL. Fcap. 8vo. cloth, 7s.

NORTHERN CIRCUIT. Brief Notes of Travel in Sweden,
Finland, and Russia. With a Frontispiece. Crown 8vo. cloth, 5s.

NORTON.—The Lady of La Garaye. By the Hon. Mrs.
NORTON, with Vignette and Frontispiece, engraved from the Author's Designs. New and cheaper Edition, gilt cloth. 4s. 6d.

O'BRIEN.—An Attempt to Explain and Establish the Doc-
trine of Justification by Faith only, in Ten Sermons on the Nature and Effects of Faith, preached in the Chapel of Trinity College, Dublin. By JAMES THOMAS O'BRIEN, D.D. Bishop of Ossory. **Third Edition.** 8vo. cloth, 12s.

ORWELL.—The Bishop's Walk and the Bishop's Times.
Poems on the Days of Archbishop Leighton and the Scottish Covenant. By ORWELL. Fcap. 8vo. cloth, 5s.

PALMER.—The Book of Praise: from the best English
Hymn Writers. Selected and arranged by ROUNDELL PALMER. With Vignette by WOOLNER. 18mo. extra cloth, 4s. 6d.; morocco, 7s. 6d.; extra, 10s. 6d. The ROYAL EDITION of this work, printed in extra fcap. 8vo. handsomely bound, 6s.

PARKINSON.—A Treatise on Elementary Mechanics.
For the Use of the Junior Classes at the University, and the Higher Classes in Schools. With a Collection of Examples. By S. PARKINSON, B.D. Fellow and Assistant Tutor of St. John's College, Cambridge. **Second Edition.** Crown 8vo. cloth, 9s. 6d.

PARKINSON.—A Treatise on Optics.
Crown 8vo. cloth, 10s. 6d.

PATMORE.—The Angel in the House.
Book I. The Betrothal.—Book II. The Espousals.—Book III. Faithful For Ever—with Tamerton Church Tower.
By COVENTRY PATMORE. 2 vols. fcap. 8vo. cloth, 12s.

PATMORE.—The Victories of Love.
By COVENTRY PATMORE. Fcap. 8vo. 4s. 6d.

PAULI.—Pictures of England. By Dr. REINHOLD PAULI.
Translated by E. C. OTTE. Crown 8vo. cloth, 8s. 6d.

PHEAR.—Elementary Hydrostatics.
By J. B. PHEAR, M.A. Fellow of Clare College, Cambridge. **Third Edition.** Accompanied by numerous Examples, with the Solutions. Crown 8vo. cloth, 5s. 6d.

PHILLIPS.—Life on the Earth: Its Origin and Succession.
By JOHN PHILLIPS, M.A. LL.D. F.R.S. Professor of Geology in the University of Oxford. With Illustrations. Crown 8vo. cloth, 6s. 6d.

PHILOLOGY.—The Journal of Sacred and Classical Philology.
Four Vols. 8vo. cloth, 12s. 6d. each.

16   MACMILLAN & CO.'S PUBLICATIONS.

PLATO.—The Republic of Plato.
Translated into English, with Notes. By Two Fellows of Trinity College, Cambridge (J. Ll. Davies M.A. and D. J. Vaughan, M.A.). **Second Edition.** 8vo. cloth, 10s. 6d.

PLATONIC DIALOGUES, THE.—For English Readers.
By W. WHEWELL, D.D. F.R.S. Master of Trinity College, Cambridge. Vol. I. **Second Edition,** containing **The Socratic Dialogues.** Fcap. 8vo. cloth, 7s. 6d. Vol. II. containing **The Anti-Sophist Dialogues,** 6s. 6d. Vol. III. containing **The Republic.** Fcap. 8vo. cloth. 7s. 6d.

PRATT.—Treatise on Attractions, La Place's Functions,
and the Figure of the Earth. By J. H. PRATT, M.A. Archdeacon of Calcutta, and Fellow of Gonville and Caius College, Cambridge. **Second Edition.** Crown 8vo. cloth, 6s. 6d.

PROCTER.—A History of the Book of Common Prayer: with a Rationale of its Offices. By FRANCIS PROCTER, M.A. Vicar of Witton, Norfolk, and late Fellow of St. Catharine's College. **Fifth Edition,** revised and enlarged. Crown 8vo. cloth, 10s. 6d.

PROCTER.—An Elementary History of the Book of Common
Prayer. By FRANCIS PROCTER, M.A. 18mo. bound in cloth, 2s. 6d.

PROPERTY AND INCOME.—Guide to the Unprotected in
matters relating to Property and Income. Crown 8vo. cloth 3s. 6d.

PUCKLE.—An Elementary Treatise on Conic Sections and
Algebraic Geometry. With a numerous collection of Easy Examples progressively arranged, especially designed for the use of Schools and Beginners. By G. HALE PUCKLE, M.A. Principal of Windermere College. **Second Edition,** enlarged and improved. Crown 8vo. cloth, 7s. 6d.

RAMSAY.—The Catechiser's Manual; or, the Church Cate-
chism illustrated and explained, for the use of Clergymen, Schoolmasters, and Teachers. By ARTHUR RAMSAY, M.A. of Trinity College, Cambridge. **Second Edition.** 18mo. 1s. 6d.

RAWLINSON.—Elementary Statics.
By G. RAWLINSON, M.A. late Professor of the Applied Sciences in Elphinstone College, Bombay. Edited by EDWARD STURGES, M.A. Rector of Kencott, Oxon. Crown 8vo. cloth, 4s. 6d.

RAYS OF SUNLIGHT FOR DARK DAYS. A Book of
Selections for the Suffering. With a Preface by C. J. VAUGHAN, D.D. Vicar of Doncaster and Chaplain in Ordinary to the Queen. 18mo. elegantly printed with red lines, and bound in cloth with red leaves. **New Edition.** 3s. 6d. morocco, Old Style, 9s.

ROBY.—An Elementary Latin Grammar. By H. J. ROBY, M.A.
Under Master of Dulwich College Upper School; late Fellow and Classical Lecturer of St. John's College, Cambridge. 18mo. bound in cloth, 2s. 6d.

ROBY.—Story of a Household, and Other Poems. By
MARY K. ROBY. Fcap. 8vo. cloth, 5s.

ROMANIS.—Sermons Preached at St. Mary's, Reading.
By WILLIAM ROMANIS, M.A. Curate. Fcap. 8vo. cloth, 6s.

MACMILLAN & CO.'S PUBLICATIONS. 17

ROSSETTI.—Goblin Market, and other Poems.
By CHRISTINA ROSSETTI. With Two Designs by D. G. ROSSETTI. Fcap. 8vo. cloth, 5s.

ROUTH.—Treatise on Dynamics of Rigid Bodies.
With Numerous Examples. By E. J. ROUTH, M.A. Fellow and Assistant Tutor of St. Peter's College, Cambridge. Crown 8vo. cloth, 10s. 6d.

ROWSELL.—THE ENGLISH UNIVERSITIES AND THE ENGLISH POOR. Sermons Preached before the University of Cambridge. By T. J. ROWSELL, M.A. Rector of St. Margaret's, Lothbury, late Incumbent of St. Peter's, Stepney. Fcap. 8vo. cloth limp, red leaves, 2s.

ROWSELL.—Man's Labour and God's Harvest.
Sermons preached before the University of Cambridge in Lent, 1861. Fcap. 8vo. limp cloth, red leaves, 3s.

RUTH AND HER FRIENDS. A Story for Girls.
With a Frontispiece. **Third Edition.** Royal 16mo. extra cloth, gilt leaves, 3s. 6d.

SCOURING OF THE WHITE HORSE; or, The Long Vacation Ramble of a London Clerk. By the Author of "Tom Brown's School Days." Illustrated by DOYLE. **Eighth Thousand.** Imp. 16mo. cloth, elegant, 8s. 6d.

SEEMANN.—Viti: an Account of a Government Mission to the Vitian or Fijian Group of Islands. By BERTHOLD SEEMANN, Ph.D. F.L.S. With Map and Illustrations. Demy 8vo. cloth, 14s.

SELWYN.—The Work of Christ in the World.
Sermons preached before the University of Cambridge. By the Right Rev. GEORGE AUGUSTUS SELWYN, D.D. Bishop of New Zealand, formerly Fellow of St. John's College. **Third Edition.** Crown 8vo. 2s.

SELWYN.—A Verbal Analysis of the Holy Bible.
Intended to facilitate the translation of the Holy Scriptures into Foreign Languages. Compiled for the use of the Melanesian Mission. Small folio, cloth, 14s.

SHAKESPEARE. — The Works of William Shakespeare.
Edited by WILLIAM GEORGE CLARK, M.A. and JOHN GLOVER, M.A. Vols. 1 and 2, 8vo. cloth, 10s. 6d. each. To be completed in Eight Volumes.

SIMEON.—Stray Notes on Fishing and on Natural History.
By CORNWALL SIMEON. Crown 8vo. cloth, 7s. 6d.

SIMPSON.—An Epitome of the History of the Christian Church during the first Three Centuries and during the Reformation. With Examination Papers. By WILLIAM SIMPSON, M.A. **Fourth Edition.** Fcp. 8vo. cloth, 3s. 6d.

SMITH.—A Life Drama, and other Poems.
By ALEXANDER SMITH. Fcap. 8vo. cloth, 2s. 6d.

SMITH.—City Poems.
By ALEXANDER SMITH, Author of "A Life Drama," and other Poems. Fcap. 8vo. cloth. 5s.

SMITH.—Edwin of Deira. Second Edition. By ALEXAN- DER SMITH, Author of "City Poems." Fcap. 8vo. cloth, 5s.

SMITH.—**Arithmetic and Algebra, in their Principles and Application**: with numerous systematically arranged Examples, taken from the Cambridge Examination Papers. By BARNARD SMITH, M.A. Fellow of St. Peter's College, Cambridge. **Ninth Edition.** Crown 8vo. cloth, 10s. 6d.

SMITH.—**Arithmetic for the use of Schools.**
New Edition. Crown 8vo. cloth, 4s. 6d.

SMITH.—**A Key to the Arithmetic for Schools.**
Second Edition. Crown 8vo. cloth, 8s. 6d.

SMITH.—**Exercises in Arithmetic.**
By BARNARD SMITH. With Answers. Crown 8vo. limp cloth, 2s. 6d. Or sold separately, as follows:—Part I. 1s. Part II. 1s. Answers, 6d.

SNOWBALL.—**The Elements of Plane and Spherical Trigonometry.** By J. C. SNOWBALL, M.A. Fellow of St. John's College, Cambridge. **Ninth Edition.** Crown 8vo. cloth, 7s. 6d.

STEPHEN.—**General View of The Criminal Law of England.**
By J. FITZJAMES STEPHEN, Barrister-at-law, Recorder of Newark-on-Trent. 8vo. cloth, 18s.

STORY.—**Memoir of the Rev. Robert Story, late Minister** of Roseneath, including Passages of Scottish Religious and Ecclesiastical History during the Second Quarter of the Present Century. By R. H. STORY. Crown 8vo. cloth, 7s. 6d.

SWAINSON.—**A Handbook to Butler's Analogy.**
By C. A. SWAINSON, M.A. Principal of the Theological College, and Prebendary of Chichester. Crown 8vo. sewed, 1s. 6d.

SWAINSON.—**The Creeds of the Church in their Relations** to Holy Scripture and the Conscience of the Christian. 8vo. cloth, 9s.

SWAINSON.—**THE AUTHORITY OF THE NEW TESTAMENT**; The Conviction of Righteousness, and other Lectures, delivered before the University of Cambridge. 8vo. cloth, 12s.

TAIT and STEELE.—**A Treatise on Dynamics, with numerous Examples.** By P. G. TAIT, Fellow of St. Peter's College, Cambridge, and Professor of Mathematics in Queen's College, Belfast, and W. J. STEELE, late Fellow of St. Peter's College. Crown 8vo. cloth, 10s. 6d.

THEOLOGICAL Manuals.
  I.—**History of the Church during the Middle Ages.**
  By ARCHDEACON HARDWICK. Second Edition. With Four Maps. Crown 8vo. cloth, 10s. 6d.

  II.—**History of the Church during the Reformation.**
  By ARCHDEACON HARDWICK. Crown 8vo. cloth, 10s. 6d.

  III.—**The Book of Common Prayer: Its History and Rationale.** By FRANCIS PROCTER, M.A. **Fifth Edition.** Crown 8vo. cloth, 10s. 6d.

  IV.—**History of the Canon of the New Testament.**
  By B. F. WESTCOTT, M.A. Crown 8vo. cloth, 12s.

  V.—**Introduction to the Study of the Gospels.**
  By B. F. WESTCOTT, M.A. Crown 8vo. cloth, 10s. 6d.

  ⁎ Others are in progress, and will be announced in due time.

TEMPLE.—Sermons preached in the Chapel of Rugby
School. In 1858, 1859, and 1860. By F. TEMPLE, D.D. Chaplain in Ordinary to her Majesty, Head Master of Rugby School, Chaplain to Earl Denbigh. 8vo. cloth, 10s. 6d.

THRING.—A Construing Book.
Compiled by the Rev. EDWARD THRING, M.A. Head Master of Uppingham Grammar School, late Fellow of King's College, Cambridge. Fcap. 8vo. cloth, 2s. 6d.

THRING.—The Elements of Grammar taught in English.
Third Edition. 18mo. bound in cloth, 2s.

THRING.—The Child's Grammar.
Being the substance of the above, with Examples for Practice. Adapted for Junior Classes. **A New Edition.** 18mo. limp cloth, 1s.

THRING.—Sermons delivered at Uppingham School.
By EDWARD THRING, M.A. Head Master. Crown 8vo. cloth, 5s.

THRING.—School Songs.
A Collection of Songs for Schools. With the Music arranged for four Voices, Edited by EDWARD THRING, M.A. Head Master of Uppingham School, and H. RICCIUS. Small folio, 7s. 6d.

THRUPP.—The Song of Songs.
A New Translation, with a Commentary and an Introduction. By the Rev. J. F. THRUPP, Vicar of Barrington, late Fellow of Trinity College, Cambridge. Crown 8vo. cloth, 7s. 6d.

THRUPP.—Antient Jerusalem: a New Investigation into the
History, Topography, and Plan of the City, Environs, and Temple. Designed principally to illustrate the records and prophecies of Scripture. With Map and Plans. By JOSEPH FRANCIS THRUPP, M.A. 8vo. cloth, 15s.

THRUPP.—Introduction to the Study and Use of the
Psalms. By the Rev. J. F. THRUPP, M.A. 2 vols. 8vo. 21s.

THRUPP.—Psalms and Hymns for Public Worship.
Selected and Edited by the Rev. J. F. THRUPP, M.A. 18mo. cloth, 2s. limp cloth, 1s. 4d.

TOCQUEVILLE.—Memoir, Letters, and Remains of Alexis
De Tocqueville. Translated from the French by the Translator of "Napoleon's Correspondence with King Joseph." With Numerous additions, 2 vols. crown 8vo. 21s.

TODHUNTER.—WORKS by ISAAC TODHUNTER, M.A.
F.R.S. Fellow and Principal Mathematical Lecturer of St. John's College, Cambridge:—

1. **Euclid for Colleges and Schools.**
   18mo. bound in cloth, 3s. 6d.

2. **Algebra for Beginners.**
   With numerous Examples. 18mo. bound in cloth, 2s. 6d.

3. **A Treatise on the Differential Calculus.**
   With numerous Examples. **Third Edition.** Crown 8vo. cloth, 10s. 6d.

4. **A Treatise on the Integral Calculus. Second Edition.**
   With numerous Examples. Crown 8vo. cloth, 10s. 6d.

MACMILLAN & CO.'S PUBLICATIONS.

WORKS by ISAAC TODHUNTER—continued.

5. A Treatise on Analytical Statics, with numerous Examples. **Second Edition.** Crown 8vo. cloth, 10s. 6d.

6. A Treatise on Conic Sections, with numerous Examples. **Third Edition.** Crown 8vo. cloth, 7s. 6d.

7. Algebra for the use of Colleges and Schools. **Third Edition.** Crown 8vo. cloth, 7s. 6d.

8. Plane Trigonometry for Colleges and Schools. **Second Edition.** Crown 8vo. cloth, 5s.

9. A Treatise on Spherical Trigonometry for the Use of Colleges and Schools. **Second Edition.** Crown 8vo. cloth, 4s. 6d.

10. Critical History of the Progress of the Calculus of Variations during the Nineteenth Century. 8vo. cloth, 12s.

11. Examples of Analytical Geometry of Three Dimensions. Crown 8vo. cloth, 4s.

12. A Treatise on the Theory of Equations. Crown 8vo. cloth, 7s. 6d.

TOM BROWN'S SCHOOL DAYS.
By AN OLD BOY. **Seventh Edition.** Fcap. 8vo. cloth, 5s.
COPIES OF THE LARGE PAPER EDITION MAY BE HAD, PRICE 10s. 6d.

TOM BROWN AT OXFORD.
By the Author of "Tom Brown's School Days." **Second Edition.** 3 vols. crown 8vo. £1 11s. 6d.

TRACTS FOR PRIESTS AND PEOPLE.
By VARIOUS WRITERS.

The First Series, Crown 8vo. cloth, 8s.
The Second Series, Crown 8vo. cloth, 8s.

Supplementary Number to the Second Series, price 1s. Nonconformity in the Seventeenth and in the Nineteenth Century. I. English Voluntaryism, by J. N. LANGLEY. II. The Voluntary Principle in America. By an English Clergyman. This number can be bound up with the Second Series.

The whole Series of Fifteen Tracts may be had separately, price One Shilling each.

TRENCH.—WORKS by RICHARD CHENEVIX TRENCH,
D.D. Dean of Westminster and of the Order of the Bath:—

1. Notes on the Parables of Our Lord. **New Edition.**
[*In the Press.*
2. Notes on the Miracles of Our Lord. **Seventh Edition.** 8vo. 12s.

3. Synonyms of the New Testament. **Fifth Edition.** Fcap. 8vo. 5s.

4. Synonyms of the New Testament. **Second Part.** F 8vo. 5s.

MACMILLAN & CO.'S PUBLICATIONS. 21

WORKS by R. C. TRENCH—continued.

5. On the Study of Words. **New Edition.** [*In the Press.*

6. English Past and Present. **Fifth Edition.** Fcap. 8vo. 4s.

7. Proverbs and their Lessons. **Fifth Edition.** Fcap. 8vo. 3s.

8. Select Glossary of English Words used Formerly in Senses different from the Present. **Second Edition.** 4s.

9. On Some Deficiencies in our English Dictionaries. **Second Edition.** 8vo. 3s.

10. Sermons preached in Westminster Abbey. **Second Edition.** 8vo. 10s. 6d.

11. Five Sermons preached before the University of Cambridge. Fcap. 8vo. 2s. 6d.

12. The Subjection of the Creature to Vanity. Sermons preached in Cambridge. Fcap. 8vo. 3s.

13. The Fitness of Holy Scripture for Unfolding the Spiritual Life of Man: Christ the Desire of all Nations; or, the Unconscious Prophecies of Heathendom. Hulsean Lectures. Fcap. 8vo. **Fourth Edition.** 5s.

14. St. Augustine's Exposition of the Sermon on the Mount. With an Essay on St. Augustine as an Interpreter of Scripture. 7s.

15. On the Authorized Version of the New Testament. In Connexion with some recent Proposals for its Revision. **Second Edition.** 7s.

16. Justin Martyr and Other Poems. **Fifth Edition.** 5s.

17. Poems from Eastern Sources, Genoveva, and other Poems. **Second Edition.** 5s. 6d.

18. Elegiac Poems. **Third Edition.** 2s. 6d.

19. Calderon's Life's a Dream: the Great Theatre of the World. With an Essay on his Life and Genius. 4s. 6d.

20. Remains of the late Mrs. Richard Trench. Being Selections from her Journals, Letters, and other Papers. **Second Edition.** With Portrait, 8vo. 15s.

21. Commentary on the Epistles to the Seven Churches in Asia. **Second Edition.** 8s. 6d.

TUDOR.—The Decalogue viewed as the Christian's Law, with Special Reference to the Questions and Wants of the Times. By the Rev. RICHARD TUDOR, B.A. Curate of Helston. Crown 8vo. cloth, 10s. 6d.

22   MACMILLAN & CO.'S PUBLICATIONS.

VACATION TOURISTS; or, Notes of Travel in 1861.
Edited by F. GALTON, F.R.S. With Ten Maps illustrating the Routes. 8vo. cloth, 14s.

VAUGHAN.—Sermons preached in St. John's Church,
Leicester, during the years 1855 and 1856. By DAVID J. VAUGHAN, M.A. Fellow of Trinity College, Cambridge, and Vicar of St. Martin's, Leicester. Crown 8vo. cloth, 5s. 6d.

VAUGHAN.—Sermons on the Resurrection. With a Preface.
By D. J. VAUGHAN, M.A. Fcap. 8vo. cloth, 3s.

VAUGHAN.—Three Sermons on The Atonement. With a
Preface. By D. J. VAUGHAN, M.A. Limp cloth, red edges, 1s. 6d.

VAUGHAN.—Sermons on Sacrifice and Propitiation, preached
in St. Martin's Church, Leicester, during Lent and Easter, 1861. By D. J. VAUGHAN, M.A. Fcap. 8vo. cloth limp, red edges, 2s. 6d.

VAUGHAN.—WORKS by CHARLES JOHN VAUGHAN, D.D.
Vicar of Doncaster, Chancellor of York, and Chaplain in Ordinary to the Queen:—

1. **Notes for Lectures on Confirmation.** With suitable
Prayers. **Fourth Edition.** Limp cloth, red edges, 1s. 6d.

2. **Lectures on the Epistle to the Philippians.**
Crown 8vo. cloth, red leaves, 7s. 6d.

3. **Lectures on the Revelation of St. John.**
2 vols, crown 8vo. cloth, 15s.

4. **Epiphany, Lent, and Easter.** A Selection of Expository Sermons. **Second Edition.** Crown 8vo. cloth, red leaves, 10s. 6d.

5. **The Book and the Life: Four Sermons Preached before**
the University of Cambridge in November, 1862. Crown 8vo. cloth, 3s. 6d.

6. **Memorials of Harrow Sundays.**
A Selection of Sermons preached in Harrow School Chapel. With a View of the Interior of the Chapel. **Third Edition.** Crown 8vo. cloth, red leaves, 10s. 6d.

7. **St. Paul's Epistle to the Romans.**
The Greek Text with English Notes. Second Edition. Crown 8vo. cloth, red leaves, 5s.

8. **Revision of the Liturgy.** Four Discourses. With an
Introduction. I. ABSOLUTION. II. REGENERATION. III. ATHANASIAN CREED. IV. BURIAL SERVICE. V. HOLY ORDERS. **Second Edition.** Crown 8vo. cloth, red leaves, 4s. 6d.

9. **Lessons of Life and Godliness.** A Selection of Sermons
Preached in the Parish Church of Doncaster. Fcap. 8vo. cloth, 4s. 6d.

VILLAGE SERMONS BY A NORTHAMPTONSHIRE
RECTOR. With a Preface on the Inspiration of Holy Scripture. Crown 8vo. 6s.

MACMILLAN & CO.'S PUBLICATIONS.

VIRGIL.—The Æneid translated into English Blank Verse.
By JOHN MILLER. Crown 8vo. cloth, 10s. 6d.

VOLUNTEER'S SCRAP BOOK.
By the Author of "The Cambridge Scrap Book." Crown 4to. half-bound, 7s. 6d.

WAGNER.—Memoir of the Rev. George Wagner, late of St.
Stephen's, Brighton. By J. N. SIMPKINSON, M.A. Rector of Brington, Northampton. **Third and Cheaper Edition.** Fcap. 8vo. cloth, 5s.

WATSON AND ROUTH.—CAMBRIDGE SENATE-HOUSE
PROBLEMS AND RIDERS. For the Year 1860. With Solutions by H. W. WATSON, M.A. and E. J. ROUTH, M.A. Crown 8vo. cloth, 7s. 6d.

WARREN.—An Essay on Greek Federal Coinage.
By the Hon. J. LEICESTER WARREN, M.A. 8vo. cloth, 2s. 6d.

WESTCOTT.—History of the Canon of the New Testament
during the First Four Centuries. By BROOKE FOSS WESTCOTT, M.A. Assistant Master of Harrow School; late Fellow of Trinity College, Cambridge. Crown 8vo. cloth, 12s. 6d.

WESTCOTT. — Characteristics of the Gospel Miracles.
Sermons preached before the University of Cambridge. **With Notes.** By B. F. WESTCOTT, M.A. Author of "History of the New Testament Canon." Crown 8vo. cloth, 4s. 6d.

WESTCOTT.—Introduction to the Study of the Four Gospels. By B. F. WESTCOTT, M.A. Crown 8vo. cloth, 10s. 6d.

WILSON.—Counsels of an Invalid: Letters on Religious
Subjects. By GEORGE WILSON, M.D. late Regius Professor of Technology in the University of Edinburgh. With Vignette Portrait, engraved by G. B. SHAW. Fcap. 8vo. cloth, 4s. 6d.

WILSON.—Religio Chemici.
By GEORGE WILSON, M.D. With a Vignette beautifully engraved after a Design by NOEL PATON. Crown 8vo. cloth, 8s. 6d.

WILSON.—Memoir of George Wilson, M.D. F.R.S.E.
Regius Professor of Technology in the University of Edinburgh. By his Sister. 8vo. cloth, with Portrait, 14s.

WILSON.—The Five Gateways of Knowledge.
By GEORGE WILSON, M.D. F.R.S.E. Regius Professor of Technology in the University of Edinburgh. **Second Edition.** Fcap. 8vo. cloth, 2s. 6d. or in Paper Covers, 1s.

WILSON.—The Progress of the Telegraph.
Fcap. 8vo. 1s.

WILSON.—Prehistoric Annals of Scotland.
By DANIEL WILSON, LL.D. Professor of History and English Literature in University College, Toronto; Author of "Prehistoric Man," &c. 2 vols. demy 8vo. **Second Edition.** With numerous Illustrations. 36s.

WILSON.—A Treatise on Dynamics.
By W. P. WILSON, M.A. Fellow of St. John's, Cambridge, and Professor of Mathematics in the University of Melbourne. 8vo. bds. 9s. 6d.

WILTON.—The Negeb; or, "South Country" of Scripture.
By the Rev. E. WILTON, M.A. Oxon. Incumbent of Scofton, Notts, and Chaplain to the Earl of Galloway. Crown 8vo. cloth, 7s. 6d.

WOLFE.—ONE HUNDRED AND FIFTY ORIGINAL PSALM AND HYMN TUNES. For Four Voices. By ARTHUR WOLFE, M.A. Fellow and Tutor of Clare College, Cambridge. Oblong royal 8vo. extra cloth, gilt leaves, 10s. 6d.

WOLFE.—Hymns for Public Worship.
Selected and Arranged by ARTHUR WOLFE, M.A. 18mo. cloth, red leaves, 2s. Common Paper Edition, limp cloth, 1s. or twenty-five for 1l.

WOLFE.—Hymns for Private Use.
Selected and Arranged by ARTHUR WOLFE, M.A. 18mo. cloth, red leaves, 2s.

WOOLLEY.—Lectures Delivered in Australia.
By JOHN WOOLLEY, D.C.L. Principal and Professor of Logic and Classics in the University of Sydney, Late Fellow of University College, Oxford. Crown 8vo. cloth, 8s. 6d.

WOOLNER.—My Beautiful Lady.
By THOMAS WOOLNER. Fcap. 8vo. 5s.

WRIGHT.—Hellenica; or, a History of Greece in Greek,
as related by Diodorus and Thucydides, being a First Greek Reading Book, with Explanatory Notes, Critical and Historical. By J. WRIGHT, M.A. of Trinity College, Cambridge, and Head-Master of Sutton Coldfield Grammar School. **Second Edition,** WITH A VOCABULARY. 12mo. cloth, 3s. 6d.

WRIGHT.—A Help to Latin Grammar;
or, the Form and Use of Words in Latin. With Progressive Exercises. Crown 8vo. cloth, 4s. 6d.

WRIGHT.—The Seven Kings of Rome:
An easy Narrative, abridged from the First Book of Livy by the omission of difficult passages, being a First Latin Reading Book, with Grammatical Notes. Fcap. 8vo. cloth, 3s.

WRIGHT.—A Vocabulary and Exercises on the "Seven Kings of Rome." Fcap. 8vo. cloth, 2s. 6d.
*** The Vocabulary and Exercises may also be had bound up with "The Seven Kings of Rome." Price 5s. cloth.

Yes and No; or, Glimpses of The Great Conflict.
3 vols. crown 8vo. cloth, 1l. 11s. 6d.

CAMBRIDGE; AND 23, HENRIETTA STREET, COVENT GARDEN,
LONDON.

R. CLAY, SON, AND TAYLOR, PRINTERS, BREAD STREET HILL.

Trieste

Trieste Publishing has a massive catalogue of classic book titles. Our aim is to provide readers with the highest quality reproductions of fiction and non-fiction literature that has stood the test of time. The many thousands of books in our collection have been sourced from libraries and private collections around the world.

The titles that Trieste Publishing has chosen to be part of the collection have been scanned to simulate the original. Our readers see the books the same way that their first readers did decades or a hundred or more years ago. Books from that period are often spoiled by imperfections that did not exist in the original. Imperfections could be in the form of blurred text, photographs, or missing pages. It is highly unlikely that this would occur with one of our books. Our extensive quality control ensures that the readers of Trieste Publishing's books will be delighted with their purchase. Our staff has thoroughly reviewed every page of all the books in the collection, repairing, or if necessary, rejecting titles that are not of the highest quality. This process ensures that the reader of one of Trieste Publishing's titles receives a volume that faithfully reproduces the original, and to the maximum degree possible, gives them the experience of owning the original work.

We pride ourselves on not only creating a pathway to an extensive reservoir of books of the finest quality, but also providing value to every one of our readers. Generally, Trieste books are purchased singly - on demand, however they may also be purchased in bulk. Readers interested in bulk purchases are invited to contact us directly to enquire about our tailored bulk rates. Email: customerservice@triestepublishing.com

You May Also Like

Hour by Hour; Or, The Christian's Daily Life

E. A. L.

ISBN: 9780649607242
Paperback: 172 pages
Dimensions: 6.14 x 0.37 x 9.21 inches
Language: eng

The University of Minnesota. The Calendar for the Year 1883-84

University Minneapolis

ISBN: 9780649057054
Paperback: 140 pages
Dimensions: 6.14 x 0.30 x 9.21 inches
Language: eng

www.triestepublishing.com

You May Also Like

Results of Astronomical Observations Made at the Sydney Observatory, New South Wales, in the Years 1877 and 1878

H. C. Russell

ISBN: 9780649692613
Paperback: 120 pages
Dimensions: 6.14 x 0.25 x 9.21 inches
Language: eng

Longmans' English Classics; Dryden's Palamon and Arcite

William Tenney Brewster

ISBN: 9780649565733
Paperback: 170 pages
Dimensions: 6.14 x 0.36 x 9.21 inches
Language: eng

www.triestepublishing.com

You May Also Like

Report of the Department of Farms and Markets, pp. 5-71

Various

ISBN: 9780649333158
Paperback: 84 pages
Dimensions: 6.14 x 0.17 x 9.21 inches
Language: eng

Catalogue of the Episcopal Theological School in Cambridge Massachusetts, 1891-1892

Various

ISBN: 9780649324132
Paperback: 78 pages
Dimensions: 6.14 x 0.16 x 9.21 inches
Language: eng

www.triestepublishing.com

You May Also Like

Three Hundred Tested Recipes

Various

ISBN: 9780649352142
Paperback: 88 pages
Dimensions: 6.14 x 0.18 x 9.21 inches
Language: eng

A Basket of Fragments

Anonymous

ISBN: 9780649419418
Paperback: 108 pages
Dimensions: 6.14 x 0.22 x 9.21 inches
Language: eng

Find more of our titles on our website. We have a selection of thousands of titles that will interest you. Please visit

www.triestepublishing.com

Lightning Source UK Ltd.
Milton Keynes UK
UKOW06f0842231017
311488UK00004B/433/P

9 780649 657537